What people are saying about …

Truth, Dare, Double Dare

"You've heard it said, 'Kids rise to the level we expect from them.' In Ann-Margret Hovsepian's latest devotional for girls, she takes this principle literally by tapping into kids' innate sense of adventure and daring them—no, double daring them—to put their faith into action with real-life challenges that will transform their faith from principles into practice. It's a book that will not only change girls' lives, but the lives of those they encounter."

Karl Bastian, founder of Kidology.org
and BeTheDadToday.com

"I dare you to let this newest book by Ann-Margret Hovsepian change your life. Get answers to the questions you have about life, the Bible, and your faith while learning about yourself in the process. *Truth, Dare, Double Dare* is written in a fun and energetic voice with truth that will challenge you an a daily basis. I double dare you!"

Nicole O'Dell, founder of Choose NOW Ministries

Truth, DARE, Double Dare

another year of dynamic devotions for girls

ann-margret HOVSEPIAN

David C Cook

transforming lives together

TRUTH, DARE, DOUBLE DARE
Published by David C Cook
4050 Lee Vance View
Colorado Springs, CO 80918 U.S.A.

David C Cook Distribution Canada
55 Woodslee Avenue, Paris, Ontario, Canada N3L 3E5

David C Cook U.K., Kingsway Communications
Eastbourne, East Sussex BN23 6NT, England

The graphic circle C logo is a registered trademark of David C Cook.

The website addresses recommended throughout this book are offered as a resource to you. These websites are not intended in any way to be or imply an endorsement on the part of David C Cook, nor do we vouch for their content.

All Scripture quotations are taken from the Holy Bible, New International Version®, NIV®. Copyright © 1973, 2011 by Biblica, Inc.™ Used by permission of Zondervan. All rights reserved worldwide. www.zondervan.com.

LCCN 2014945711
ISBN 978-1-4347-0211-1

Published in association with the literary agency of Credo Communications, LLC, Grand Rapids, Michigan

The Team: Susan Tjaden, Jamie Chavez, Amy Konyndyk, Nick Lee, Kathy Mosier, Karen Athen
Cover Design: Luke Flowers
Gecko photo: © Thomas Marent / ardea.com

Printed in the United States of America
First Edition 2014

1 2 3 4 5 6 7 8 9 10

080114

To my parents, Joseph and Jessie, and late grandparents, Vartevar, Osanna, Vehazoun, and Zabel—my very own daring heroes. Thank you for your faithful examples of following Jesus no matter what.

INTRODUCTION

When kids play together, there's usually someone in the group who is a little more mischievous than the others and enjoys taking risks. She may get a thrill from trying things that are a bit dangerous or even things that the rest of you know are against the rules. Maybe you're that person in your group of friends.

Whether you're the brave one among your friends or one of the timid ones, you've probably heard someone say, "I dare you to do that!" It's a challenge that basically means, "If you do that, it means you're cool. If you don't, it means you're a chicken."

And then there are times someone will call out, "I double dare you!" Usually that means, "Ha! I really don't think you have the guts to do it." For a timid girl, those words can create feelings of fear or confusion. For a girl who's up to the challenge, those words may be fun to hear.

In this devotional, *Truth, Dare, Double Dare*, you will be challenged every day, but in a positive way! The Bible is full of wonderful truths, and we're going to discover those together by reading different Bible verses. Some of them might be difficult to understand at first, so I'm going to help you and, more importantly, show you how you can find treasures in the Bible on your own.

Then, at the end of each day's chapter, you'll be *double dared* to apply what you've just learned to your everyday life. The more dares you take as you go through this book, the stronger and braver you'll grow in your faith, and the more you'll know the awesome God who created and loves you!

If you ever thought that being a Christian is tough or boring, *Truth, Dare, Double Dare* will help you see that it can be exciting and full of blessings.

Are you ready? I dare you—no, I *double dare* you—to get started! Each day, flip to the next page and look up and read the Bible verse listed before reading the "Truth" and "Dare" sections for that day. It's a good idea to pray before and after you do each day's devotion, asking God to help you focus on and understand what He wants to teach you through His Word. Also, take time to answer the journaling questions (you're allowed to write in this book!) or to jot down whatever thoughts come to mind as you work on the devotion. You might want to keep a blank journal with your Bible for those days when you want to write more or there's an activity to complete.

Hang on tight … Here we go!

Ann-Margret Hovsepian

Are You a Double-Dare Dynamo?

Some Christian girls are daring when it comes to living out their faith in Jesus. Most are not. And then there are some who are *double daring*. (Yes, I just made up that word. It's fun to do that sometimes!) Answer the questions in this quiz to see if you're *dull, daring*, or a *double-dare dynamo*! Circle the letter that is closest to what you would actually do (not what you think you *should* do).

1. Your older sister, who is often mean to you, comes home with a new haircut. She thinks it makes her look funny, so she's pretty grumpy. You ...

   a. stay out of her way. You don't want her yelling at you!
   b. tell her she looks nice and that she shouldn't worry about it.
   c. bring her favorite snack to her room, give her a hug, and tell her all the things that are special about her.

2. Your science teacher says that believing God created the earth is stupid because science can prove He didn't. You ...

   a. sit quietly and hope no one in your class looks at you.
   b. tell your friends afterward that you believe in God and in the Bible.
   c. ask your teacher if you can make a presentation in class next week explaining why you believe God *did* create the world. If she says yes, you ask your pastor or another teacher at church to help you prepare your speech.

3. You're allowed to spend a Saturday at your friend's house. You know that no one in her family is a Christian. When her mom calls you both into the kitchen for lunch, you sit at the table with your friend and her mom and ...

   a. start eating right away, just like they do.
   b. bow your head and say a silent prayer of thanks.
   c. ask, "Would it be okay if I said grace before we eat?"

4. A cute boy from school walks by your church just as your family is getting ready to go inside. He sees your Bible and asks what you're doing. You ...

   a. try to hide your Bible and shrug like you're bored.
   b. confidently tell him that you and your family go to church there every week.
   c. tell him you're going to church and ask him if he wants to come too.

If you answered

... *mostly a's*, you don't seem very excited about being a Christian. Maybe you haven't really learned how to take what you read in the Bible and practice it in your everyday life. Or maybe you're just afraid of how people will treat you if you do what the Bible says.

... *mostly b's*, you're pretty brave! Good for you for not hiding your faith in Jesus and for being obedient in tough situations. But maybe you try not to attract extra attention to yourself because you don't want people to think you're a religious nut.

... *mostly c's*, wow! You are definitely a double-dare dynamo! Way to go on having the courage to speak up about your faith in Jesus and for caring about other people the way Jesus would. Keep up the good work—but don't forget to always ask God for wisdom and humility so you don't do anything without thinking or praying first.

In your journal, write a prayer to God telling Him how you would like to change this year. If you need to go from dull to daring or from daring to double daring (or from dull to double daring!), ask Him to give you courage and wisdom. Make a commitment to work on this every day.

Excited? Me too! Let's go!

DOUBLE DARE

Look up these Bible verses and choose one to memorize this weekend as a reminder to be double daring:

Deuteronomy 31:6   *Joshua 1:9*   *1 Chronicles 22:13*

1 Corinthians 16:13   *Romans 1:16*   *1 Peter 4:16*

What are your thoughts?

The First Step Is the Hardest

BIBLE READING *1 Peter 2:21*

TRUTH

God is only one step away!

I have a strange condition that I call pickupthephonephobia. In my many years as a writer, I've done hundreds of interviews and tackled lots of difficult projects. But do you know what the hardest part of my job is? It's picking up the phone to make a business call. Weird, right?

It gets worse. I have another condition that I call putonmysneakersphobia. I love walking. When I get going, I can put in a great workout, speeding around a big park with lots of energy. That's if I can manage to put my sneakers on and actually walk out the front door.

Sometimes I keep myself from accomplishing great things because I can't get over the first hurdle on the track. This happens in our spiritual lives too. We know we should read the Bible and pray, but we get distracted by other things and put off our quiet time until "later." But later doesn't come because we run out of time. Until we simply sit down and close our eyes, that quiet time won't happen.

The only way we can take the second, third, fiftieth, and last steps is to start with the first step.

DARE Take that first step!

DOUBLE DARE

1. What are some of your own *ican'tdothisphobias* that keep you from getting things done? Ask God to help you have the courage to take the first step and get started.

2. If you struggle to get your devotions done, think about what distracts you. Come up with a plan to sit with your Bible, devo book, and journal at a certain time each day.

PROMISE TO REPEAT

How did it go? What did you learn?

Feel the "Pull"

BIBLE READING *Ecclesiastes 3:11 and Colossians 3:2*

TRUTH

You don't have to see God to know He's real.

I don't know anything about Mary Burns Warmenhoven except that she wrote one poem many, many years ago called "The Pull." It's about a boy who was out flying his kite one day, so high that you couldn't even see it as a speck in the sky. The boy stood holding the string, feeling calm and happy, when a stranger walked by and asked him how he knew he still had a kite.

> "You had a kite, and you have a string,
> But where is the kite? You see not a thing!
> Maybe it's gone, blown far from here.
> How do you know it's still up there?"
> "I know it's there!" laughed the boy aloud,
> His keen eyes fixed on a lacy cloud,
> "I don't have to see it; the wind is full
> And my kite's up there—I feel the pull!"

That's how it is with Christians. People may laugh at us for believing in God because they don't see Him, but when we trust in Him, we feel the "pull" of His Spirit in our hearts, and we feel just as peaceful and confident as that little boy did.

DARE   Don't be discouraged by people who can't "see" God.

DOUBLE DARE

1. Think of some ways God shows you He's real. Ask Him to give you courage to share this with someone who doesn't believe God exists.

2. Draw a colorful picture of a kite and write the words to Colossians 3:2 on it. Ask if you can post your picture on the fridge for your family to see.

PROMISE TO REPEAT

How did it go? What did you learn?

God ...or the World?

BIBLE READING *Luke 16:13 and Deuteronomy 5:7*

TRUTH

We must love God more than the world.

Have you ever seen a balance scale? It's not like the flat scales that you either stand on or put an object on to measure weight. A balance scale has two shallow bowls hanging on opposite ends of a beam that is attached in the center to a stand. You place the object you want to measure in one bowl and then slowly add standard weights (objects with their exact weight marked on them) to the other bowl until the two are exactly even. Adding up the totals of the standard weights tells you how much the object weighs.

When you use a balance scale, the more one side goes down, the more the other side goes up. It's kind of like a seesaw: When the person at one end pushes down, the person at the other end pops up!

The balance scale can help us understand Luke 16:13. The more we love material things, the less we can love God. But the more we love God, the less we will love everything else. In Deuteronomy 5:7, God commanded us not to worship anything more than Him. That means the "scale" of our love must always tip to His side and not the world's.

DARE Love God more than anything else!

DOUBLE DARE

1. Being completely honest, think about how much you enjoy other things compared to the time you spend with God. Ask God to help you love Him more.

2. Give up something today to spend extra time praying or reading your Bible. Then write in your journal how it felt to do that.

PROMISE TO REPEAT

How did it go? What did you learn?

BIBLE READING *Joshua 1:8*

TRUTH

True success comes from knowing and obeying God's Word.

Besides doing these daily devotionals, it's important for you to get into the habit of reading the Bible on your own. Many of these devos ask you to read only one verse—so if that's all you do this year, it'll be like having one lick of the icing on a huge piece of delicious chocolate cake, or watching only the first thirty seconds of your favorite movie. To do more, you can either start from the beginning (Genesis 1) and read a chapter a day, or you can choose different parts of the Bible. Whatever you do, try to read more than just a few verses each day.

As you read, look for one or more of these five clues that will help you grow as a Christian. Write your discoveries in a special notebook or your journal.

S – Sins to confess (reminders of a sin in your life)
P – Promises to keep (something you want to do for God)
A – Actions to avoid (warnings you want to remember)
C – Commands to obey (instructions from God you must follow)
E – Examples to follow (people in the Bible who showed you how to live)

For example, in Joshua 1:8 we see a **Command to obey**: meditate on God's Word every day.

DARE Make S.P.A.C.E. in your heart for God's Word.

DOUBLE DARE

1. Make a bookmark or index card with the S.P.A.C.E. Bible study guide above. Keep it in your Bible as a reminder of what to look for as you read.

2. Read Matthew 7:24–27. In your journal write the "Actions to avoid" and the "Examples to follow."

PROMISE TO REPEAT

How did it go? What did you learn?

Pray, Pray, and Pray Some More!

BIBLE READING *1 Thessalonians 5:17 and Colossians 4:2*

TRUTH

Without prayer, a Christian has no power.

As an author, I often have friends and even strangers ask me for advice about writing. There are so many things I could tell them about proper grammar, punctuation, and spelling. I could explain how to send their stories to magazine or book editors. I could suggest books, websites, or classes that would help them. But the advice I give them most of all is surprisingly simple. Can you guess what it is?

I tell people who want to become successful writers to do two things:

1. Read, read, and read some more. Reading good books is a great way to learn about good writing.

2. Write, write, and write some more. The best way to get better at writing is to practice as much as possible.

You know, growing as a Christian is a bit like that. We have to read, read, and read our Bible to learn what God's will is for us. But what really helps us in our Christian life is prayer. We have to pray, pray, and pray some more to connect with God and receive His strength and help.

DARE Pray continually!

DOUBLE DARE

1. Think of an activity you enjoy or something you take lessons for where you have to practice to get better (for example, playing guitar, swimming, or drawing). Try to put just as much (or more!) effort into growing as a Christian.

2. How much time do you spend praying each day? Ask God to help you spend more time talking and listening to Him.

PROMISE TO REPEAT

How did it go? What did you learn?

Yes, No, or Wait

Karen was born in Sri Lanka (an island country south of India), lived in Nigeria, Africa, when she was a teenager, and now lives in Canada. When she was fifteen years old and still in Nigeria with her two brothers, her mother had already moved to Canada to make preparations for her children to join her. During that time, life was difficult for Karen and her brothers, but she got to know about God and learned to trust Him with her problems.

One Thursday, Karen got a message saying that if her mother did not return home by Monday, she and her brothers would be deported (sent away) from Nigeria. There was nothing Karen could do but pray. She didn't have any money to call her mother in Canada to tell her the problem. So she prayed and waited.

Friday came and nothing happened. Karen felt scared, so she prayed again, asking God to bring her mother home. This time she felt calm and happy. She went to bed around 11:00 p.m. and fell asleep. About three hours later, there was a knock on the door. Karen was very scared because it was 2:00 a.m. and she didn't know who was at the door. The knocking continued, so she opened the door. There was her mother, standing right in front of her! It was like a dream.

Karen's brothers were still sleeping, so she woke them up. They were stunned to see that their mother was home. Before the kids could say anything, their mother explained that the day before—even before Karen had prayed—she felt as though a voice was telling her that her children needed her at home. So she left Canada right away and made the long trip all the way to Nigeria. And she got there before Monday!

A few years later, when Karen told this story in her new church in Canada, she said, "Time and time again, over the years, God has answered our prayers many times, even before we asked Him. God has been wonderful to us, and He continues to love us every day. He loves you too."

God answers prayers in three different ways. He may say:

1. Yes.

2. No.

3. Not right now.

When Karen prayed, she got a yes answer so fast it showed that God knew what she needed *before* she even prayed about it. We don't always get that kind of answer to our prayers, but we can still trust that God's answer is exactly what is best for us. If He says no, it's always because He has something better planned for us. So instead of feeling disappointed, we can trust Him and say thank you even though we didn't get what we asked for.

YOUR TURN

- Read John 16:24.

- In the boxes below, write the first letter of each of the objects in the picture frames above.

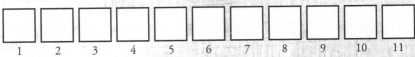

1	2	3	4	5	6	7	8	9	10	11

- Using the code you just made, fill in the missing letters below and you'll discover today's simple reminder. An answer key for this, and all activities throughout the devotional, is found on pages 428–30.

___ ___   ___ ___ ___ ___ ___ ___ ___   ___ ___ ___ ___ ___ ___.
 4 6 2   1 5 9 10 3 8 9   7 8 1 11 3 8

- In your journal, write about one or two things you would like to ask God to help you with. Spend some time talking with Him about them this weekend, remembering to ask Him for His will and not yours. Also ask Him to help you patiently trust Him to answer whenever it's the right time. Don't forget to thank Him for answering your prayer, even if you don't know what that answer will be yet.

BIBLE READING   *Colossians 3:16*

TRUTH

Jesus should be more than a visitor in your heart.

On a piece of paper, write down as many things as you can think of that you do on a normal weekday. For example, *brush my teeth, feed the cat, ride on the school bus, learn math, or watch TV.* As you look at your list, how much information do you think your brain gets in one day? It could be from your teacher, your parents, your friends, TV shows, songs you listen to, and so on.

Children today receive so much information in one day that it can be difficult for them to handle it all, so sometimes the information gets pushed aside or doesn't get enough attention to really be understood. The problem with this is that a lot of good stuff is forgotten or ignored.

Today's verse says that Jesus and His words should dwell (or live) inside a Christian. That means we have to make a special place for Jesus in our hearts where He gets the attention and honor He deserves—not just for a few minutes each week.

DARE   Make sure there's enough room for Jesus in your life.

DOUBLE DARE

1. In your journal, draw a house that's shaped like a heart (use your imagination!) and then write Colossians 3:16 somewhere on the house. While you draw, ask God to forgive you for not giving Him enough time out of your day.

2. Try to review each day's devo at least twice—once in the afternoon and once before going to bed—to make sure you've learned that day's "Truth."

PROMISE TO REPEAT

How did it go? What did you learn?

A Recipe for Love

BIBLE READING *1 Timothy 1:5*

TRUTH

You can't love without a pure heart.

Draw a line from each meal on the left to three ingredients it needs in the lists on the right.

Meal	Ingredient 1	Ingredient 2	Ingredient 3
Tuna sandwich	oranges	ice cream	spaghetti noodles
Fruit salad	sprinkles	bread	apples
Spaghetti	tuna	meat sauce	chocolate syrup
Ice cream sundae	cheese	grapes	mayonnaise

The apostle Paul gave his student Timothy a "recipe" for love. Just as you can't pick a fruit salad off a tree or grow spaghetti in a field, you can't make yourself be loving. Love is more than something you *feel*, like sadness or anger. It's something you decide to *do*. No one ever says, "Okay, I want to feel angry right now." Anger just shows up when something happens to upset us. Even happiness is like that. But not love. We need God's help to develop love in our hearts.

What three things did Paul say love comes from?

1.   2.   3.

And where do we find those things?
A pure heart comes from asking God to forgive and wash away our sins.
A good conscience comes from obeying God and doing what He asks us to do.
A sincere faith comes from spending time with God in prayer and Bible study.

DARE Grow love in your heart.

DOUBLE DARE

1. Use an index card to make a "recipe card" for love. List the three "ingredients" and then write the instructions for finding them. Write "1 Timothy 1:5" at the bottom. Stick the card on your fridge as a daily reminder.

2. Make a second recipe card and share it with a Christian friend.

PROMISE TO REPEAT

How did it go? What did you learn?

BIBLE READING *2 Chronicles 1:9–12*

TRUTH

Asking God for wisdom is wise!

When I was a little girl, my grandparents used to tell me Turkish folktales about a man named Hodja. Sometimes Hodja did silly things, and other times he was very clever.

One day, his friends saw him riding his donkey and noticed he was carrying a heavy sack on his back. Surprised, they asked him why he was carrying it instead of putting it on the donkey's back.

Hodja replied, "Well, the poor animal is tired and now he's carrying me. I felt sorry for him and didn't want him to carry extra weight."

See the problem? Hodja forgot that even if he put the sack on his own back, the donkey still had to carry all the weight! It would have been wiser for Hodja to put the sack on the donkey so that they wouldn't both get tired.

Sometimes we are not very wise in life, but there is a way for us to become wiser. Like Solomon in today's Bible reading, we can ask God to give us wisdom. God loves to give wisdom because He knows we can use it to honor Him and to help others.

DARE   Add wisdom to your wish list.

DOUBLE DARE

1. What are some things Solomon could have asked God for? (Read the verses again if you don't remember.) What are some things you wish for? Take time today to ask God for wisdom.

2. Tell a friend the story about Hodja and see if she figures out why he was foolish. Then share about how you're asking God to make you wiser.

PROMISE TO REPEAT

How did it go? What did you learn?

Keep Your Sponge Wet

BIBLE READING *2 Timothy 3:14–17*

TRUTH

Studying God's Word keeps us wise, soft, and useful.

Have you ever seen or touched a dried-up sponge? Dry sponges are usually hard and rough. You can't bend them, and if you put only a bit of water on them, they don't soak it up very well. To make a dry sponge soft and useful, you have to really soak it in water and wring it out a few times. And if a sponge soaks up lots of water, squeezing it makes the water ooze out. You could actually use the water from one sponge to wet another dried-up one, right?

As Christians, it's important for us to "soak in" God's Word and spend time in prayer every day. This keeps our spiritual sponges (our hearts) soft. If we're only a little bit damp, we don't have enough to share with others, but if our hearts are overflowing with God's love and truth, then we can also begin sharing it with others around us. And then they can begin to soak it in too.

But just as a wet sponge will eventually dry up if you don't keep it wet, we also dry up spiritually if we don't have our quiet time with God each day. Today's verses remind us to "continue in what you have learned."

DARE Fill up on God's Word!

DOUBLE DARE

1. Ask your mom if you can have a little piece of sponge to pin to your bulletin board as a reminder of today's devo.

2. Memorize 2 Timothy 3:16–17. Write it in your own words in your journal (or here).

PROMISE TO REPEAT

How did it go? What did you learn?

BIBLE READING *Ezekiel 11:12*

TRUTH

We can't make up our own standards for life.

Write what tools you would need to measure the following things:

Your weight
The length of your thumb
How fast your sister runs
How warm it is in the house
How much milk is in your glass

How do we know these tools will tell us the right measurements? Because they are all made by matching them up with a standard—a measurement that never changes. What do you think would happen if people made their own rulers by taking a piece of wood and marking off what they thought was an inch? Do you think everyone's rulers would have the same measurements? Probably not.

In the same way, we can't make up our own standards in life, and we shouldn't trust the standards of the world. The Bible is our standard and the perfect tool to measure our lives by. We can always check what God says in the Bible to know if we're living as He wants us to.

DARE Live by God's standards.

DOUBLE DARE

1. List a few "standards" or rules in the Bible that the world says aren't such a big deal. For example, respecting your parents. Write down why you think God gave us those standards.

2. What are some things you find difficult about obeying God? Talk to Him about it and ask Him to help you.

PROMISE TO REPEAT

How did it go? What did you learn?

Ready for an experiment?

1. Turn off the lights in your room.

2. Turn off any music that's playing or shut your bedroom door to block out sounds from other rooms in the house.

3. Sit on your bed.

4. Close your eyes (after you finish reading the instructions, of course!) and block your ears with your fingers.

5. For about one minute, imagine you are sitting in the middle of the floor during drama class while your classmates are acting and talking and singing. But you can't see them and you can't hear them.

6. Open your eyes and unblock your ears.

How did that feel? Was it a bit scary? Upsetting? Sad?

Helen Keller was born in Alabama in 1880. She was not even two years old when a terrible illness left her blind and deaf. Because she was so little, she hadn't learned to speak yet, so she had no way of communicating with the people around her. She couldn't see. She couldn't hear. She couldn't talk. Suddenly she was all alone in a dark, quiet world. She was small and afraid. Her fear made her wild and angry, and this made some people think she was crazy and dangerous. But her loving parents were patient with her and believed she could learn to communicate and have a normal life.

Just before Helen's seventh birthday, a teacher named Anne Sullivan came to live with her. Using a perfect mix of love and discipline, it took Miss Sullivan only two weeks to get the wild little girl under control. Anne had been blind too when she was younger, but a few operations helped her see again. During her time of blindness, she had learned a type of alphabet that uses different finger positions to spell out letters. She used this to start teaching Helen simple words. Helen was a clever girl, and in just a few months, she learned three hundred words!

After a very difficult and stressful beginning to her life, Helen grew up, and her faith in God helped her keep a positive attitude through all the challenges she faced. Her favorite book became the Bible, and she also found ways to help others the way she had been helped. She spent most of her life fighting for the rights of people who were deaf or blind or had other disabilities, until she died at the age of eighty-eight.

YOUR TURN

- If someone asked you what your favorite book is, what would you say?

- How did you feel when you read that Helen Keller's favorite book was the Bible, even though she was blind?

- How do you think you would feel about God if you were deaf and blind? How easy would it be to trust Him?

- Read Isaiah 35 (it's only ten verses). Find the verse that you think would have encouraged Helen Keller and given her hope about her future in heaven. Write it here:

- Is there something in your life that you use as an excuse not to serve God? Take time to pray about it this weekend. Ask God to help you have Helen Keller's courage to serve Him and bless others no matter how difficult it is.

What are your thoughts?

It's Not About You

BIBLE READING   *1 Chronicles 16:29*

TRUTH

Worship is for God's pleasure, not ours.

After church one Sunday, a young man complained about the music. He said to the pastor, "I didn't like the songs you chose today." The pastor answered, "That's okay. We weren't singing them for you."

Some people go to church the same way they go to a concert or movie. They want a good show. They want comfortable seats. They want cool music. They want to hang out with friends. Basically, they just want to feel good. They figure that if they're going to go through the trouble of going to church, it better not be boring.

What's wrong with this picture? We're forgetting that going to church is something we do for God! Sure, He blesses us when we participate, but our main goal should be to honor God. Worship is thinking about how holy God is and telling Him how much we love Him. It's offering our hearts and time and talents and money and strength to Him.

During worship, if you're thinking, *Oh, I love this song!* or concentrating on the voices of the worship leaders, you're missing the point. Your focus should be only on connecting your heart with God's. It's not about the music. It's not about the people around you. It's not even about you. It's about God and God alone.

DARE   Go to church for God, not for yourself.

DOUBLE DARE

1. In your journal, write five things you like about your church and five things you don't. Cross out any that are about you and not God.

2. Write about how you will change the way you worship God.

PROMISE TO REPEAT

How did it go? What did you learn?

A Good Leader

BIBLE READING *1 Corinthians 11:1*

TRUTH

When we follow Jesus, others can also follow Him.

Imagine you're at camp and everyone is getting ready for a big hike in two groups. The two leaders introduce themselves before you choose which group you want to join.

Ali is wearing long pants and sleeves, a cap, and hiking boots. Her backpack has a first-aid kit, a flashlight, and water. She calmly explains exactly what route her team will follow. She explains some boring safety rules and then talks about some of the plants and animals she has seen on past hikes.

Olivia is wearing shorts, a tank top, and flip-flops. She has scratches all over, and her nose is sunburned. She is full of energy, has a huge smile on her face, and talks very loudly about how much fun her team is going to have because she's a great leader with awesome ideas of what to do on the hike.

Which team would you choose? A good leader is someone whose example and experience you can trust. When Christians really love and follow Jesus—instead of just drawing attention to themselves—then the people who follow their example will be able to find Jesus too.

DARE Be wise when you follow—and lead.

DOUBLE DARE

1. In your journal, describe a Christian who would be a good leader to others. Ask God to help you be careful about whom you follow or listen to.

2. Are you a good example to your friends of what it looks like to follow Jesus? If not, start making changes that will help them see Jesus in your life.

PROMISE TO REPEAT

How did it go? What did you learn?

The Lip Balm Mix-Up

BIBLE READING *Ezekiel 20:19 and James 1:16*

TRUTH

If we're not careful, we may be deceived.

Do you have friends who always seem to have funny things happen to them that you later share a good laugh over? My life doesn't seem to be that interesting, but my friend Susan makes me giggle at least once a week with something amusing she writes on Facebook. Sometimes she tells us about some clumsy thing she did (I don't laugh if she got hurt, of course!); other times it's something funny about her children, pets, or the forest animals that visit her backyard.

One day, Susan wrote on her Facebook page: "Almost too embarrassing to admit. I just put on what I thought was lip balm. Nope. It was a small glue stick. True story.... Sigh."

Susan's mistake wasn't dangerous—just annoying. But if we're not careful, we may get mixed up about much more serious things. For example, some people call themselves Christians but teach things that aren't in the Bible. Some people pretend to like you just to get you to do something for them. Some people try to make you believe your parents don't understand you and tempt you to disobey them.

Make sure you follow Jesus only, and you won't be deceived by others.

DARE Don't be deceived.

DOUBLE DARE

1. In your journal, write about a funny mix-up that happened to you. Then write a prayer asking God to help you not be fooled by things that can harm you.

2. Stick a small piece of paper that says "James 1:16" onto your glue stick. See if you can remember the verse whenever you use it.

PROMISE TO REPEAT

How did it go? What did you learn?

Goldfish Lesson #1

BIBLE READING *John 15:5*

TRUTH

When we remain in Christ, He remains in us.

Goldfish are great pets! You obviously can't cuddle and play with them like you can with a puppy or a cat, but they're still pretty cool. They're fun (and relaxing) to watch, and if you look closely, you can see how remarkable God's creativity is. And fish—like many other things God created—can also teach us about being Christians.

Fish depend completely on water. They need it to breathe, to swim, for their food, and more. The fish is surrounded by water, and water also flows in and out of the fish through its gills. A good word to describe this is *immersion*. Think of a sponge in a bowl of water. When you immerse a sponge, the sponge is in the water, and the water is also inside the sponge.

Jesus told His followers that if they remain in Him, He will remain in them. That means that as we spend time with Jesus and in His Word, His Spirit fills us. If we don't stay connected to Jesus, it's like a goldfish jumping out of its bowl. It wouldn't survive for long without water, and we can't truly live without Jesus.

DARE Immerse yourself in Jesus.

DOUBLE DARE

1. In your journal, draw a picture of a goldfish in a bowl of water. Write today's verse next to it and explain, in your own words, what it means to be *immersed* in Jesus.

2. Think of at least two ways you can get closer to the Lord this week and stay connected to Him. Ask God to help you.

PROMISE TO REPEAT

How did it go? What did you learn?

BIBLE READING *2 Timothy 2:15*

TRUTH

God's children have "homework" to do!

There's a joke about a college student who was lazy and didn't study for a difficult exam that he had to take just before Christmas break. After a few minutes of struggling with the questions, he wrote, "Only God knows the answers to these questions. Merry Christmas!"

When he got his test papers back, he saw that the teacher had written on it, "God gets 100 percent. You get 0. Happy New Year!"

The student thought he was being funny, but that didn't help him get a passing grade. The result of his laziness was that he failed his exam.

As Christians, we're disciples—or students—of Jesus. That means we need to study His Word (the Bible) and prepare ourselves to live the way God wants us to. When we do our best to please God, we won't be put to shame like that college student was!

DARE Do your best to learn God's truth—and obey it.

DOUBLE DARE

1. How much time do you take to read the Bible every day? Make a plan to change up some of your activities so that you can spend more time with God.

2. Do you have a friend or brother or sister who is struggling with school? Offer to help him or her study, and share today's devo too!

PROMISE TO REPEAT

How did it go? What did you learn?

The Sheep, the Coin, and the Child

Read Luke 15.

In this weekend's reading, Jesus told one parable with three parts:

1. A shepherd who lost one of his sheep

2. A woman who lost a precious coin

3. A father who lost his son

These three stories are similar, but there are a few differences we should look at:

1. The sheep was a living, conscious creature, but she didn't mean to get lost and she couldn't help herself. The only thing she could do was cry out and hope the shepherd would find her.

2. The coin was just an object. It didn't even know it was lost, so it could do nothing to help the woman find it.

3. The son made a decision to leave his home and his father. He knew what he was doing and he chose to be "lost." When he realized the mistake he had made, he had to make another choice. He knew the way home. The only thing he couldn't do was make his father forgive him and accept him back home.

People can be like all three of the examples above, which may be why Jesus told this lesson in three different ways.

LOST SHEEP

The lost sheep might have been left behind because she was busy drinking from a stream or looking for nicer grass. Even though we love God, our Shepherd, sometimes we get distracted. Our minds wander in church, we laugh at a dirty joke, we make fun of someone, or we tell a "small" lie to our parents. *It's not a big deal*, we think. But when we get off the right path, it's easy to get lost if we don't get back on it right away. We begin to wander further and further away.

LOST COIN

The coin didn't do anything to get lost. It probably got dropped and rolled off into a corner of the room. Sometimes things happen in life that make us stumble, and we don't realize what we're doing. We feel lost and stuck where we are, but no one seems to notice for a long time.

LOST CHILD

The son who left home wasn't satisfied with his life. Even though his father had given him everything he needed, he wanted more. He wanted the freedom to live his life however he wanted. So he rejected his father and went to live on his own. But instead of being happier, he became miserable. He no longer had the comfort and safety of home. He was alone, hungry, and scared. When people reject God and His love, they end up just like this young man. They don't want to live by God's rules because they think it won't be fun. But you know what? Life without God is boring, sad, lonely, and dangerous. When the young man in this story realized his mistake, he was humble enough to go home. Sadly, some people never turn back to God. They prefer to be lost.

YOUR TURN

- Which of the three stories could describe your life and your relationship with God? Are you still lost, or did God find you? Write about it here:

- If you feel like you're still lost, take a look at page 426 of this book. It explains how you can have a relationship with Jesus.

What are your thoughts?

Three Rules for Prayer

BIBLE READING *Colossians 4:2*

TRUTH

Prayer is the most important thing we can do each day.

How do you keep track of your homework assignments? Maybe you have a planner where you write down the subjects you have to study or work on. Grown-ups may not have homework to do, but most of them have a list of things they know they need to get done each day. Some will write these tasks on a calendar, in a planner, or on a list they keep on the fridge. Others will keep track of their to-do list on a computer or cell phone.

How many people do you think have "pray" on their lists? Probably not too many, right? Of course, some won't write it down because it's something they do anyway. A Christian who truly loves God knows that she should pray. But sometimes we forget that it is absolutely the most important thing we do as Christians.

A man named Andrew Bonar made himself three rules for daily quiet time with God that I'd like to remember. I hope you will too:

1. Don't speak to *anyone* before speaking to *Jesus*.
2. Don't do anything with your *hands* before you've been on your *knees* (praying).
3. Don't read *anything* until you've read your *Bible*.

DARE Make prayer your first priority.

DOUBLE DARE

1. Write the three rules on a piece of paper and put it somewhere you'll see it every morning. Try to follow the rules and see how your day goes. Write about it in your journal.

2. Do you have a friend who has a hard time remembering to pray? Tell her what you learned today.

PROMISE TO REPEAT

How did it go? What did you learn?

BIBLE READING   *James 4:7*

TRUTH

The closer we get to God, the farther we'll be from the Devil.

Many people believe that a goldfish's memory lasts only about three seconds. I used to believe that too because I had no way of checking if it was true. I figured, "What does a goldfish have to remember anyway? It doesn't have to do homework or pick up its toys or mail its mom's letters."

Well, some scientists did a study to figure out how long a goldfish could actually remember something. In a fish tank, they made an area that gave out tiny electric shocks. Then they watched the goldfish and found that if a goldfish went near that area and felt the shock, it didn't go back to that spot for at least twenty-four hours! That's pretty smart for such a little fish, isn't it?

Humans must be smarter than that, right? But it's shocking how foolish we can be sometimes. When we sin, we usually experience some kind of bad consequences, whether it's feeling guilty, getting in trouble, or even being punished. Worst of all, we feel far from God. And yet we seem to forget, and we go back to those sins instead of staying away from them.

DARE   Stay close to God.

DOUBLE DARE

1. Is there a sin that you seem to do over and over again? Spend time today praying about it and asking God to help you the next time you're tempted.

2. Memorize today's verse. If you're allowed to have goldfish-shaped crackers, ask your mom if you can have a few. Try to recite the verse every time you eat a cracker.

PROMISE TO REPEAT

How did it go? What did you learn?

BIBLE READING *Psalm 34:10*

TRUTH

God blesses those who seek Him.

Remember Hodja, the silly man from the Turkish folktales? Here's another story about him.

While in his basement one day, Hodja lost his gold ring. It was valuable, so he started looking for it but didn't see it. Then he went out the front door of his house and started looking around there.

A neighbor saw Hodja and asked what he was doing. "I lost my ring," Hodja answered. "Where did you lose it?" asked the neighbor. Hodja said that he had dropped it in his basement. Surprised, the neighbor asked, "Then why aren't you looking for it there?" Hodja shook his head sadly and said, "Well, it was so dark in there I couldn't see a thing. So I'm looking for it here."

That might seem like a funny story, but sometimes people are like that when it comes to looking for the important things in life, such as truth, wisdom, help, and peace. Many people look for something or someone to trust, someone to give them hope, but they look in the wrong places.

The Bible promises that when we turn to God for the things we need, He will provide!

DARE   Seek the Lord!

DOUBLE DARE

1. Write down a few things you feel nervous or confused about. Who do you think is the best person to help you with those situations? Ask God to help you trust *Him*.

2. Think of a friend who is going through a hard time. Write her an encouraging note with today's Bible verse, and promise to pray for her.

PROMISE TO REPEAT

How did it go? What did you learn?

Gain Prudence

BIBLE READING *Proverbs 8:5 and Proverbs 26:4–5*

TRUTH

God wants us to grow in wisdom.

Some quotes make me think, and others make me giggle. Sometimes I find quotes that do both! Here are two:

"Never wrestle with a pig; you both get dirty and the pig likes it."
"Never try to teach a pig to sing; it wastes your time and annoys the pig."

The Bible tells us that arguing with a fool makes us one too. Sometimes we get tangled up trying to explain ourselves to someone who just wants to argue and isn't really interested in listening. It's better to just end the conversation instead of wasting our time. It would be like trying to teach a pig to sing!

You may have noticed that Proverbs 26:5 seems to say the opposite of the verse before it. That's because one verse is telling us not to argue about things that don't matter, while the other one is telling us that sometimes, if it's an important matter, we might need to speak up about what's right, even if the other person doesn't accept what we say.

Prudence is another word for wisdom. God can help you be prudent when an argument starts so that you'll have the maturity to know when to speak and when to stop.

DARE Be prudent!

DOUBLE DARE

1. Think about a time you argued with someone recently. What was the result of the argument? Ask God to help you not get caught up in foolish conversations that waste your time and do no good.

2. Have you disrespected someone during an argument lately? Apologize to him or her as soon as you can.

PROMISE TO REPEAT

How did it go? What did you learn?

Be Careful What You Wish For

BIBLE READING *Psalm 37:4*

TRUTH

God loves to grant us wishes that honor Him.

Three men got shipwrecked on a desert island. As days went by with no rescue, they dreamed of being at home again with their friends and family. One day, one of the men found a bottle that contained a genie. He opened the bottle, and the genie said he would grant each of them one wish.

One man said, "I want to be back in Seattle with my wife and kids." POOF! He was gone. The second said, "I want to be back in Portland with my brother." In a flash, he was gone. The third man was left all alone. He said, "Boy, it really is lonely with my friends gone. I sure wish they were back here with me again." POOF!

Foolish man! He wasted all three wishes, and they all ended up back where they started. But, you know, most of us are like that in life. We wish for things that are nothing compared to what God has for us. We think only about what we want right now instead of what's good for us in the long run. But when we get to know God and trust Him, we begin to wish for the things that are best for us.

DARE   Take delight in the Lord.

DOUBLE DARE

1. In your journal, write down five things you wish for. Next to each one, write what you imagine God might have planned for you that's even better.

2. Share today's devo with your family. Together, talk about what it means to "take delight in the LORD."

PROMISE TO REPEAT

How did it go? What did you learn?

H.O.W. (Hero Observation Weekend) #1

Weekend

Ready for something different? This weekend and every fourth weekend, *you* will get to choose your devo to work on during Saturday and Sunday. You've done a great job being daring for the past four weeks, and your reward is getting to decide on a Bible "hero" to read about and learn from.

Here's H.O.W. it works. Look through the list of names below and choose *one* character you'd like to observe over the next two days. Write the name on the blank line below. You'll see there are Bible verses about that hero to get you started. After you read from the Bible, answer the three questions listed under "Question Time." Don't forget the Double Dare at the end of the devo too!

Next month, you'll get the same list and will be able to choose a different hero to observe.

Don't be discouraged if you see a long reading list. You've got all weekend to read the verses, and these exciting stories are worth reading! There are more than twelve in the list, so you won't have to do them all.

HERO LIST

Choose ONE of these heroes to observe this weekend:

Name	Bible Verses
Esther	Esther 3:1–11; 4:4–17; 5:1–8; 7:1–10; 8:1–11
Stephen	Acts 6–7
Ruth	Ruth 1–4
David	1 Samuel 17
Abigail	1 Samuel 25:1–42
Gideon	Judges 6–7
The Bleeding Woman	Mark 5:25–34
Joseph	Genesis 37; 39–41
The Widow of Zarephath	1 Kings 17:8–24; Luke 4:25–26
Noah	Genesis 6–8
Miriam	Exodus 2:1–10
Daniel	Daniel 6
Mary of Bethany	John 12:1–8
Abraham	Genesis 22:1–18

Your hero for this weekend: _____

QUESTION TIME

1. How did this weekend's hero show courage and faith in God?

2. What happened because of his or her courage and obedience?

3. What did you learn from this hero's life that will help you in your own walk with God?

DOUBLE DARE

Choose at least one of these ways to dig a little deeper into your hero's life this weekend:

1. See if you can find other Bible verses about him or her. Write the reference (or the "address" of the verses) here and also anything new that you learned.

2. Ask your parents or another Christian what they have learned from this hero's life and example.

Tell a friend or your family about your new hero!

What are your thoughts?

BIBLE READING *Isaiah 26:3*

TRUTH

When you trust in God, you can face any situation.

There's a funny story about a little old lady who looked in the mirror one morning and saw that she had only three hairs left on her head. She thought for a moment and then said, "Hmm, I think I'll braid my hair today." She happily braided the three hairs together and then went out.

The next morning, she saw that she had only two hairs left. "Cool! I guess I'll part my hair in the middle today," she said. And that's what she did.

The next day, she had only one hair left! So she wore it in a ponytail and had a fun day.

You can guess what happened next. Yep, she didn't have a single hair left. "Yay!" she cheered. "I don't have to fix my hair today!"

Wouldn't it be great if we all had such a positive attitude about the troubles in our lives? The thing is, we can! God will help us find something to rejoice about in every difficulty when we fully trust that He's taking care of us.

DARE   Be optimistic even when it doesn't make sense.

DOUBLE DARE

1. Think of a situation you're facing right now that would be easy to complain about. Now try to find something funny or positive about the situation that can help you get through it. Ask God to help you if you're struggling to have a good attitude about it.

2. Know someone who needs cheering up? Tell her the story of the lady with the three hairs and then share today's verse with her.

PROMISE TO REPEAT

How did it go? What did you learn?

BIBLE READING *Isaiah 26:4*

TRUTH

God can be trusted now and forever.

A man and his wife were invited to spend a weekend at his boss's beautiful country home. The wife was a little nervous at first because her husband's boss was very wealthy, but soon she was enjoying herself. On the second evening, they all drove to an expensive restaurant together. Just before going in, the boss stopped and silently looked down at the ground for a few minutes. The woman saw only a dirty penny.

Finally, he reached down and picked it up, smiling. The woman was surprised. This man was rich! Why did he need a penny? But she didn't say anything. After dinner, she couldn't suppress her curiosity anymore so she asked him if the coin he had picked up was valuable.

He showed her the writing on the coin. In America, all coins and bills say, "In God we trust." He told her that every time he saw a penny, it reminded him to stop and pray and to think about whether or not he was trusting God at that moment.

What a great idea! Instead of ignoring pennies, this man thought of them as little conversations with God. He knew the importance of trusting God at all times.

DARE Trust in God.

DOUBLE DARE

1. Put a penny in one of your pockets today as a reminder to trust in God. Whenever you feel it there, pause and talk to God. (If you don't live in the United States, use any coin. You'll still remember the lesson.)

2. In your journal, write about something that is worrying you. Then write a prayer asking God to help you trust Him.

PROMISE TO REPEAT

How did it go? What did you learn?

One Thing God Forgets

BIBLE READING   *Hebrews 8:12*

TRUTH

When God forgives our sins, He also forgets them.

Remember the devo about a goldfish's memory (page 36)? Today we're going to talk about squirrels. Can you guess whether squirrels have good or bad memories? I was surprised to learn that squirrels are actually kind of, well, scatterbrained. Scientists have found that when squirrels collect and bury nuts to store up food for the winter, they remember only about one out of five of their hiding places. They may bury an acorn one day and forget where it is the very next day.

This doesn't mean squirrels don't have enough food during the winter. They actually collect five times more food than they need. And all that extra work is not wasted, because the buried nuts and seeds are good for the survival of trees and plants.

We don't usually think of a bad memory as a good thing, but it turns out not to be a problem for squirrels. There's one other unexpected example of how forgetting something is great—great for us.

God promises us that when we confess our sins and ask for forgiveness, He doesn't only forgive us. He also forgets our sin. That means He never makes us feel bad about it again. Wouldn't it be nice if we could forget each other's sins too?

DARE   Trust God to forgive and forget.

DOUBLE DARE

1. Do you feel guilty about sins even after confessing and asking God to forgive you? Focus on doing better in the future instead of remembering the past.

2. Are you still angry with someone who asked you for forgiveness? Ask God to help you let it go.

PROMISE TO REPEAT

How did it go? What did you learn?

Don't Do What Doesn't Work

BIBLE READING _James 2:14–17_

TRUTH

If your actions don't match your faith, saying you believe in Jesus is useless.

Remember my friend Susan, who used glue stick instead of lip balm? A few weeks later, she told me another funny story.

While driving to work one morning, the sun was glaring in her eyes. To solve the problem, she did something. Something strange. She reached over and turned down the radio. "It didn't help," she told me. Susan obviously had too much on her mind and didn't realize what she was doing. It's normal to turn down the radio when the music is too loud, but it was a useless action that morning because it didn't match her need.

What if Susan had said, "I believe the sun is too bright!" without doing anything? Would that have been any better? No. Susan needed to put on her sunglasses or bring down the car's sun visor.

As Christians, what we do must match what we say. Saying "I believe Jesus is the Savior" doesn't do any good if people can't see how your life is different because of Jesus. If we have true faith, there are two things we should not do: nothing and the wrong things.

DARE Make your actions match your faith.

DOUBLE DARE

1. In your journal, list ten qualities that should be obvious in a Christian's life (for example, patience or respect). How well do you think people see those qualities in your life? Ask God to help you live out what you believe.

2. Think of at least two Christians you know whose actions match their faith. Make an effort to thank them for their good examples.

PROMISE TO REPEAT

How did it go? What did you learn?

Watch Out for Sin

BIBLE READING *Genesis 4:7*

TRUTH

We're surrounded by temptations to disobey God.

One way to understand how the Devil tempts us to sin is to think about fishing. The Devil often tempts us the way fishermen catch fish. He shows us something we like (for fish it's worms) and we "bite" the bait. The Devil may tempt us with things like popularity, money, or the chance to have fun. And, just like the fish doesn't know the worm is attached to a hook that will trap him, we sometimes don't realize that what tempted us will get us into big trouble.

For example, imagine you and a couple of other girls are at a friend's house. When she goes to the bathroom, the other girls start looking through her things. One finds a bracelet that she knows you really like and tells you to take it. You say no at first, but she says, "Don't worry. She'll think she just lost it. And you can sneak it back into her drawer the next time you're here. That's not stealing." So you take it and put it in your pocket. That is stealing!

This story can end in different ways, but do you see how easy it is for sin to trap you? We need God's help to always do what's right.

DARE Do what is right.

DOUBLE DARE

1. Write two different endings to the example above (for example, you get caught or you break the bracelet). Then write how the story would end if you didn't give in to the temptation.

2. What's your biggest temptation? Take extra time to talk to God about it and ask for His help.

PROMISE TO REPEAT

How did it go? What did you learn?

Whatever Is TRUE

For the next several weekends, we're going to take a close look at **Philippians 4:8–9**, which says,

> Finally, brothers and sisters, whatever is **true**, whatever is noble, whatever is right, whatever is pure, whatever is lovely, whatever is admirable—if anything is excellent or praiseworthy—think about such things. Whatever you have learned or received or heard from me, or seen in me—put it into practice. And the God of peace will be with you.

What are the six types of things this passage tells us to think about?

1.   4.

2.   5.

3.   6.

Starting with #1 (true) this weekend, we'll look at one "think" each weekend.

Read John 18:28–38.

At the end of this conversation between Jesus and the Roman governor, what question did Pilate ask? He felt confused at that moment, so he asked, "What is truth?" Sometimes we can be confused too when we hear different messages that all sound like they could be true but are opposite from each other. We may wonder, *What is truth?*

Now read John 14:6 and John 8:31–32.

The good news is that Jesus, who said that *He* is the Truth, will help us know what's true and what's false if we ask Him for wisdom and guidance. We also learn what's true by studying the Bible, which is God's Word. When Jesus was praying in the garden before He was arrested, He said, "Your word is truth" (John 17:17).

Once we know what's true, we have to concentrate on the truth instead of thinking and wondering about and maybe even enjoying the *untrue* things that the world tries to make us believe.

YOUR TURN

- What are some things the world tells you that aren't true? (We've given a couple of examples to get you started.)

  ♦ There is no God, so don't worry about how you live.

  ♦ It's okay to steal or lie a little as long as you're not hurting anyone.

  ♦ People will love you more if you're beautiful.

- For each of the *untrue* things listed, write an opposite and *true* statement:

- If you're not sure whether something on these lists is true or not, check with one of your parents or another mature Christian.
- Pick one truth from the second list that you want to think about this weekend. Choose something you may be struggling to believe. Circle it so you'll remember. Then ask God to help you believe that truth instead of believing what's not true.

DOUBLE DARE

Memorize Philippians 4:8.

God Sees and Knows Everything

BIBLE READING *Hebrews 4:13*

TRUTH

Nothing is hidden from God's eyes.

Try this: See how many different animals you can name in exactly one minute. Write the number here:

Humans started keeping track of earth's different living species in 1758. Since then, can you guess how many species have been discovered? Would you say about 4,000? How about 21,300? Maybe 735,912? Does that seem impossible? Would you believe the number is actually close to two million? Do you think anyone would be able to memorize a list that long?

In 2007 alone, 18,516 species were discovered for the first time. Besides tiny things like bacteria, that list includes 9,411 insects; 2,830 mammals, birds, amphibians, reptiles, and fish; 1,194 spiders, ticks, and scorpions; and 1,807 snails, clams, and other shellfish. Biologists believe we've discovered only a small part of everything that's out there.[1]

This is exciting because it shows how awesome God's creation is. Of course, God knows every creature on that list—and the ones that haven't been discovered yet! And God also knows everything about you and me. We may be able to hide things in our hearts from other people, but not from God. That's why we need to humbly ask Him every day to forgive our sins.

DARE Be honest with God.

DOUBLE DARE

1. Do you have secrets that you hope no one will discover? Remember that God already knows them. Ask Him to forgive you for any sins you've been trying to hide.

2. With your friends, see how many animals you can think of in five minutes. Afterward, share today's devo with them.

PROMISE TO REPEAT

How did it go? What did you learn?

Victory Over Sin

BIBLE READING *1 John 5:3–5*

TRUTH

We can win the battle against sin when we love and obey God.

Imagine you're playing catch in the park and your ball rolls under a fence. You stick your hand under the fence and grab the ball, but now you can't get your hand out. There's just enough room for the ball or your hand to fit through, but not both. The only way you can get your hand out is to let go of the ball.

That's like sin in a Christian's life. You can't follow Jesus and experience His joy if you're still holding on to sins. For example, you can't …

- watch TV after school when you should be studying and then ask God to help you do well in school;

- daydream during Sunday school and then complain that the Bible is too difficult to understand; or

- spend all your allowance on candy and then say you don't have enough money to help a poor family.

We can't grow spiritually if we're trying to hang on to sins and bad habits we enjoy. But when we ask God for help, He gives us victory. He helps us drop the sin and replace it with love and obedience.

DARE Let go of your sins.

DOUBLE DARE

1. What are some sins in your life that keep you from growing as a Christian? Confess them to God and ask Him to help you have victory over them.

2. In your journal, draw a picture of sins falling out of your hand. (Use your imagination!) Then write "Jesus gives me victory over sin" on the drawing of your hand.

PROMISE TO REPEAT

How did it go? What did you learn?

Sin Is Sin

BIBLE READING   *1 John 5:17*

TRUTH

There is no such thing as a sin that doesn't matter.

Can you imagine walking from New York City to San Francisco? The cities are almost three thousand miles apart, and it would take someone forty-two hours to drive that distance in a car. According to Google Maps (an Internet site that gives directions), it would take someone over nine hundred hours to walk all that way. That's about thirty-eight days if you don't stop to sleep, rest, and eat.

Astonishingly, more than sixty people have walked across the United States! One man, after finishing his long journey, was asked what the hardest thing about it was. He said it wasn't climbing mountains or going through hot deserts. What almost made him quit was the sand in his shoes.

That's how sin is. We might think something we did wasn't so bad. We might think of a sin as "small"—like a grain of sand. But the Bible warns us that all wrongdoing is sin. Telling your mom you ate only two cookies when you really had three is a sin. It may not seem as bad as stealing money or cheating on a test, but it's still disobedience and it spoils your relationship with God.

DARE   Confess all your sins—even the "small" ones.

DOUBLE DARE

1. In your journal, write why you think God doesn't look at sins as "big" or "small." Take time today to confess all your sins to Him.

2. Place something small, like a pebble, in your shoe and walk around like that for a while. How does that help you understand today's devo? Write about it in your journal.

PROMISE TO REPEAT

How did it go? What did you learn?

No Fishing from the Balcony!

BIBLE READING *Isaiah 55:7*

TRUTH

God forgives those who turn to Him.

There once was a hotel in Texas called the Flagship, built right near the Gulf of Mexico. Large windows around the dining room on the first floor gave a beautiful view of the water, but the hotel was spending a lot of money replacing the windows. Can you guess why? Some guests thought it would be a good idea to go fishing from their balconies! It was such a long way from their balconies to the water that they would put heavy weights on the fishing lines. Then they would cast their lines and WOOOSH ... CRASH! The weights would smash into the windows below.

The hotel tried to stop people from doing this, but nothing worked. Finally, they took down the signs that said "No Fishing from the Balcony," and no one fished from them again!

People always seem to want to do what they know they're not allowed to. Babies do it. Children do it. Even adults do it! That's called rebellion. Humans can be very stubborn, not wanting to obey God even though we know His commands are good and right. But the Bible promises that if we stop rebelling and turn to God, He will forgive us.

DARE Stop rebelling against God.

DOUBLE DARE

1. What is a sin you're tempted to do the more you're told you can't? Talk to God about it. Ask Him to help you trust that His reason for saying no is for your own good.

2. Put a little "No Fishing from the Balcony" sign on your balcony at home (or hang it somewhere else if you don't have a balcony). Share today's lesson with anyone who asks about the sign.

PROMISE TO REPEAT

How did it go? What did you learn?

A Little Can Hurt a Lot

BIBLE READING *James 2:10*

TRUTH

Breaking one of God's laws is just as bad as breaking all of them.

Let's pretend you're at my house and we're going to make tuna sandwiches for lunch. First I get a loaf of sliced bread. Then I open a can of tuna and empty it into a bowl. I like to chop up a bit of tomato and green onions and add those to my tuna, but if you don't like those, that's okay. Now, let's see. What's next?

I get a bottle of chocolate syrup, open the top, and start to pour the syrup into the bowl. What? You seem a little upset. What's wrong with putting chocolate syrup into a tuna sandwich?

Gross! Some things just don't go together. Like cereal and ketchup. Or ice cream and pickles. (Okay, that one sounds really yucky.) Even just a little bit of the wrong thing can spoil what you're eating.

That's just like sin, except that sin is much more serious. We can't say, "Oh, but it's just a little sin. What harm can it do?" The Bible warns that even one sin can separate us from God. We need to ask for His forgiveness for all our sins, whether we think they're big or small.

DARE Keep all of God's laws.

DOUBLE DARE

1. Are there any sins you haven't confessed to God because you don't think they're so bad? Talk to Him about them before they spoil your relationship with Him.

2. Tell a friend about today's devo and see if the two of you can think of other examples of things that don't go together.

PROMISE TO REPEAT

How did it go? What did you learn?

Whatever Is NOBLE

Finally, brothers and sisters, whatever is true, whatever is **noble**, whatever is right, whatever is pure, whatever is lovely, whatever is admirable—if anything is excellent or praiseworthy—think about such things. Whatever you have learned or received or heard from me, or seen in me—put it into practice. And the God of peace will be with you. (Philippians 4:8–9)

Do you know what *noble* means? Look it up in a dictionary and write the definition here: _____

Here are a few examples of things we normally consider to be noble because of their importance or the respect they deserve:

royalty (e.g., kings)   bravery   good deeds   honesty

Can you think of any other examples?

In our key verses for this weekend, the Bible tells us to think about things that are noble. That doesn't mean we have to sit there and daydream about the queen of England, but it does mean that our hearts and minds should be more interested in:

1. **People** who deserve our admiration and respect because of their pure character and good deeds, instead of people who are popular only because of their beauty, money, or "coolness."

2. **Things** or **actions** that please and honor God, that bless others, or that help us grow as Christians, instead of things that waste our time, take our attention from God, or go against what the Bible teaches.

YOUR TURN

- Complete this puzzle by looking up the verses next to each row of squares and, for each one, finding the word that has a similar meaning to the word *noble*. (Note: We used the New International Version of the Bible for this puzzle.)

Matthew 11:29									N					
1 Kings 1:46									O					
1 Chronicles 12:21									B					
1 Timothy 3:2									L					
Ruth 3:11									E					

DOUBLE DARE

Under each heading below, list some of your favorite things in that category.

Things I talk about with friends

_____

_____

_____

_____

Things I do when I have free time

_____

_____

_____

_____

Things I daydream about

_____

_____

_____

Things I like to spend money on

_____

_____

_____

Now go through each list and put a star next to anything you think is _noble_ and an _X_ next to anything you know _isn't noble_.

Ask God to help you keep your mind on things that are noble.

What are your thoughts?

Water for the Thirsty

BIBLE READING *Isaiah 44:2–4*

TRUTH

God satisfies spiritual thirst.

Have you ever heard the saying "You can lead a horse to water, but you can't make him drink"? It's another way of saying you can try to show people what they need to do, but you can't force them to do it—it's their choice.

For example, you can teach your little sister an easier way to do math, but that doesn't mean she's going to do it that way. Or you can give your friend good advice on how to save her money, but you can't change her habits for her. You can tell someone about Jesus, but you can't make her believe in Him.

Someone once said, "Your job isn't to make the horse drink water. It's to make the horse thirsty." That's very wise! If a horse is thirsty enough, it will drink when you lead it to water, right? But what does that have to do with telling someone about Jesus?

Some people think they don't need Jesus because they believe that other things can satisfy their hearts. You can show people how much joy and peace you have in your relationship with God. As they watch your life, they will realize they're spiritually thirsty and will want what you have. Then you can lead them to the water—Jesus—and they will drink!

DARE Make people thirsty for Jesus.

DOUBLE DARE

1. Does your life attract people to Jesus? If not, ask God to show you how you can create a spiritual thirst in your friends who don't know Him.

2. Memorize Psalm 63:1.

PROMISE TO REPEAT

How did it go? What did you learn?

Know the Truth

BIBLE READING *John 8:31–32 and Philippians 4:6*

TRUTH

Knowing the truth can help us overcome fear.

One day I was talking with my parents when I heard a small crash in the kitchen. I looked around but couldn't see that anything had fallen. Then I heard a rustling noise from inside one of the lower cabinets. It kept starting and stopping and it sounded like … Uh oh! It sounded like a mouse with some paper.

We didn't want the mouse to run into the house, so I carefully opened the cabinet door just enough to slide in a mousetrap.

The next morning, my mom needed a pot, so we opened the cabinet door carefully to see if the mouse was still there … And then we started laughing!

There was no mouse. The big knob on the glass cover of a frying pan had somehow broken and fallen into the pan (the crash), and then the little bits of shattered glass had slowly been crumbling down (the rustling noise). Boy, did we feel silly for thinking it was a mouse.

Sometimes we're afraid of a situation in our lives because we don't have all the facts about it. We often worry for nothing! But Jesus taught us that knowing the truth will set us free, so we don't need to be anxious.

DARE Always look for the truth.

DOUBLE DARE

1. Think of a situation that's worrying you. Ask God to help you not to feel anxious about the things you don't understand.
2. Memorize Philippians 4:6 and make a bookmark with the verse.

PROMISE TO REPEAT

How did it go? What did you learn?

Walk in Truth

BIBLE READING   *1 John 1:6–7*

TRUTH

Our lives—not just our words—must be full of truth.

A high school student named Sam decided to try out for track just to make his father happy. He wasn't athletic and didn't like running, but his father had been a strong runner when he was Sam's age. The first race was between two students: Sam and the fastest runner in the school. Of course, Sam lost the race.

Later, Sam told his dad, "Guess what? I ran against Bill Williams, the fastest runner in the school. He came in next to last and I came in second!"

Do you see what he did there? Did Sam lie? Not exactly. Bill did come in next to last, and Sam did come in second, but that's because there were only two runners! If Sam's father didn't know that and thought there were five or ten or twenty runners, he'd have the wrong idea about how the race went. Sam purposely tricked his father into believing something that wasn't true (that he did well in the race), but he felt good about himself because he didn't exactly lie.

Truth isn't just what we say with our words. Truth is how we live and behave. The Bible says that followers of Jesus have to walk in His light, without hiding secret sins in darkness.

DARE   Be honest, inside and out.

DOUBLE DARE

1. Can you think of a time when you didn't lie but still weren't completely honest? Ask God to help your heart and actions match your words.

2. Make up your own ending to Sam's story, after the race was over. Write it in your journal.

PROMISE TO REPEAT

How did it go? What did you learn?

Only One True God

BIBLE READING *1 Kings 18:26–29*

TRUTH

There is only one living and loving God.

I love all the stories in the Bible, but this is one of my favorites because it shows how God is the only true and living God.

If you read the whole story later (as one of your Double Dares), you'll see that Elijah boldly went to face King Ahab to warn him about disobeying God and worshipping Baal, a false god. He said that Ahab and the people had to choose—they could not believe in God and also follow Baal. Then he set up a competition to prove which god was real and which was fake.

An altar was prepared for Baal, but Elijah said not to light the fire. If Baal was real, he should start the fire by a miracle. For hours, Baal's worshippers prayed, danced, cried out, and even cut themselves, but nothing happened. Elijah began teasing them, saying that Baal must be sleeping or too busy to answer them. The Bible says, "There was no response, no one answered, no one paid attention."

Next, Elijah set up an altar for God and even made things difficult by soaking the firewood with water three times. When he prayed, God answered immediately and set the altar on fire. Then the people believed in Him!

DARE Don't waste your time on things that leave you spiritually empty.

DOUBLE DARE

1. Read the whole story about Elijah and the worshippers of Baal in 1 Kings 18:16–39.

2. What are some things that people worship instead of God? Ask God to help you remember that nothing on earth can bring you joy like He can.

PROMISE TO REPEAT

How did it go? What did you learn?

You Ought to Be Like an Otter

BIBLE READING *1 Peter 3:8*

TRUTH

We all need each other!

Have you ever seen sea otters sleeping? It's the cutest thing! They float on their backs, staying very close together and often crossing their paws with each other, which looks like they're holding hands.

You might think, *Aww, look how much they love each other!* Well, maybe. But their linked paws are about more than friendship. Otters do this to keep from drifting away from each other while they're asleep.

This is a good lesson for Christians. The Bible tells us we should treat each other with compassion (sharing in how someone is feeling), with love, and with humility. That means we need to look around to see if someone needs our help, our time, our prayers, or just a listening ear. Just as sea otters keep each other close by as they sleep, we must care for the people around us.

DARE Give someone a helping hand.

DOUBLE DARE

1. Ask one of your parents to help you find a picture (on the Internet or in a book) of sea otters sleeping with their paws linked. Print it out or make a photocopy and write today's verse somewhere on the page (or on the back). Keep the picture in your Bible near 1 Peter 3:8.

2. Think of a friend or someone you know at church who is going through a hard time and write an encouraging note or card to give to him or her.

PROMISE TO REPEAT

How did it go? What did you learn?

Finally, brothers and sisters, whatever is true, whatever is noble, whatever is **right**, whatever is pure, whatever is lovely, whatever is admirable—if anything is excellent or praiseworthy—think about such things. Whatever you have learned or received or heard from me, or seen in me—put it into practice. And the God of peace will be with you. (Philippians 4:8–9)

Circle the answer you think is right for each question below:

5+3=   9   12   8   2

If you mix red paint with yellow paint, you get …

purple   orange   green   black

The capital of France is …

tomorrow   zebra   Paris   bread

Okay, I'll admit it. That last question's answers were a bit silly. But all three questions were very easy, weren't they? The right answer was easy to spot because, for each question, there is only one possible answer. No matter how much you try, you can't prove that five plus three equals two because it's not possible. You'll never get purple paint by mixing red paint with yellow paint. And, no matter how much people in France like fresh bread, it will never be their capital!

Let's try three more questions:

What do you have to do to go to heaven?

    a. Pray five times a day.
    b. Ask Jesus to forgive your sins and promise to follow Him.
    c. Do your very best to be a good girl.

You don't feel like hanging out with a friend so you say you have to study. You are …

    a. being polite.
    b. stretching the truth a little.
    c. lying.

The commandments in the Bible …

    a. must all be obeyed.
    b. are just good advice.
    c. are old-fashioned and don't need to be followed anymore.

You probably chose the right answer for each of the last three questions, but do you think everyone would answer them the same way? Probably not, and yet each of those questions has only one right answer, just like the first three questions. But many people don't believe in God or don't want to live by what the Bible says. They make their own decisions about what's right or wrong.

That's a little like saying mixing orange juice with marshmallows will give you bacon. It just doesn't make sense! You can choose to believe it, but that doesn't make it right. Believing that it's okay to lie as long as you're not hurting anyone doesn't make it right. Believing that it doesn't matter who you worship as long as you're kind to everyone doesn't make it right. Believing that it's okay to keep the extra change you got at a store because it wasn't your mistake doesn't make it right.

The Bible gives us very clear guidelines about what's wrong and right. The problem is we are surrounded by messages about things that are wrong, and it can get confusing. That's why Philippians 4:8 tells us to focus our minds on what is right. The more we know what is right and what honors God, the better we will be at recognizing what's wrong and saying no to it.

YOUR TURN

- Spend some time asking God to give you wisdom to know when something is wrong or right. Remember that reading your Bible regularly will be a huge help in learning what's right.

- Think ahead. For each of the following situations, write down how you can keep your mind on what's right. By coming up with solutions ahead of time, you'll be prepared if any of these situations happen to you.

  ◆ Your friend always talks about a TV show you are not allowed to watch at your house. What do you do?

  ◆ A boy you think is cute starts paying attention to you, but he also makes fun of a girl who doesn't have a lot of friends. He encourages you to pick on her too. What do you do?

  ◆ Your friends at church pass notes to each other and to you during class or during the worship service. What do you do?

- If you're not sure what to do in these situations, ask your mom or dad or another Christian you trust to help you figure out what's right.

What are your thoughts?

You're Not a Plastic Doll

BIBLE READING *Psalm 135:15–18*

TRUTH

God wants you to LIVE for Him!

When I was a little girl, I had a few Barbie dolls that I liked to play with. I would dress them up, fix their hair, and make up stories about their lives. How about you? Maybe you have a brother who has action figures. It can be fun to move around the arms and legs of these dolls and make them do whatever we want them to do.

Some plastic dolls are made with so much detail that they look very much like humans, but, of course, they're not. They can't see or hear, they can't move on their own, and they certainly can't think or feel.

God warns us in the Bible that if we want things in the world—such as our toys, clothes, or TV shows—more than we want Him, then we become like our plastic dolls. We stop worshipping Him the way He deserves and living the way He wants us to. But God wants us to be real Christians who live what we believe.

DARE   Don't just say you believe in God—live for Him too!

DOUBLE DARE

1. Think about the activities you do when you have free time. Do they help you get closer to God, or do they take your mind off Him? Ask God to help you make enough time to spend with Him and grow in your relationship with Him.

2. Write today's Bible reading on a piece of paper and keep it somewhere near your dolls so you'll be reminded of today's devo whenever you play.

PROMISE TO REPEAT

How did it go? What did you learn?

Secretly Generous

BIBLE READING *Matthew 6:1–4*

TRUTH

God blesses those who don't boast about their good deeds.

Charles Spurgeon was a well-known preacher in London, England, in the 1800s and is still greatly respected today. He wrote many sermons and books that have been translated into dozens of languages. Like anyone who wants to serve God, he wasn't always respected, but he continued working for God no matter what people said.

I once read that Mr. Spurgeon and his wife used to sell eggs laid by their chickens. They never gave them away, even to their relatives, and they told people, "You may have them if you pay for them." What do you think people said about the Spurgeons? They thought this couple was greedy for money and not very kind. But the Spurgeons never tried to explain why they only sold their eggs. They just quietly listened to people's hurtful comments.

Years later, after Mrs. Spurgeon died, the whole story came out. The couple sold the eggs and gave all the money they collected to two elderly widows. The Spurgeons obeyed Matthew 6:3 and didn't let other people know about the good they were doing.

They were willing to be good in secret, with only God knowing what they were doing! This is how we all should live.

DARE Be generous, but do it secretly.

DOUBLE DARE

1. Find ways to secretly help or encourage others. For example, bake cookies for a family at church going through a hard time. Ask your pastor to give them the cookies without saying who they're from.

2. Talk to God about how it feels to do good when no one knows about it.

PROMISE TO REPEAT

How did it go? What did you learn?

Don't Turn Them Away

BIBLE READING *Matthew 5:42*

TRUTH

God's children should always be ready to help others.

There once was a pastor named Tom Erickson who often received "wrong number" phone calls. The public library had a special phone number that children could call to hear a story read to them, and this phone number had only one number that was different from Pastor Tom's. Little kids with inexperienced fingers would sometimes punch in the wrong number and end up calling Pastor Tom.

At first he tried to explain to them that they had the wrong number and not the one for Dial-A-Tale, but they were too young to understand, so finally he decided it would be easier to read to them. He got a copy of *The Three Little Pigs*, left it near his phone, and read from it whenever a child called for a story. Pastor Tom could have become annoyed and changed his phone number. Instead, he chose to be kind and make the children happy, even if it meant giving up some of his own time.

The Bible tells us not to reject people who need our help. This verse doesn't mean that we should give without thinking but that our hearts should be ready to give, help, and care.

DARE Be generous!

DOUBLE DARE

1. When your mom asks you to do a chore, make her day by finding a way of doing double the work she expects. For example, after cleaning your room, clean the bathroom too.

2. Is there a girl who is usually alone at recess or lunchtime? Invite her to play or eat with you and your friends.

PROMISE TO REPEAT

How did it go? What did you learn?

Love Your Friends

BIBLE READING *Leviticus 19:18*

TRUTH

A true friend trusts and loves.

A group of turtles decided to go on a hike one day. They wore their sneakers, put on their caps, and tucked some sandwiches and canned soup in their backpacks for lunch. Halfway into the woods, one of them remembered that he'd forgotten to bring a can opener. All the turtles looked at Henrietta, the youngest turtle, and told her to go back for the can opener.

Henrietta said, "No! You'll eat all the sandwiches while I'm gone!" The other turtles promised not to eat the sandwiches while they waited, and Henrietta went on her way.

The turtles sat and waited. And waited. And waited. For hours. And days. And weeks. Finally, they were so hungry that they decided to eat the sandwiches. As they each took their first bite, Henrietta suddenly jumped out from behind a tree and shouted, "Aha! That's why I didn't want to go!"

Henrietta didn't trust her friends, and she thought only about herself instead of doing what would be good for everyone. But the Bible tells us to love others as much as we love ourselves.

DARE Don't be a Henrietta!

DOUBLE DARE

1. Take a few minutes to think about whether you have any grudges or bad feelings in your heart toward anyone. If you do, how is that affecting your relationship? Ask God to help you forgive and love this person.

2. Memorize today's verse and see if you can remember it whenever you see someone use a can opener.

PROMISE TO REPEAT

How did it go? What did you learn?

Do What's Right

BIBLE READING *1 John 3:7*

TRUTH

God wants you to be righteous.

I once came across a cute video of a little boy flipping through a magazine. He was obviously trying to copy what grown-ups do because he was licking the tips of his fingers on his right hand before turning the magazine pages. But there was one little problem …

Instead of turning the page with the fingers he had just licked, the boy flipped the page with his left hand! It took me a moment to figure out what he was doing, and then I started giggling. He looked like he was doing the right thing, just like an adult, but it actually made no sense at all. He was licking his fingers for nothing.

As Christians, we, too, sometimes think we're doing the right thing because we copy others without taking time to pray or think about our actions and words. But the Bible reminds us not to be led the wrong way; instead, we should concentrate on doing what's right, which makes us righteous in God's eyes.

DARE   Don't be fooled into thinking you're doing right when you're not.

DOUBLE DARE

1. Ask your parents for some examples of ways that Christians may think they're doing what's right when they're actually not. Then pray and ask God to help you not to be deceived but to know what's right in His eyes.

2. When you're hanging out with a friend, act out what the boy in the story was doing and see how long it takes her to notice. Then share today's devo with her.

PROMISE TO REPEAT

How did it go? What did you learn?

HERO LIST

Choose ONE of these heroes to learn about this weekend:

Name	Bible Verses
Esther	Esther 3:1–11; 4:4–17; 5:1–8; 7:1–10; 8:1–11
Stephen	Acts 6–7
Ruth	Ruth 1–4
David	1 Samuel 17
Abigail	1 Samuel 25:1–42
Gideon	Judges 6–7
The Bleeding Woman	Mark 5:25–34
Joseph	Genesis 37; 39–41
The Widow of Zarephath	1 Kings 17:8–24; Luke 4:25–26
Noah	Genesis 6–8
Miriam	Exodus 2:1–10
Daniel	Daniel 6
Mary of Bethany	John 12:1–8
Abraham	Genesis 22:1–18

Your hero for this weekend: _____

QUESTION TIME

1. How did this weekend's hero show courage and faith in God?

2. What happened because of his or her courage and obedience?

3. What did you learn from this hero's life that will help you in your own walk with God?

DOUBLE DARE

Choose at least one of these ways to dig a little deeper into your hero's life this weekend:

1. See if you can find other Bible verses about him or her. Write the reference (or the "address" of the verses) here and also anything new that you learned.

2. Ask your parents or another Christian what they have learned from this hero's life and example.

Tell a friend or your family about your new hero!

What are your thoughts?

God's Arm Around Your Neck

BIBLE READING *Matthew 11:28–30 and Psalm 55:22*

TRUTH

God doesn't ask us to do anything He won't help us with.

One day, when a Sunday school teacher wanted to explain the verses you just read in Matthew, she asked her young students what a yoke was. A little boy put his hand up and correctly answered, "That's what you put around animals' necks when they have to plow a field."

Then the teacher asked what the class thought the Bible means when it talks about the yoke God puts on us. After thinking for a moment, a little girl raised her hand and said, "I think that's when God puts His arms around our necks!"

That's a pretty good way to think about it! Yes, life can be hard sometimes and it's not always easy to obey God or to live according to what the Bible teaches us, but Psalm 55:22 reminds us that God is always there to support us. His instructions in the Bible are there to help us, not hurt us.

DARE Trust God's arm around your neck.

DOUBLE DARE

1. Write down a few things about following Jesus that you find difficult or confusing. Ask God to help you trust that He'll give you strength and wisdom as you choose to obey Him.

2. Pay attention to see if a family member or friend seems down today. Gently put your arm around her (or his) neck and share Psalm 55:22. If you have time beforehand, write the verse on a blank card or piece of paper, decorate it, and have it ready to give.

PROMISE TO REPEAT

How did it go? What did you learn?

The Courage to Do Right

BIBLE READING *1 Chronicles 28:20*

TRUTH

It takes more courage to be right than to be popular.

Many years ago, students from grade school up to university level were given an unusual test. Groups of ten were put into a classroom where, on the board in front of them, there were three lines drawn: one long, one medium, and one short. In each group, nine students were told ahead of time to raise their hands when the professor pointed to the medium line. The other student was told nothing.

The professor asked the students to raise their hands when he pointed to the longest line. When he did, only one student raised his hand, looked around at the others who didn't have their hands up, and then slowly lowered his hand.

This happened three-quarters of the time. It shows us that most people prefer to be popular than to be right.

King David encouraged his son not to be afraid to obey God and do His work. You, too, can be courageous and do what's right even when no one else around you does.

DARE Do the right thing even if you're the only one doing it.

DOUBLE DARE

1. In your journal, write about a time when you wanted to say the truth or do something good but hesitated because you were the only one. Ask God to help you be more courageous next time.

2. Do you have a friend who doesn't have the courage to do what she knows is right? Write today's verse in a nice card and give it to her. Then tell her about today's devo.

PROMISE TO REPEAT

How did it go? What did you learn?

BIBLE READING *Matthew 5:20*

TRUTH

No one can enter heaven without being righteous.

Years ago, researchers asked high school students what they would do in an emergency: Save a stranger or save their dog? Most of them said they would save their dog because they loved their dog, not the stranger. Surprised? Were these students right in answering the way they did? What influenced their decision to want to save their dog instead of the stranger? It was their feelings.

Many people decide what's wrong or right by paying attention to how they feel. They might say, "Well, I feel that it's okay to do this or I feel that it's bad to do that." What they're saying might even seem to make sense. But we can't make up our own morality or rules about what's good and what's bad. That's God's job.

Think of the most moral person you know—someone who is good, fair, honest, generous, and so on. Could you be as good as he or she is, or do you think, *Well, I don't need to be that good, as long as I do my best?*

The Bible says our goodness has to be better than what we feel is good. Of course, only God can help us be that moral, so we need to ask Him to teach and guide us.

DARE   Be more moral than the most moral person you know.

DOUBLE DARE

1. Ask your best friend the same question the high school students were asked. Afterward, talk about what the Bible says about morality, or righteousness.

2. Pray and ask God to help you make decisions according to what His Word says and not your own feelings.

PROMISE TO REPEAT

How did it go? What did you learn?

BIBLE READING *Luke 9:23*

TRUTH

Following Jesus means going where He goes and doing what He says.

In about twenty verses in the New Testament, we see Jesus telling His disciples or others to follow Him. Of course, He didn't mean, "Follow Me to that tree over there," or "Follow Me to the boat and we'll go fishing." Jesus was asking these people to give up whatever they had been doing until then, trust Him, and start living their lives only for Him. And many of them did!

Our world today says it doesn't matter what religion you follow or who you believe in as long as you're pretty good and don't hurt anyone. The world says, "Follow your own mind and whatever you think is right." That's like getting behind a wheelbarrow, pushing it wherever you want to go, and then saying, "I'm following this wheelbarrow!" That's not really following, is it? In the same way, making up your own beliefs is not truly following anything or anyone.

The only way we can make sure we are on the right path, the one that will lead us to eternal life in heaven, is to follow Jesus. That means we trust His wisdom more than our own and let Him guide us each day.

DARE   Start each day with the decision to follow the Lord Jesus.

DOUBLE DARE

1. Read John 12:26. In your journal, write what you think it means to follow Jesus. Then write how you will follow Jesus today.

2. If there are things in your life that keep you from following Jesus, ask God to help you give them up.

PROMISE TO REPEAT

How did it go? What did you learn?

Trusting in the Dark

BIBLE READING *Psalm 91:1–5*

TRUTH

We can trust God even when we can't see Him.

Have you ever thought about how babies don't seem scared of the dark? When it's nighttime, they simply go to sleep, not at all worried about not being able to see anything in the dark. It's as if they somehow understand that they're safe because Mommy and Daddy are nearby.

Baby chicks are a little like that too. When they're afraid or sense danger, they quickly run over to their mother hen and hide under her wings. Even though it's dark there and they can't see anything, they know they're protected by their mother.

When life seems dark and confusing and we can't see any hope or solutions, we can have that kind of faith in God. In Psalm 91, the Bible uses the example of a bird covering her chicks with her wings. God loves us even more than a mother hen, even more than our own mothers. He promises to watch over us even in the worst situations.

DARE Hide under God's "wings."

DOUBLE DARE

1. In your journal, write down three things that frighten or worry you. Then write out a prayer to God asking Him to help you trust Him even when you can't see a solution to your problems.

2. Create a bookmark or card with the first two phrases of Psalm 91:4 and a drawing of a chick hiding under its mother's wing. Give it to a friend who is going through a hard time.

PROMISE TO REPEAT

How did it go? What did you learn?

Finally, brothers and sisters, whatever is true, whatever is noble, whatever is right, whatever is **pure**, whatever is lovely, whatever is admirable—if anything is excellent or praiseworthy—think about such things. Whatever you have learned or received or heard from me, or seen in me—put it into practice. And the God of peace will be with you. (Philippians 4:8–9)

Cross out all the letters above *even* numbers and then write the letters that are left in the spaces below to see what Psalm 119:9 says about being pure.

R	H	E	B	O	W	L	C	H	A	N	Y	M	A	Y
2	3	6	8	7	9	8	1	4	3	5	2	4	9	3
O	U	R	N	E	G	P	A	E	Z	R	S	J	O	N
1	5	2	3	4	7	9	4	9	8	3	1	6	7	5
U	S	T	X	I	A	N	Y	O	R	N	A	T	K	H
2	3	3	2	8	7	6	9	7	4	1	4	5	2	5
E	D	G	P	A	R	T	L	P	H	O	F	W	P	S
1	4	4	5	3	2	5	6	8	9	7	9	4	7	6
F	U	R	B	I	R	T	Y	G	B	B	O	Y	L	I
6	3	1	2	7	2	7	9	4	8	1	8	5	3	9
V	I	M	N	F	G	A	R	C	C	P	O	S	R	D
5	1	8	7	6	3	1	2	3	5	4	5	2	7	9
H	I	V	N	G	O	T	R	O	Y	H	S	O	X	N
8	5	2	9	7	4	7	6	7	3	8	2	1	6	8
T	E	U	C	I	R	W	A	G	O	L	R	E	D	Y
2	2	7	6	8	1	3	4	8	5	2	9	2	9	6

" ___ ___ _ _____ _____ ____ __ ___ ____ __ _____? __ _____ _____ __ ____ ____. "

Purity is another word for *clean*, except it means even more than just clean. When you rinse a plate or wipe crumbs off it, it's clean. But purity means there isn't even a speck of dirt or bacteria in (or on) it.

If you put one drop of clear poison into a glass of water, the water would still look clean, but would you want to take a drink from it? No, because it would not be pure anymore. That little bit of poison would have *contaminated* the water and made it dangerous. Nowadays, depending on where you live, many people prefer to drink filtered water, which means that the water has gone through a system to remove minerals and to make it as pure as possible.

For just about anything you want to clean, you can find the solution somewhere. Magazines, books, and websites can tell you how to get candle wax out of a table-cloth, crayon off a wall, baked-on grease off an oven door, paint off your hands, or spaghetti sauce off your favorite shirt. But what they can't tell you is how to make your heart and mind pure.

Thankfully, we have the Bible to answer that question. The verse in Psalm 119 tells us we can remain pure by living according to God's Word. The verse in Philippians 4 tells us to keep thinking about pure things. That brings peace into our lives.

YOUR TURN

• Write down some examples of *impure* things that we should not spend time thinking about and also *pure* things that are good to think about. We've given a couple of examples to get you started.

Impure Thoughts	Pure Thoughts
things you don't like about someone	*things you're thankful for*
things you're tempted to lie about	*Bible verses you've memorized*
sexy or inappropriate messages or images	*ways you can make your parents happy*
_____	_____
_____	_____
_____	_____
_____	_____

• Ask God to be your spiritual "filter" and to help you keep your mind on things on the second list. Keep adding to these lists (use your journal if you need more space) as you think of other ideas.

What are your thoughts?

BIBLE READING *John 15:12–13*

TRUTH

Real love is willing to make sacrifices.

Dana and I were great friends when we were preteen girls. We went to the same church, and our families enjoyed spending time together. Now Dana is married and lives with her family in San Diego, California, which is about three thousand miles from Montreal, Quebec, so we get to see each other only on Facebook. But we still rejoice about the great things happening in each other's lives.

In September 2013, about ten months after she found out she needed a kidney transplant because of a disease she was suffering from, Dana received a very special gift from her best friend, Melissa, the softball coach at the University of San Diego. Melissa, who is terrified of hospitals and needles, volunteered to donate one of her kidneys to Dana. She had the right blood type and was a perfect match for Dana, so with God's help, she mustered up her courage to give her friend a gift that would save her life.

Melissa was inspired by John 15:12–13, which she wrote out and stuck on a can of kidney beans that she gave to Dana three weeks before the surgery. Even though she didn't have to give up her life, Melissa had to overcome her fears and was willing to give up one of her kidneys.

Dana and Melissa are both healthy and enjoying their friendship now because they trusted God!

DARE   Love someone the way God loves you.

DOUBLE DARE

1. Ask your parents to help you find out if there's someone at your church or school who is going through a difficulty that you might be able to help with. Ask God to show you what to do.

2. Memorize today's verse and share it with a close friend.

PROMISE TO REPEAT

How did it go? What did you learn?

The Chicken with Three Legs

BIBLE READING *Ephesians 5:15–17*

TRUTH

True wisdom is following God's way, not our own.

One day, a man was driving along a country road when he noticed something very strange. Up ahead of him was a chicken walking very quickly, and it had three legs! The surprised man slowed down a little and followed the chicken all the way to a farm. When he got there, he got out of his car and noticed that all the chickens had three legs.

The man found the farmer and asked, "What's up with these chickens?" The farmer answered, "Well, I know how much everyone likes chicken legs, so I found a way to breed a three-legged chicken. I'm going to be rich!" The man asked the farmer how these strange chickens tasted.

"I don't know," the farmer replied. "I haven't been able to catch one yet!"

Of course, this isn't a true story, but it's a good example of how people sometimes think that doing things their own way, instead of the way they should be done, is smart. But the Bible teaches us to be wise and to understand what God's will is. We will always have better results if we obey God!

DARE Live God's way instead of your own.

DOUBLE DARE

1. Have you ever thought you were smarter than your parents or a teacher? Confess your pride to God and ask Him to help you be humble and obedient.

2. Draw a picture of a three-legged chicken and write out Ephesians 5:17 next to it. Put it on your fridge and share today's devo with your family when they ask about the drawing.

PROMISE TO REPEAT

How did it go? What did you learn?

BIBLE READING *Ecclesiastes 5:2 and Ecclesiastes 10:2*

TRUTH

Wisdom can help us speak words that please God.

Have you ever said something and, the second you said it, wish you hadn't? Our careless words can be more damaging than punches and kicks. For example:

- Talking back to your dad shows you don't respect him as you should.

- Telling others a secret that a friend shared with you means she can't trust you.

- Chattering about silly things while your sister is doing her homework says you don't care about wasting her time.

- Telling your teacher you lost your assignment when you actually forgot to complete it is being dishonest.

Today's Bible verses remind us to be careful about the words that come out of our mouths. God hears everything we say and He will judge us for the way we speak if it is hurtful, disrespectful, foolish, or dishonest.

Here's a good way to check your words to make sure they would please God. Remember the word *THINK* and, before you speak, THINK about whether what you're going to say is **true** (T), **honest** (H), **inspiring** (I), **necessary** (N), or **kind** (K). If it is none of those, you might want to find something else to say!

DARE T-H-I-N-K, don't sink!

DOUBLE DARE

1. Make a poster that says "Before you speak, THINK," with the letters of the word *THINK* going down the left side of the poster. Next to each letter, write "Is it" and the matching word. (For example, "Is it TRUE?") Put the poster somewhere you'll see it often.

2. Every morning before you start your day, ask God to help you not be too quick to speak.

PROMISE TO REPEAT

How did it go? What did you learn?

Watch What You Say!

BIBLE READING Ephesians 5:4

TRUTH

Our words show what's in our hearts.

Before we start today's devo, I want you to do a few things and then answer a question. Ready?

1. Say "milk" (out loud).
2. Say "milk milk milk" (out loud).
3. Spell the word *milk* (out loud).
4. What do cows drink?

Did you say "milk" again? ☺ I've had this trick played on me a few times, and I always fall for it!

This is a fun little prank, but it also teaches us an important lesson. We can be easily influenced by the things we see and hear around us. If we watch TV shows that make sin look innocent and fun, we may forget what the Bible teaches us about sin. If we listen to music with bad words in the lyrics, we may start using those words without realizing it. If we hang around people who are rude or disrespectful, we may start behaving like them.

Today's Bible verse reminds us that bad words, dirty jokes, and foolish conversations are out of place for Christians. A good way to make sure the things you say are appropriate is to ask yourself, "Would Jesus tell this joke, sing this song, or talk to His Father that way?"

DARE Make sure your words honor God.

DOUBLE DARE

1. Try the "milk" joke on your family members and friends. Afterward, tell them what you learned in today's devo.

2. Is there anything in your life that influences your words in a bad way (for example, a CD or TV show)? Try replacing it with something that honors God.

PROMISE TO REPEAT

How did it go? What did you learn?

BIBLE READING *Psalm 65:1–3; 9–11*

TRUTH

God is the gardener of our hearts.

My friend Carol knows a lot about gardening (and knitting and cooking and lots of other creative things!). One day she was talking about how she has to pull out the same weeds in her garden every year. No matter how well she pulls them out one summer, they come back the following summer.

Then she said, "I wonder if God says that when He weeds my heart."

What a great way to picture the work God does in our hearts when we follow Him. When we confess our sins to Jesus and ask Him to be our Savior, He forgives us and makes our hearts clean—just like Carol gets rid of weeds in her garden to make room for flowers or vegetables. But then our hearts seem to start getting messy again when we disobey God and do wrong things.

The good news is that we have a loving Gardener who will help us with those weeds. But wouldn't it be much better if we loved God so much that we did our best to keep the weeds out in the first place?

DARE Don't let your heart get full of "weeds."

DOUBLE DARE

1. Did you know that the longer you leave weeds in a garden, the harder they are to pull out? Try to confess sins to God right away so that your heart will remain pure for Him.

2. Confessing sin isn't just saying sorry because you have to; it's also believing that what you did is wrong. How does knowing that change the way you will pray today?

PROMISE TO REPEAT

How did it go? What did you learn?

Finally, brothers and sisters, whatever is true, whatever is noble, whatever is right, whatever is pure, whatever is **lovely**, whatever is admirable—if anything is excellent or praiseworthy—think about such things. Whatever you have learned or received or heard from me, or seen in me—put it into practice. And the God of peace will be with you. (Philippians 4:8–9)

A little girl was out for a walk with her dad one evening, and they stopped to look up at the stars in the sky. After staring awhile with wide eyes, the little girl said with excitement, "Oh, Daddy! If the *wrong* side of heaven is this beautiful, I wonder how beautiful the *right* side is!"

This little girl's comment sounds cute and childish, but if you think about it, it's also very wise. In her innocence, she saw earth and the sky above as the "wrong" side of heaven because she understood that heaven, where we will spend eternity with God, is the best place to be. Not only that, but she appreciated the beauty of the sky and stars that God has created. Some people never take time to look around them and enjoy all the magnificent blessings God has given us because they're too busy on their computers, watching TV, and even wasting time doing nothing. And those people usually don't have a lot of joy or peace.

Remember Helen Keller? She once said, "Keep your face to the sunshine and you cannot see the shadow. It's what sunflowers do." When you face the sun, can you see your shadow behind you? No, you see it only when you turn away from the sun and look behind you. In the same way, when we keep our eyes and thoughts on God, on His creation, on His love for us, and on all the other lovely things He brings into our lives, we won't be bothered by the "shadows" of negative and bad things.

How we feel and act depends on our attitude (where we look) more than it does on our circumstances (what we're going through).

YOUR TURN

- What are some things most people in the world think are "lovely"? We've given a few examples:

    - trendy clothes

    - perfectly white and straight teeth

    - a nicely decorated house

    - _____

    - _____

    - _____

    - _____

- What kinds of things do you think the Bible means when it tells us to think about whatever is lovely?

    - a forgiving heart
    - spending time with someone who's sick
    - noticing and thanking God for blessings
    - _____
    - _____
    - _____
    - _____
    - _____

- Look at both your lists and put a little star next to the things you spend a lot of time thinking about. Be honest! If you have more stars in the first list, ask God to help you turn your mind toward things that are *truly* lovely and not just what fits the world's description of beautiful or attractive.

DOUBLE DARE

If your friends spend most of their time shopping, looking at pictures of celebrities, or fixing their hair and makeup, try to get them to start thinking more about things that are really lovely—things that have a deeper beauty and can bring joy and peace into their lives.

What are your thoughts?

Don't Answer the Door!

BIBLE READING   *1 Corinthians 10:13*

TRUTH

Jesus can help you say no to sin.

A little girl was once asked what she did when she felt tempted to sin. I love her answer:

"When Satan knocks on the door of my heart, I send Jesus to answer the door. That way, when Satan sees Jesus, he says, 'Oops, I must have the wrong house!'"

Of course, that's not exactly how it works, but this young girl understood very well that we don't have to give in to temptation. Sometimes we open the door of our heart just a little and say, "Go away, Devil!" That does not work because the Devil isn't afraid of us. He just pushes the door open wider and starts to come in, and then it becomes harder to kick him out. The longer we wait to ask for God's help when we're tempted, the easier it is to give in and sin.

The best thing to do when we feel tempted is to pray right away. Jesus promised that He will always give us a way out if we ask Him for help.

DARE   When temptation knocks, don't answer the door.

DOUBLE DARE

1. In your journal, write about five sins that you are often tempted by. Write out a prayer to God asking for His help to say no to each one.

2. Tie a ribbon or bandana around your bedroom doorknob. Memorize today's verse and repeat the verse to yourself whenever you see the ribbon.

PROMISE TO REPEAT

How did it go? What did you learn?

Are You a Carrot or a Kiwi?

BIBLE READING *1 Peter 1:14–16*

TRUTH

Holiness means being a Christian on the inside—not just the outside.

What color is the outside of a kiwi? _____

What color is the inside? _____

What does the outside of a kiwi feel like? _____

What about the inside? _____

Do the outside and inside of a kiwi taste the same? _____

Imagine someone says she is a Christian and loves Jesus. Now imagine that she is always rude to her parents, she doesn't pay attention in church, and she cheats on her math test. Would you say that who she is on the inside matches what she tries to look like on the outside?

What color is the outside of a carrot? _____

What color is the inside? _____

Do the outside and inside of a carrot feel the same? _____

Taste the same? _____

God wants our holiness to be like a carrot and not like a kiwi. We need to be holy (obeying God and becoming more like Him) inside and out!

DARE Don't just say you follow Jesus. Do it!

DOUBLE DARE

1. Ask God to show you if you're the same on the inside and outside. Then ask Him to help you be holy in your heart as well as in your words and actions.

2. In your journal, write some things you need to change in your life to become more holy. Try to work on at least one of those changes today.

PROMISE TO REPEAT

How did it go? What did you learn?

Copper Nails

BIBLE READING *1 Peter 2:1*

TRUTH

When we love God, we want to do what's right.

After hearing a preacher talk about the importance of confessing our sins and making things right with people we have wronged, a young Christian man felt troubled. He had been telling his boss about Jesus, but his boss wasn't interested. At the same time, the young man had been stealing copper nails from his boss to use on a boat he was building. He knew that he was a thief and had to confess to his boss, but he was worried that his Christian testimony would be ruined. His boss would know he was a hypocrite for saying he was a Christian and then stealing. But the younger man didn't want to also lie.

Finally, he got the courage to confess what he had done. His boss surprised him by saying, "If Christianity can make you humble enough to admit what you did wrong, then maybe it's something I should pay attention to!"

By being honest about his sin, the young man showed what being a Christian really means. Pretending we're perfect or better than others won't attract people to Jesus. But when we're humble and let people see how God changes us, that's a good testimony!

DARE Don't pretend to be something you're not.

DOUBLE DARE

1. Have you lied to someone or covered up a sin lately? Ask God to give you the courage to admit what you did wrong and ask for forgiveness.

2. Read Matthew 23:25–26. In your journal, write what you think these verses mean.

PROMISE TO REPEAT

How did it go? What did you learn?

BIBLE READING *1 John 1:9*

TRUTH

When you confess your sins to God, He takes them away.

Where I live, we collect our trash from all around the house into one or two large plastic bags and place them outside our back gate every Monday and Thursday evening. A collection truck drives down the back lane, picks up the garbage, and takes it away. If you live in the country or a small town, you may get rid of trash a bit differently.

There's one thing we probably all do the same: Wherever we put our trash bags (or cans) for pickup, we leave them there. Can you imagine saving some garbage in a bin just in case you needed it later? Or how about running after the garbage truck and asking for your trash back? No way!

In a sense, that's how it is with sin. We need to search through our hearts for wrong that we've done and take that "trash" to God (confess our sin) so that He can take it away (forgive us). If we hang on to our sin, it'll just stink up our lives.

DARE Take out the "trash" in your life!

DOUBLE DARE

1. Are there any sins you haven't admitted to God yet? Take time today to think about it and talk to Him. Ask Him to forgive you and help you to obey Him in the future.

2. Memorize today's verse. Tape a piece of paper that says "1 John 1:9" somewhere on your garbage can so you'll remember the verse often.

PROMISE TO REPEAT

How did it go? What did you learn?

BIBLE READING *1 Corinthians 10:31*

TRUTH

No matter what we do, God should get the applause.

It's tough for people to stay humble in a world with so many talent competitions, beauty pageants, sports competitions, and awards shows. Even Christian writers, singers, and speakers usually like to be recognized or win awards for their talents. It can be tempting to feel good about ourselves when we know people admire us.

But there are many reminders in the Bible that our talents, beauty, or intelligence are things that God gives us. We could not have created them on our own. We can only develop and use those gifts. For example, it would be silly for a beautiful bird to feel proud, because God gave it its lovely feathers. The bird didn't make them! And a flower shouldn't feel good when we admire it, because God created its petals, not the flower itself.

The famous German composer Johann Sebastian Bach, who was born in 1685, once said that the goal of all music should be to bring glory to God and to comfort people's souls. He didn't want his music to make people admire him but, instead, to worship God.

We, too, should have Bach's attitude: That whatever we do should bring praise to God, not ourselves.

DARE Do everything for God's glory.

DOUBLE DARE

1. What are some things you do with the hope of getting people's attention or making them admire you? Confess this to God and ask Him to help you live your life so others will look at Him instead.

2. Does the music you listen to glorify God (as Bach said it should)? Try to find music that does.

PROMISE TO REPEAT

How did it go? What did you learn?

Whatever Is
ADMIRABLE

Finally, brothers and sisters, whatever is true, whatever is noble, whatever is right, whatever is pure, whatever is lovely, whatever is **admirable**—if anything is **excellent** or praiseworthy—think about such things. Whatever you have learned or received or heard from me, or seen in me—put it into practice. And the God of peace will be with you. (Philippians 4:8–9)

There's a website called Pinterest that I like to go to when I have free time. It allows people to find photos of things they like and make their own "pinboards," where they can collect and share their favorite pictures. My pinboards are mostly about crafts, gift ideas, art, decorating, healthy snacks, nature, cute animals, and so on.

Before I worked on this devo, I did a search on Pinterest using the word *admirable*. I wanted to see what kinds of things people admire. The results were interesting! Here are some examples of what I found:

a bracelet	a designer dress	patio furniture
a pillow	a vintage action figure	a few quotes
a hotel	a couple of actors/actresses	a purse

A few people had a picture of Philippians 4:8 designed as a pretty poster or sign, but most people had pictures of "stuff," while others had photos of famous people they admire.

To see what the dictionary definition of *admirable* is, cross out every second letter in the puzzle below and write the remaining letters on the blank lines.

DJEKSQEWRXVZIPNRG HRLEWSCPVESCNTK OYRK
ALPKPLRVOWVRAZLY

_____ _____ __ _____

Many people (and things!) are admired even though they haven't done anything to deserve it. The Bible tells us to focus our thoughts on things that are truly admirable—not on things that are just popular, trendy, or cool.

In the list below, check off the scenarios you think deserve respect or approval:

❑ A girl in your class who dresses like an older teenager most of the time gets a lot of attention from the boys.

❑ When your older brother crashes his bike into your dad's car, he admits what he did as soon as your dad gets home and offers to pay for the repairs out of his allowance.

❑ In gym class, your best friend is one of the captains who has to choose kids to play on her team. The first person she picks is a shy, awkward girl who usually gets picked last.

❑ One of the worship leaders at your church always talks about what a great voice he has.

❑ Your mom comes home from work feeling exhausted. When she finds out your neighbor broke her arm that morning, she cooks extra for supper and takes some next door before your family eats.

When you think about people or actions that are admirable, doesn't it make you want to do the same? The more our thoughts are on things that please and honor God, the more we will also live in a way that pleases and honors Him.

YOUR TURN

• Here's an easy way to remember the six "thinks" (plus the word *excellent* in the verse at the top of this devotion) you've learned about in the last several weeks. Your goal is to replace bad thoughts with thoughts that are true, noble, right, pure, lovely, admirable, and excellent. Another word for *replace* could be *replant*—such as when you *replant* your garden with new flowers. The letters are not in the same order as the words are in the verses, but you'll still remember the key words:

R – right
E – excellent
P – pure
L – lovely
A – admirable
N – noble
T – true

• Make a bookmark or sign that says "REPLANT" and decorate it. Add "Philippians 4:8" in small letters so you'll remember where to find the verse in the Bible. Use the bookmark in your planner so you'll see it often and be reminded to keep your thoughts right, excellent, pure … Well, you know the rest by now!

What are your thoughts?

Useless!

- -

BIBLE READING *1 Samuel 12:20–22*

TRUTH

Anything we worship instead of God is useless.

There are a lot of useful things in the world, such as clocks, bicycles, hairbrushes, and forks. But how useful do you think these things would be?

Inflatable dartboards
Lace umbrellas
Waterproof teabags
Fireproof matches
Braille driving instruction books
Screen doors for submarines

Those are all silly ideas, of course, but sometimes we're not very wise in the way we live our Christian lives. We may get preoccupied with our activities, friends, TV shows, money, and other things that take our attention away from God. None of those things can fill up our hearts or help us the way God does, so they become useless when we don't stay close to God.

In today's reading, the prophet Samuel reminds us to serve the Lord with all our hearts. Let's do it!

DARE Make God No. 1 in your life.

DOUBLE DARE

1. Share today's devo with a friend, and then see if the two of you can come up with some more useless inventions like the ones listed above.

2. Ask God to show you if there are things in your life that you "worship" more than Him. Make a plan for putting those things aside and focusing more on Jesus.

PROMISE TO REPEAT

How did it go? What did you learn?

He Created It

BIBLE READING   *Isaiah 45:18*

TRUTH

God is the awesome designer behind all of creation.

Let's try something. Before you continue this devo, go and get another book (with at least thirty pages). Turn to page 22. In your journal, write the first word on the page. Then write every fifth word on that page until you have fifteen to twenty words. When you're done, read what you've written.

Here's what I came up with when I grabbed *The Tale of Peter Rabbit* from my shelf: **He a locked room rabbit old and door-step to wood way she pea she only him then**.

Well, that doesn't make sense! Next I tried it with *A Little Princess*: **Always done my papa French older being she in but felt her very and sure whatever felt be her.** Huh?

These two sentences are pure nonsense because they're just random words put next to each other with no purpose or meaning. Some people believe the earth and the universe around us are the result of an accident or "big bang." The possibility of an accident resulting in the perfectly detailed and awesome world we live in is zero. We would have a better chance of dumping a bag of Scrabble letters on the ground and finding a sentence that makes sense!

DARE   Tell someone about our great Creator!

DOUBLE DARE

1. Read Genesis 1 (and 2 if you have time).
2. Try the book activity with your friends and see what sentences they come up with. Then tell them about how God created the earth.

PROMISE TO REPEAT

How did it go? What did you learn?

BIBLE READING *Psalm 27:4*

TRUTH

The heart always finds what it looks for.

Can you think of two types of birds that fly over deserts? One is the hummingbird and another is the vulture. They're both birds, but do you know how they're different?

Vultures circle around and around looking for rotting meat. They love to find dead animals and eat what's left of them. (Gross, I know!) But hummingbirds don't like rotting meat. Instead, they look for beautiful flowers on desert plants so they can suck the sugar out of them.

You could say that vultures feed on what was past, while hummingbirds look for new life. Both these birds find what they're looking for. So do humans.

Some people always think about days and years that have passed and don't experience the good things happening in their lives today or the hope that God gives us for the future. But Christians should be more like King David, who told God that what he wanted more than anything was to be with Him and enjoy His beauty forever.

When our hearts seek God, we always find Him!

DARE   Make sure you're looking for the right thing.

DOUBLE DARE

1. Being as honest as you can, think of the five things you want or hope for more than anything and write them in your journal. If God's not at the top of that list, ask Him to help you want to want Him. (I've done it. It works!)

2. Quiz your family about the two desert birds, and then tell them what you learned today.

PROMISE TO REPEAT

How did it go? What did you learn?

It's How You Look at It

BIBLE READING *Hebrews 12:2*

TRUTH

God's creation is always beautiful—even when we don't see it.

Riding in a cab on my way home from the airport one evening, I felt tired and had a lot on my mind. It was a rainy day in May and was dull outside, but, with my head tipped back, I noticed the trees on the side of the street. The newly budding branches were wet and dark against the pale gray sky and were oddly beautiful. The tiny light green buds were almost shiny, and I couldn't stop staring at the sky as we drove along.

Down at street level, all I could see was cement sidewalks littered with garbage, cars rumbling down the road, cluttered balconies, and chained-up bicycles. It was a bit depressing. But up above … now that was a whole other thing! When I looked up at God's creation instead of down below at the mess created by humans, I couldn't help but smile and relax.

This is just how it is in our spiritual lives. We're not always going to have sunny, happy days with everything going right. But, just as a cloudy sky doesn't make flowers and trees disappear, difficulties in our lives don't cancel out the blessings we receive from God. We just have to change what we're looking at!

DARE Focus on your blessings instead of on your troubles.

DOUBLE DARE

1. What are three things bugging you right now? Think of three things God has blessed you with and take time to praise Him for them.

2. Whenever you catch yourself complaining, think of one positive thing to say.

PROMISE TO REPEAT

How did it go? What did you learn?

The Best Name

BIBLE READING *Psalm 8 and Philippians 2:9–11*

TRUTH

God's name deserves honor more than any other name.

Can you unscramble these common girls' and boys' names?

Nifjeren	Antjohan	Limey
Shipoe	Wander	Sonila
Mange	Ashjou	Masoth

Where I live, most of the people I know came to Canada from other countries (or their parents did), so I hear a lot of really neat but uncommon names. For example, I have friends and relatives with names such as Delina, Gerthsie, and Koushika (girls), and Vehazoun, Shubroto, and Ferrere (boys).

Sometimes a person's name can influence how she's treated. For example, studies show that people with common, easy-to-pronounce names sometimes get picked for a job more quickly than someone with an unusual, difficult-to-pronounce name. When someone has the same name as a famous person, we might think she's cool, just because of her name. Some people are so famous that they're known only by their first names, like Beyoncé, Adele, Pink, and Shakira. There's an older actress known by her first name. Know what it is? Ann-Margret! (No, really. It's true.)

The Bible says no one on earth, no matter how famous his or her name is, deserves the honor and praise that God does. As Christians, our favorite name (and person) should be Jesus.

DARE Honor God's name.

DOUBLE DARE

1. Are you shy to talk about God or say the name of Jesus around your friends? Pray that God will give you courage to honor His name in front of others.

2. In your journal, write the name JESUS in large bubble letters. Fill each letter with words that tell why you love Jesus.

PROMISE TO REPEAT

How did it go? What did you learn?

HERO LIST

Choose ONE of these heroes to learn about this weekend:

Name	Bible Verses
Esther	Esther 3:1–11; 4:4–17; 5:1–8; 7:1–10; 8:1–11
Stephen	Acts 6–7
Ruth	Ruth 1–4
David	1 Samuel 17
Abigail	1 Samuel 25:1–42
Gideon	Judges 6–7
The Bleeding Woman	Mark 5:25–34
Joseph	Genesis 37; 39–41
The Widow of Zarephath	1 Kings 17:8–24; Luke 4:25–26
Noah	Genesis 6–8
Miriam	Exodus 2:1–10
Daniel	Daniel 6
Mary of Bethany	John 12:1–8
Abraham	Genesis 22:1–18

Your hero for this weekend: _____

QUESTION TIME

1. How did this weekend's hero show courage and faith in God?

2. What happened because of his or her courage and obedience?

3. What did you learn from this hero's life that will help you in your own walk with God?

DOUBLE DARE

Choose at least one of these ways to dig a little deeper into your hero's life this weekend:

1. See if you can find other Bible verses about him or her. Write the reference (or the "address" of the verses) here and also anything new that you learned.

2. Ask your parents or another Christian what they have learned from this hero's life and example.

Tell a friend or your family about your new hero!

The Cleaning Lady's Name

BIBLE READING *Zephaniah 2:3*

TRUTH

Followers of Jesus must be humble.

One day, a college student went to class and discovered that the professor had prepared a pop quiz. The student wasn't too worried because she always paid close attention in class and did well on her assignments. She answered all the questions on the quiz easily until she got to the last one. The question was:

What is the first name of the woman who cleans the school?

The student thought this must be a joke. She had seen the cleaning lady many times and knew what she looked like, but why would she know her name? So she left the last question blank and handed in her quiz. At the end of class, another student asked if that question would count toward the quiz grade. "Absolutely," said the professor. "In your future jobs, you will meet many people. All of them are important and deserve your attention, even if you only smile and say hello."

The student never forgot that lesson. And she later learned the cleaning lady's name: Dorothy.

Being humble means not thinking you're too important to give others your time and care.

DARE Bless someone with your humility.

DOUBLE DARE

1. Do you know the name of the person who cleans your school (or church)? Try to find out, and the next time you see him or her, smile and say, "Hello!" Remember to pray for this special person too.

2. In your journal, write what you think it means to "seek the Lord," "seek righteousness," and "seek humility." Ask for help if you get stuck.

PROMISE TO REPEAT

How did it go? What did you learn?

Your Offering to God

BIBLE READING *Romans 6:13*

TRUTH

The best thing you can give to God is yourself.

In the list below, circle the things that can be used for good *and* for bad.

a knife	wind	money	fire
hands	paper	mud	water

Actually, *all* of those things can be used for something good or for something bad. For example, fire can help you roast yummy marshmallows, or it can burn a house down. Money can be used to help a family in need, or it can make someone greedy. Mud can cool off a pig, or it can stain your clothes.

Did you know that *you* can also have either a good purpose or a bad purpose? The choice is yours. The Bible warns us not to use our bodies, brains, or any part of us to do evil or to harm others. Instead, we should be willing to use everything God has given us to honor and serve Him. You can use your hands to hit your little brother or to give him a high-five. You can use your voice to lie to your parents or to thank them. You can use your eyes to watch bad things on TV or to read your Bible. It's up to you!

DARE Offer yourself completely to God.

DOUBLE DARE

1. Write at least three more examples of ways you can use parts of yourself either for bad or for good.

2. If you haven't been cheerfully obeying God, ask Him to change your heart and to help you *want* to serve and follow Him.

PROMISE TO REPEAT

How did it go? What did you learn?

Be an Encourager

BIBLE READING *Romans 14:19*

TRUTH

Christians should find ways to encourage others.

There once was an elderly lady in Oakland, California, whose husband had died; she was all alone. She couldn't do very much, but she really wanted to serve the Lord. She prayed about it for a while, wondering what she could do.

Finally, she realized she could cheer people up by playing the piano for them, so she put a small advertisement in her local newspaper offering to play hymns (Christian songs) over the phone for anyone who was sick and feeling down, and she would do this for free. She added her phone number at the bottom and waited to see what would happen.

Soon, people started to call her. She always asked them what hymn they would like to hear, and then she'd play the song for them. Some of them would also share their troubles with her and she would try to help. In the next few months that followed, she encouraged hundreds of people!

This lady is a good example of what today's Bible verse teaches. You, too, can help others and encourage them if you make the effort.

DARE Build someone up today.

DOUBLE DARE

1. What is a special talent you have? In your journal, write out a plan for how you will use it to bring joy or comfort to others. Ask your parents for their advice too.

2. Share today's devo with a friend and encourage her to find a special way to serve God too.

PROMISE TO REPEAT

How did it go? What did you learn?

Whine, Whine, Whine

BIBLE READING *Philippians 2:14–15*

TRUTH

God is pleased when we don't complain.

When I was a young girl, I heard this joke that still makes me chuckle:

One day, a young man decided to become a monk, so he joined a monastery and took a vow of silence. After ten years of not speaking, the head monk asked him, "Do you have anything to say?" The younger man answered, "Food bad."

Ten years later, he was allowed to speak again, and he simply said, "Bed hard."

Another ten years passed, and again the head monk asked him if he wanted to say anything. The answer was, "I quit." When he heard this, the head monk said, "I'm not surprised. Ever since you got here, you've done nothing but complain!"

Although the younger monk said only four words in his first twenty years at the monastery, it's true that he only complained instead of saying something positive. We all know people like that, right? No matter what's happening—even in good situations—they always find things to complain about. If we're honest with ourselves, we have to admit that sometimes we're like that too.

The Bible warns us not to have complaining spirits. Instead, we should be a good example to others.

DARE Don't be a whiner!

DOUBLE DARE

1. Think back on the past day and, in your journal, write down all the things you can remember complaining about. Ask God to forgive you for each complaint.

2. Whenever you feel like complaining, try to pause and think of something positive first. You'll get better at this with practice!

PROMISE TO REPEAT

How did it go? What did you learn?

BIBLE READING   *Mark 12:41–44*

TRUTH

How you give is more important than what you give.

We don't know the name of the woman in today's Bible story. It's possible that the disciple who wrote it, Mark, never learned her name. And yet this woman's example has been passed on to us over two thousand years later!

Anyone sitting in the temple near Jesus that day, watching as people gave their offerings, would probably have admired those who brought in large bags of shiny coins. Those watching might have thought, *Wow! Look how generous he is. He gave so much. He must really love God.* But they might not have felt the same way when they saw a poor lady come in and drop two small coins into the offering box. They might have secretly made fun of her or judged her for giving so little.

But Jesus knew how much it cost this woman to give those coins, considering she had so little to start with. Her sacrifice was great because she was left with nothing. Jesus knew that she really loved the Lord because she was willing to give all she had.

DARE   Give from your heart.

DOUBLE DARE

1. Don't help others just when you have nothing else to do. This week, give up at least two activities you enjoy and offer your time to someone in your family who could use an extra hand.

2. Keep two pennies in your pocket for the rest of this week so that you'll remember this devo. Each time you reach in your pocket and feel them, ask God to help you be more generous.

PROMISE TO REPEAT

How did it go? What did you learn?

More Than We Can Imagine

Gloriana's mother was a hero. A few weeks after the doctors told her she had stage-four breast cancer (that means the cancer has spread to other parts of the body and the patient doesn't have much hope of getting better), she found out that she was also going to have a baby. She made the tough decision to continue with her pregnancy even though she knew she would not be able to receive any chemotherapy treatments (to fight the cancer) until the baby was born. The doctors warned her that she had only a few years to live, but she ignored them. She focused instead on praying every day that she would live to see her baby girl (Gloriana) become a young woman.

Growing up, Gloriana never heard her mother complain about her pain, which was quite terrible. Her mom worked hard at cleaning, cooking, gardening, and doing laundry, and she also homeschooled her five rowdy little children. She taught them about Jesus and His love through her actions. Gloriana said, "I grew up in a family where God was the center of our lives."

After some time, her mom's breast cancer spread even more, and she also got bone cancer. Never complaining, she continued to stay busy as if nothing had changed. But when Gloriana was ten years old, things definitely changed. Her mom now had a disease in her liver too. The end had come. The night before she died, the family sat together in the living room and prayed. Gloriana asked God to rescue her mother, but she knew in her heart that it was time for her mom to go. She had suffered for thirteen years (much longer than the doctors had said she would live), and now God was going to take His faithful servant to heaven. Gloriana cried, but in her heart, she let go of her mom and gave her to God. She also prayed a very courageous prayer:

> "Lord, if only one person comes to know Jesus through You taking away Mommy, then all of this will be worth it. I know we experienced this pain for a reason."

Later that night, Gloriana's mother died, but her soul went up to be with Jesus in heaven.

One year later, Gloriana's aunt called and told her family an extraordinary story. She had told a little girl at vacation Bible school about Gloriana's mom and her battle with cancer. A few minutes later, the little girl asked Jesus to be her Savior. That girl went and told her friend, and her friend accepted Jesus as her Savior too! Gloriana didn't realize it right away, but God had answered the prayer she said as her mother was dying.

"I never even learned the name of that little girl or how old she was," said Gloriana. "All I know is that her story changed my life. God has a purpose and reason for everything, and we have no idea of the awesome plan He has."

YOUR TURN

- List all the examples you can find in this story of ways people trusted and obeyed God.

_____

_____

- How do you think you would have felt or acted if you were in Gloriana's situation?

_____

_____

- Read Ephesians 3:20–21. How does Gloriana's story help you understand these verses?

_____

_____

- In your journal, write down all the ways you would change your life if you had the power to. Then take time to pray and ask God to help you trust that _His_ plans for your life are even greater than yours. But remember: You can only receive these blessings from God if you trust Him instead of doing things your own way.

What are your thoughts?

Keep Your Saw Sharp!

BIBLE READING *Mark 1:32–35*

TRUTH

Without lots of prayer time, we won't be "sharp" Christians.

There was only one person in the world who could have said, "I don't need to pray," but this person got up very early each morning to spend time with His heavenly Father. I'm talking about Jesus, of course. He could have said, "I'm God. I'm strong. I'm wise. I don't need prayer." But Jesus knew how important it was to connect with God and to focus His mind on God's plan for Him each day.

If Jesus spent time in prayer, don't you think it's even more important for us to make prayer a regular part of our daily schedules? We may think, *I don't have time to pray!* But we need to make time. Here's why:

Praying does for us what sharpening a saw does for someone cutting wood. Only a foolish person would use a saw for hours and hours without sharpening it, because the longer you use a saw, the duller it gets and the less it works. A wise person knows that it's better to stop and sharpen the saw and then continue. The time spent sharpening the saw is gained back by being able to cut the wood faster!

Taking time for prayer makes the rest of our day go better.

DARE Don't skip your prayer time.

DOUBLE DARE

1. Write down five ways people prepare to accomplish different tasks (for example, chop vegetables to make stew). How do you prepare yourself spiritually? Take time to pray about this today.

2. Whenever you spend time in prayer (more than five minutes!), write in your journal about how that helped you.

PROMISE TO REPEAT

How did it go? What did you learn?

Are You Listening?

BIBLE READING *Proverbs 16:20*

TRUTH

God blesses those who truly listen to Him.

Have you ever had a friend ask you a question or ask for some advice, but, after you responded, she went and asked someone else the same thing? Or maybe she listened to you and then asked, "Are you sure?" I don't know about you, but I find that annoying because it shows that the person who asked me the question doesn't really trust me. And it makes me wonder why he or she asked me in the first place.

I know people who go to the doctor and are given special instructions (for example, lose ten pounds, take this medicine, stop eating salt, and so on), but they don't really like what the doctor said so they discuss the problem with friends instead. And sometimes their friends will say, "Oh, you don't need to do that. Just do what I did (for example, skip breakfast every day or take this other medicine) and you'll be fine."

The problem is that sometimes those friends give advice that's not only wrong but even dangerous!

In your Christian life, be careful that you don't take someone's advice just because you like it better than what the Bible says. Instead, listen carefully to God and trust Him.

DARE Take God's advice!

DOUBLE DARE

1. Write about a time when someone told you to do something that sounded better than what you learned from your parents or the Bible. Whom did you listen to? Pray for a heart that always listens to God.

2. Memorize today's Bible verse.

PROMISE TO REPEAT

How did it go? What did you learn?

Knowing Isn't Enough

BIBLE READING *James 1:22–25*

TRUTH

Reading the Bible is useless if you don't let it change your life.

Imagine a warm, fresh loaf of bread sitting on the counter in a bakery. A hungry customer walks in, sees the bread, and thinks, *Oh, that looks good.* She looks at the bread for a while and reads the little card that explains what's in the bread. If she goes home without buying the bread, does it do her any good? No, because she only knows about it.

What if the customer buys the bread, smells it, and then takes it home and leaves it on her kitchen table? Now is she getting anything out of it? Not much. The nice smell might make her happy for a little while, but it won't satisfy her hunger.

What does this lady have to do to really enjoy the bread? She has to eat it! That will take away her hunger and satisfy her.

The Bible is spiritual food for our souls. If we only look at it sometimes, it won't help us at all. If we read it but don't do what it says, nothing much changes. But when we study it eagerly and obey it, then our lives begin to change and our souls are satisfied.

DARE Don't just read the Bible. Live it!

DOUBLE DARE

1. In your journal, write about what has changed in your life since you started doing daily devos. If there isn't much change, ask God to help you live out what you learn in the Bible.

2. Make a bookmark with the words of James 1:22. Use it in your Bible as a reminder.

PROMISE TO REPEAT

How did it go? What did you learn?

Just the Core?

BIBLE READING *Leviticus 27:30 and Luke 12:15*

TRUTH

God deserves more than our leftovers.

Once upon a time there was a man who had nothing. God gave the man ten apples and told him that three apples were for him to eat, three were for him to trade for shelter, three were for him to trade for clothes, and the last apple was for him to give back to God as a way of saying thanks for the other nine.

So the man ate the first three apples, traded the next three for shelter, and then traded the next three for clothes. Then he looked at the last apple, which seemed so much bigger and shinier and juicier than the others. He thought, *God has all the apples in the world!* So he ate the tenth apple ... and then He gave the core to God.

You might think, *I would never do that!* Sadly, most people don't think of God first. We want to spend our money—and our time—on ourselves, and sometimes there's nothing left for God.

The Bible teaches us to give to God first, with a grateful heart. We can trust that He will give us everything else we need.

DARE Be generous when you're giving to God.

DOUBLE DARE

1. If you get an allowance, ask your parents to help you figure out how much you should save for God before you spend it. Put that amount in an envelope to put in the offering at church on Sunday.

2. Write a list of things that God has generously given to you. Now think of ways you can use your "wealth" to be a blessing to others. And then do it!

PROMISE TO REPEAT

How did it go? What did you learn?

Puffed-Up Pride

BIBLE READING *Luke 18:9–14*

TRUTH

God won't honor us when we honor ourselves.

Aren't balloons fun? They make great decorations at birthday parties, they're fun to toss when you fill them with water, and, if you know how to twist the long, skinny ones, you can make all kinds of neat animals and objects. No matter what size or shape balloons are, they all have something in common: They're stretchy and pliable (that means you can squish them around in your hands) when they're flat, and they're firm and unpliable when they're full of air.

In the story Jesus told in today's reading, we see a good example of someone with a soft heart and someone with a hard heart. The Pharisee was proud of being religious on the outside, and the only thing his prayer did was puff himself up. Read his prayer again (verses 11 and 12). Doesn't it sound like he's worshipping himself instead of God? His heart was so full of himself that there was no more room for God!

But the tax collector, the kind of man most people hated and judged as being dishonest, prayed very differently. He didn't puff himself up. In fact, he called himself a sinner and begged God to forgive him. His soft and empty heart was ready for God to fill with His Spirit.

DARE   Humble yourself when you talk to God.

DOUBLE DARE

1. Think about how you usually pray. Which man in Jesus's parable do you sound more like? Try to be more like the tax collector: humble and honest.

2. Use a balloon to explain today's devo to a friend or one of your siblings.

PROMISE TO REPEAT

How did it go? What did you learn?

Why?

Have you ever heard young kids asking "Why?" almost every time a grown-up says something? If you have younger brothers or sisters, maybe you're used to this. Or maybe *you* did it when you were younger. It usually goes something like this ...

Mom: Zoe, please turn the TV off.
Zoe: Why?
Mom: Because I need you to go get dressed.
Zoe: Why?
Mom: Because we're going to Aunt Julia's in half an hour.
Zoe: Why?
Mom: Because they're having a party for your cousin Andrew.
Zoe: Why?
Mom: Because he's going away to college next weekend!
Zoe: Why?

If you were Zoe's mom, would you keep answering her questions, or would you be pretty exasperated by now? It can be frustrating when someone continually asks questions. It's fine to ask questions when you need help, want to learn something, or are concerned about someone. For example:

How are you feeling?
What is the homework for tomorrow?
What kinds of hobbies did Grandma have when she was my age?
Why did Jesus have to die on the cross?

But when we ask questions just because we're nosy or we don't trust someone or we're trying to waste time, that's not good. When something happens and we ask God, "Why?" it's usually because we're not happy. We feel like if *we* were God, we would have done things differently. That's like telling God we're smarter than Him.

Believe it or not, there were people in the Bible who did the same thing! Look up each Bible verse and write down the "Why" question.

1. Genesis 25:22: Rebekah asked, "Why _____?"

2. Exodus 17:3: The Israelites asked Moses, "Why _____?"

3. Exodus 32:11: Moses asked God, "Why _____?"

4. Job 3:11: Job asked, "Why _____?"

5. Job 21:7: Job also asked, "Why _____?"

6. Psalm 42:9: David asked, "Why _____?"

    "Why _____?"

It's not wrong to ask "Why?" if we're asking with a real desire to understand and if we're ready to accept the answer. But it's not good if we ask "Why?" with anger and don't wait for an answer.

Here's something to think about. If we want to ask God "Why?" then maybe we should be willing to answer some of His questions too. Look up each Bible verse and write the "Why?" question God is asking you.

1. Matthew 6:28: "Why _____?"

2. Matthew 7:3: "Why _____?"

3. Matthew 8:26: "You of little faith, why _____?"

4. Matthew 9:4: "Why _____?"

5. Matthew 15:3: "Why _____?"

The next time you want to ask "Why?" take a moment to ask yourself why you're asking.

YOUR TURN

• Write down a few "Why?" questions you wish you could ask God.

Why _____?

Why _____?

Why _____?

• Ask God to help you have patience and trust if you can't have the answer to those questions right now.

What are your thoughts?

BIBLE READING   *1 John 4:1*

TRUTH

False teachers are hard to spot if you don't know the Bible well.

In the New Testament, there are many warnings about false teachers—people who sound like they're telling the truth but are actually twisting it into something dangerous. With many different kinds of churches and Christian groups, it's not always easy to know if the difference is something that doesn't matter too much to God (for example, should you sit or stand or kneel when you pray?) or something that really does (for example, if there if such a place as hell).

Some false teachers convince the people listening to them that if you believe in Jesus, you'll never get sick or you'll become rich or you can stop asking God to forgive your sins. But they say so many other things that sound right that people who don't study God's Word don't notice the wrong messages.

The Bible warns that this will become a worse problem as years go by, so we must do our very best to study the Bible well. The quick devos in this book aren't enough, my friends. Start studying the Bible now while you're young and you'll be ready to spot false teachers when you're older.

DARE   Make studying your Bible a priority.

DOUBLE DARE

1. How many minutes do you spend each week reading your Bible? How many minutes do you spend watching TV or surfing the Internet? Which activity will help you more in your life? Write down changes you think you should make.

2. Ask your parents or another Christian adult to quiz you on your Bible knowledge, and see how well you do.

PROMISE TO REPEAT

How did it go? What did you learn?

Two Foolish Cats

BIBLE READING *James 1:5*

TRUTH

Without God's wisdom, we do foolish things.

Two cats were walking one day when they found a big piece of cheese. Excitedly, they agreed to share it. They tried to cut it in half, but one piece ended up bigger than the other. Both cats wanted the larger piece, so they weren't sure what to do.

They asked a monkey for his advice. He said, "I'll make the pieces equal for you," and he took a little bite out of the bigger piece. That made the other piece a bit bigger, so he took a nibble out of that one. That made the first piece bigger again. He did this until the two pieces of cheese became quite small. Finally, the cats cried out, "Stop! We'll have the pieces the way they are now."

But the monkey said, "Wait. This is my payment for helping you with your problem." And he popped the last little bits of cheese into his mouth and gobbled them up!

Sometimes, when we're not sure what to do, we look for wisdom in the wrong places and end up worse off than we were before. The Bible promises that God will give us His wisdom generously if we ask Him for it.

DARE Ask God for wisdom.

DOUBLE DARE

1. Do you have a friend who always asks the wrong people for advice? Share today's devo and verse with her and encourage her to turn to God for help.

2. Think of a situation you're facing today. How would your friends' advice be different from what God would want you to do? Ask Him to give you His wisdom.

PROMISE TO REPEAT

How did it go? What did you learn?

Where's Your Loyalty?

BIBLE READING *James 4:4*

TRUTH

We can't say we love God and then be loyal to the world.

In the 1960s, at the same time Lyndon Johnson was president of the United States, there was an economist (an expert on money matters who can give advice to the government) in Canada named John Kenneth Galbraith. One day, President Johnson called Mr. Galbraith's home and asked to speak to him.

"I'm sorry, Mr. President," said the housekeeper, Emily, "but he is sleeping and said not to disturb him."

"Well, wake him up! I want to speak with him," said the president. "No, Mr. President," she said. "I work for him, not you. When he wakes up, I'll ask him to call you."

Later, when Mr. Galbraith called the president back, the president was very pleased! He was so impressed with Emily's loyalty to her boss that he said, "Tell that woman I want her here in the White House!"

As Christians, we will often be tempted or pressured by people around us or messages that we get from TV and magazines to do things that go against what the Bible teaches. Like Emily, we have to remember who we belong to. We belong not to the world but to God. He's the only One we must obey.

DARE Don't give in to the world's pressure.

DOUBLE DARE

1. What are some things you feel pressured to do that you know wouldn't please or honor God? How do you deal with it? Ask God to help you stay loyal to Him more than to anyone or anything else.

2. Write a story that would explain today's Bible verse. Get a friend to help you!

PROMISE TO REPEAT

How did it go? What did you learn?

The Best Way to Pray?

BIBLE READING *Matthew 6:5–7*

TRUTH

When you pray, the posture of your heart matters more than the posture of your body.

One day, four Christians were trying to agree on the best way to pray. One said, "The proper way is to get down on your knees." The second one said, "No, no! It's much better to stand with your arms stretched out and your eyes looking up." The third one said, "I think you have to bow your head, close your eyes, and hold your hands together in front of you."

The last one, after listening to the others, said, "Well, last week I fell into my neighbor's well headfirst, with my feet sticking up. Believe me, the best prayer I ever said was right there, standing on my head!"

It's definitely important to honor God when we pray by sitting (or standing or kneeling) in a way that shows respect and humility. For example, I wouldn't lie on the couch chewing gum and playing with my hair while I pray. But it's even more important for our hearts to be humble and respectful. There's no point in sitting properly if you're thinking about going shopping when you should be talking to God. Being able to talk to God is a privilege. Let's not be careless about it.

DARE Respect God when you pray.

DOUBLE DARE

1. You can pray anytime, during any activity, but it's important to also put aside special time to pray. When you do that, try to find a quiet spot by yourself and think about your posture.

2. Ask your parents or another Christian about their posture when they pray.

PROMISE TO REPEAT

How did it go? What did you learn?

BIBLE READING *Psalm 24:3–4*

TRUTH

We can't get to heaven unless Jesus "washes" our hearts and hands.

There has probably never been another time in history when people were as concerned about being clean as they are today. Some people, especially in North America and Europe, worry so much about germs and dirt that we could say they're germophobes. They may wash their hands every hour or so, wash their towels and sheets every day, shower twice a day, scrub their toilets twice a day, and do whatever they can to get rid of germs in their homes or on their bodies. The problem with being a germophobe is that it can actually be harmful because our bodies don't get used to fighting germs and we get sick more easily.

Of course, there is nothing wrong with being clean. It keeps us healthy, looking good, and smelling fresh. But what about being pure and clean on the inside? The Bible says that only those whose sins have been washed away by Jesus (when we ask Him to forgive us and promise to follow Him) can enter heaven. Also, when the Bible talks about clean hands, it's not talking about our physical hands, but about our actions and the things we do.

When it comes to our hearts and actions, we should be germophobes!

DARE Stay pure, inside and out.

DOUBLE DARE

1. How often do you ask God to make your heart pure? If you haven't done it for a while, ask Him today to forgive your sins.

2. Try to develop this habit: Whenever you wash your hands, pray and ask God to help you keep your actions and words clean too.

PROMISE TO REPEAT

How did it go? What did you learn?

"Oh What a Happy Soul"

If you go to a church where they sing traditional hymns (older Christian songs), you may recognize some of these lyrics (or at least you might recognize the tunes if we could somehow play them on this page):

> "To God be the glory, great things he hath done!"
> "Blessed assurance, Jesus is mine!"
> "Jesus, keep me near the cross …"

These hymns were all written by a woman named Fanny Crosby. Even if you've never heard a song written by Fanny Crosby, I think you'll find her story very encouraging. She was an extraordinary woman! Here are some interesting facts about her life:

1. She was born in New York in 1820.

2. Her full name was Frances Jane Crosby.

3. At the age of six, Fanny went blind because of sickness in her eyes that wasn't taken care of properly.

4. She wrote her first poem when she was eight years old:

> Oh what a happy soul am I!
> Although I cannot see,
> I am resolved that in this world,
> Contented I will be.
> How many blessings I enjoy,
> That other people don't.
> To weep and sigh because I'm blind,
> I cannot and I won't!

5. Fanny became so well known for her poems that, starting at age twenty-three, she became friends with some of the presidents of the United States.

6. When she was twenty-seven, she became a teacher at her old school, the Institute for the Blind. Her gentleness, patience, and friendliness made her well loved.

7. She got married when she was thirty-eight to another blind teacher. Her married name became Frances van Alstyne.

8. She wrote many poems and songs, but her first "hymn" came much later in life, when she was forty-four years old.

9. She wrote an unbelievable number of hymns in her lifetime: nine thousand of them!

10. Fanny died at the age of ninety-five.

One day, someone told Fanny Crosby it was too bad that when God gave her so many talents, He didn't also give her sight. Fanny gave an answer I'll never forget. She said she was thankful she was blind because when she got to heaven, the first face she would see would be the face of God, her Savior. Wow! What a great attitude.

YOUR TURN

Fanny Crosby didn't let her young age or her blindness stop her from using her talents to serve and honor God. Nearly one hundred years after her death on February 15, 1915, we still sing her songs. God is still using her life and her work to touch people's hearts!

- Can you match the Bible verses on the left with the hymn lyrics on the right? Look up the verses, and then find the song lyrics they go with. Check the answer key at the end of the book for the answers.

Verses	Hymn Lyrics
Ecclesiastes 12:6–7	"Praise him! Praise him! Jesus, our blessed Redeemer!"
Luke 23:49	"To God be the glory, great things he hath done!"
Hebrews 10:22	"Jesus, keep me near the cross."
Hebrews 3:15	"He hideth my soul in the cleft of the rock."
Psalm 150:2	"Take the world, but give me Jesus."
Exodus 33:22	"Jesus is tenderly calling you home."
Psalm 29:2	"Draw me nearer, nearer blessed Lord."
Mark 8:36	"Some day the silver cord will break."

- Is there something in your life that makes you feel as though you can't be useful to God? Write about it here or in your journal, and then take time to talk to God about it. Ask Him for the courage to use your talents *and* your weaknesses to serve Him.

_____

_____

_____

DOUBLE DARE

Ask your parents or your pastor at church to help you find some songs written by Fanny Crosby. Choose one that you like and try to learn to sing it, even if it's just to sing it by yourself.

What are your thoughts?

BIBLE READING *John 15:18–21*

TRUTH

Jesus was treated badly, and His followers will go through hard times too.

In each list below, circle the letters that appear three times. Then unscramble the circled letters in each list to find two words from today's Bible reading.

List 1	List 2
OVAL	FRY
TREES	TYPE
SOAP	MASK
NUT	SURF
VAN	MIX
REST	ROPE
IVY	TOAST
RING	GAME

_ _ _ _ _ _ _   _ _ _ _ _ _

When we go through hard times, we may sometimes feel like no one understands. It can be even more confusing when we try to be good and obey God and then people make fun of us or treat us badly because of our faith in Jesus. Don't give up! Jesus knew it would happen, because it happened to Him. Remember: "A servant is not greater than his master." Jesus will give you strength. Just trust and remember that our troubles on earth aren't forever, but heaven is!

DARE   Hang on to Jesus when being a Christian seems tough.

DOUBLE DARE

1. In your journal, write down some ways the world shows it hates Jesus. Ask God to help you not to feel afraid when people treat you badly and to give you peace and courage.

2. Do you have friends who make fun of you for being a Christian? Pray for them to understand that they need Jesus too and continue to show them love.

PROMISE TO REPEAT

How did it go? What did you learn?

BIBLE READING *John 15:4*

TRUTH

Jesus is our only source of power.

What is the difference between a clock that plugs into the wall and one that needs batteries?

They both tell the time, with the minutes changing every sixty seconds and the hours changing every sixty minutes. The way they work is pretty much the same, but what makes them work is different—the source of power.

A clock that you plug into the wall gets its power from electrical wires that run through the walls of your house. As long as it's plugged in, it will work. The clock doesn't need to produce electricity. The electricity goes through the plug and makes the clock work.

A clock that uses batteries will not run forever. The batteries will eventually drain and need to be replaced (or recharged). So the power for a battery-operated clock comes from inside the clock, but it doesn't last forever.

As Christians, we always need to be plugged into Jesus. If we try to live on "batteries" (our own strength and power), we won't last for long. We also lose power if we unplug ourselves from Jesus (for example, when we stop praying). We need His "electricity" (the Holy Spirit) to give us strength to follow Him every day.

DARE Plug yourself into Jesus.

DOUBLE DARE

1. Think of five ways (we already talked about praying) that you can stay connected to Jesus. Consider the ones you need to work on and ask God to help you.

2. How is the example of the clocks similar to the example of tree branches in today's Bible verse?

PROMISE TO REPEAT

How did it go? What did you learn?

BIBLE READING   *Matthew 5:46–47*

TRUTH

God isn't impressed when you love only people who are easy to love.

At recess, if you wanted to play a game of hopscotch or tag, whom would you ask to play with you? Your closest friends and the girls you really like? Or would you ask the school bully, the kid who always has a runny nose, and the girl who talks about herself all the time?

For most of us, our first thought is to be nice to other people we think are nice. But does that make us nice people? God doesn't think so.

The Bible teaches us that loving people who are easy to love is not a big deal, and we shouldn't feel proud about it. What is true goodness and love in God's eyes is when we reach out to people who aren't necessarily nice or smart or pretty or rich or talented, people who may not even be nice to us in return.

Jesus gave us a perfect example of this when He died on the cross for all those who sinned against Him. That includes me. And that includes you.

DARE   Love those who are harder to love.

DOUBLE DARE

1. Instead of talking only to your close friends today, find a way to show God's love to someone who is unpopular or difficult to love. Ask God for help. Later, write about the experience in your journal.

2. Do you think you're ever difficult to love? Take time to thank God that there are people in your life (such as your parents) who love you anyway.

PROMISE TO REPEAT

How did it go? What did you learn?

God Gives What We Need

BIBLE READING Matthew 6:34

TRUTH

When God asks us to do something, He also gives us what we'll need to succeed.

My family has always lived in a neighborhood where there are many shops just a few minutes' walk from our house, so when I was a young girl, sometimes my mom would ask me to run to the store to buy some milk or bread or to pick up clothes from the cleaners. Before I left, she gave me the money I would need to pay for whatever I was getting. It didn't matter to me if I needed just a dollar or if I needed twenty dollars, because my mom always made sure I had enough. If she didn't, it would have been difficult for me—even impossible—to do what she'd asked.

God asks us to do things too. We're told to honor our parents, love our enemies, be patient, give generously, and so on. You know you have to do your best in school, keep your room tidy, and be nice to your little brother. You may worry sometimes that you don't have the strength or courage to do all these things.

But God promises to give us everything we need in life, so we can stop worrying.

DARE Trust God to provide.

DOUBLE DARE

1. Think of times when you've been asked to help someone or when you had a job to do. Were you given everything you needed to get it done? Thank God for always giving you what you need.

2. Memorize today's verse and share it with someone who's worried about a problem.

PROMISE TO REPEAT

How did it go? What did you learn?

BIBLE READING   *2 Corinthians 5:21 and Romans 5:8*

TRUTH

Jesus understands what it's like to be treated unfairly.

Has anything like this ever happened to you?

> You get into trouble because the kids sitting behind you are fooling around and your teacher thinks you were involved too.

> You do most of the work on a project with a friend and she gets the same grade as you.

> You do extra chores without being asked to and no one notices. Instead, your little brother gets rewarded for just making his bed.

How do you react in situations like these? If you're like me, you might say, "It's not fair!" It's normal to feel upset when you think you should have been treated better. You may even try to explain to your teacher or parents why you think they're being unfair.

As you go through life, you'll realize that unfair things happen all the time. You can fix *some* situations but not all. What you can always control is your attitude. Jesus was treated more unfairly than anyone in history. He was perfect and holy, but He was willing to die on the cross because He loved us so much. So He understands how you feel when life is unfair, and He can give you strength to carry on.

DARE   Be patient when life is unfair.

DOUBLE DARE

1. In each of the three situations above, how do you think Jesus would react? Ask God to help you become more like Jesus (patient and humble) when life seems unfair.

2. Think about how unfair it is to God when we disobey Him. Take time to thank Him for forgiving your sins.

PROMISE TO REPEAT

How did it go? What did you learn?

Hosanna!

I miss my grandma. She died a few days after Christmas in 2004, and I still think of her often because we were very close. My grandparents lived next door to us, so I saw them a few times each week, and throughout grade school and high school I used to sleep over on Saturday nights. Grandma's name was Osanna, which is the Armenian way of saying "Hosanna"—a word that's in the Bible.

My grandma's father died before she was even born, and her mother got married again when Osanna was just four years old. At the time, her family lived in Turkey, but because of a terrible war that was going on, Armenian families weren't safe. While her stepfather stayed to fight in the war, Osanna and her mother, who was pregnant, joined others who ran away. It was very dangerous. They had to walk for about a month through a mountain area, with very little food and no shoes.

Along the way, they discovered a pile of food and clothing that others had left behind. Osanna found a bottle of pills and put it in her pocket. Later, when they were on a ship with many other refugees (the people who had to run away to be safe), the pills that Osanna had found helped all the people who became sick with fever.

Many weeks later, Osanna and her mother arrived in Greece, and soon baby Stephen was born. Her new dad also joined them, and the family was all together at last! But life remained hard. Osanna never went to school, and she got her first job when she was just eight years old. She worked hard and got tired, and she started to get a pain in her left foot. One Sunday after church, her foot hurt so badly and it was so swollen that her mother took her to the doctor. They put her foot in a cast and sent her home. But her foot got worse and worse, and three months later, the doctors discovered that the cast had caused a terrible infection in her leg. Three months after that, they had to amputate (cut off) her leg below the knee.

She was just a tween—nine years old! For one year, Osanna used crutches, and then she was able to get a prosthesis (a fake leg). At twelve years old, she began her own business, sewing for people.

Osanna had lost a lot in a very short time, but when she was twenty years old, she found Jesus while reading John 3:16 in the Bible my grandpa had given her (they were just friends at that time). My grandma's life began to change as she followed Jesus and told others about Him. Although she always struggled physically, God blessed her with a wonderful husband, two children, four grandchildren, and six great-grandchildren! Osanna was never shy to tell people how wonderful God is. She didn't care if they laughed at her, because God gave her strength and courage every day.

YOUR TURN

- In your journal, write down how hearing a story like Osanna's makes you feel about the difficulties you face in your life. How did this story help or encourage you?

- If your grandparents are still alive, ask them to tell you about their experiences when they were your age. Write their stories in your journal or another notebook so that you'll remember them when you're older.

- Do you remember where the word *Hosanna* was used in the Bible? If not, read John 12:12–16.

- Memorize John 3:16, the verse that helped Osanna understand that she needed Jesus to be her Savior.

What are your thoughts?

BIBLE READING *John 15:13*

TRUTH

Nothing is bigger than God's love for you.

Sophie had a bad habit of coming home late from school every day. One day, her parents warned her that she must be home on time that afternoon. But Sophie came home later than ever. When she walked in, her mother looked at her but didn't say anything. At supper that evening, Sophie looked at her plate and saw only a piece of bread. She looked at her dad's full plate of food and then at her dad, but he didn't say anything. Sophie felt awful.

A few quiet minutes passed while Sophie thought about how she had disobeyed and disappointed her parents. Then her dad took her plate and placed it in front of himself. He took his own plate of chicken and rice, put it in front of Sophie, and smiled at her.

Sophie's father showed her an example of God's love. Even though we have all sinned and deserve punishment, God loves us. His love is so great that He was willing to be punished in our place. In fact, Jesus allowed Himself to be killed so that we can have eternal life. The father in the story gave up only his meal to show his love to his daughter. But Jesus gave His life. That is the greatest love of all!

DARE Thank God for His great love.

DOUBLE DARE

1. In your journal, write down as many things as you can remember that God has forgiven you for. Thank Him for His love and forgiveness.

2. Knowing how much God loves you, think of some ways you can love Him back.

PROMISE TO REPEAT

How did it go? What did you learn?

Put That Burden Down

BIBLE READING *1 Peter 5:7*

TRUTH

Jesus wants to help carry your burdens.

Have you ever watched people lifting weights, either in a gym or during an Olympic competition? Some athletes can lift more than 105 kilograms, which is more than 220 pounds! That's like lifting a large grown man. But a competitive weight lifter keeps those heavy barbells up in the air for only a few seconds, until the referee sees that he did it right and blows the whistle. As strong as he is, the weight lifter can't hold that weight up for too long; otherwise he might seriously injure himself.

A science teacher once asked a student to hold a glass of water during class. The first few minutes were fine, but the longer the student held the glass, the more difficult it became. The teacher wanted to show the class that even something as light as a glass of water can become extremely heavy if you hold it for too long. The weight of the glass doesn't change, but the pressure on your arm becomes worse as time passes, until you either drop the glass or cause damage to your arm.

That's how the troubles in our lives are. They may seem small at first, but if we don't take care of them by asking for God's help, they become heavier burdens, or weights, in our hearts and minds.

DARE Take what's troubling you to God.

DOUBLE DARE

1. Try this with a friend: Find two things that are the same (for example, two tennis balls) and each of you hold one in one hand. See who can hold it the longest without having to put it down. (Make sure it's not breakable!) Talk about the experience and today's lesson.

2. Write out 1 Peter 5:7 on a piece of paper and tuck it into your schoolbag's pocket as a reminder.

PROMISE TO REPEAT

How did it go? What did you learn?

A Is Still A

BIBLE READING *Hebrews 13:8*

TRUTH

People change, but Jesus never changes.

Have you ever seen a tuning fork? It's not a utensil you eat with; it's a tool that musicians use to tune their instruments. A musical scale (there's an example of one in the picture of piano keys) uses the letters A to G, one for each note. Tuning forks are made to give the perfect sound of the note A, so musicians tune the A on instruments such as guitars and violins to match the tuning fork, and then they can tune the rest of the notes. That way, when many musicians play together, they don't make your ears hurt by playing different tones of the same note.

Long ago, when a music teacher was asked if he had good news, he tapped his tuning fork gently and the sound of the note filled the room. Then he said, "A is still A. It is A today, it was A five thousand years ago, and it will still be A ten thousand years from now!" He also talked about how singers and pianos get out of tune sometimes, but the A note would never change.

That's what the Bible says about Jesus! It promises that Jesus is the same yesterday, today, and forever. Now that's good news!

DARE Put your hope in Jesus, not in people, who change.

DOUBLE DARE

1. What does it mean to you that Jesus is the same "yesterday and today and forever"? Take time to thank God that you can always depend on Him.

2. Are you dependable? If people never know what to expect from you, ask God to help you become more trustworthy.

PROMISE TO REPEAT

How did it go? What did you learn?

Food for Your Soul

BIBLE READING *John 6:26–27, 35*

TRUTH

Jesus is the "bread of life."

In the list below, circle the eleven foods you think are the healthiest for us (and are easy to find in grocery stores):

beets	oranges	bananas
cabbage	yogurt	eggs
swiss chard	oatmeal	raisins
cinnamon	grapes	carrots
pomegranates	cucumbers	olives
prunes	eggplant	tomatoes
pumpkin seeds	cheese	green peppers
sardines	avocadoes	spinach
turmeric (a spice)	oregano (a spice)	thyme (a spice)
frozen blueberries	peas	corn on the cob
canned pumpkin	green beans	apples

You might be surprised that the eleven healthiest foods in that list are all in the first column. But you won't see those items very often in people's carts at the grocery store. Sometimes people don't eat healthy because they don't know what's good for them. Others don't want to change their diet.

As important as it is to eat healthy, it's even more important to eat good spiritual food. We keep our souls and hearts healthy and alive when we spend time with Jesus and study our Bibles.

DARE Eat good spiritual food.

DOUBLE DARE

1. In the middle of a piece of paper, write out John 6:35. Around the verse, draw pictures of the eleven healthiest foods from the list. Ask your parents to help you find pictures if you're not sure what they are.

2. How much time do you spend reading the Bible or praying? If you think you might be starving spiritually, eat up!

PROMISE TO REPEAT

How did it go? What did you learn?

BIBLE READING *John 3:19, John 9:5, and Matthew 5:14*

TRUTH

Jesus is the solution to the world's darkness.

Do you ever feel angry or frustrated with people who don't believe in God or think the Bible isn't true? We live in a world that makes fun of Christians, is disrespectful toward God, and hates following the rules in the Bible. We might wonder why some people don't understand the truth. We might even be tempted to think bad thoughts about people who are against God and the Christian faith.

But the Bible never tells us to hate the spiritual darkness that people live in. It tells us to bring them the light of Jesus. Imagine being in a room that is completely dark. There are no windows, and you can't find a light switch. If someone got angry because you didn't know there was a red chair, flowery curtains, and a big-screen TV, how would you feel? What if someone turned on the lights for you instead? Then you would see what they were talking about.

As Christians, we need to patiently and gently tell people about Jesus—the light of the world—so that they can see Him and believe too. We can show them through our actions and words how much God loves them.

DARE Turn on the lights for someone.

DOUBLE DARE

1. Do you know someone who doesn't want to believe in Jesus? Ask if you can share why you do believe and how Jesus helps you.

2. If someone doesn't want to listen to you talk about Jesus, don't push. Just pray for her and ask God to soften her heart.

PROMISE TO REPEAT

How did it go? What did you learn?

HERO LIST

Choose ONE of these heroes to learn about this weekend:

Name	Bible Verses
Esther	Esther 3:1–11; 4:4–17; 5:1–8; 7:1–10; 8:1–11
Stephen	Acts 6–7
Ruth	Ruth 1–4
David	1 Samuel 17
Abigail	1 Samuel 25:1–42
Gideon	Judges 6–7
The Bleeding Woman	Mark 5:25–34
Joseph	Genesis 37; 39–41
The Widow of Zarephath	1 Kings 17:8–24; Luke 4:25–26
Noah	Genesis 6–8
Miriam	Exodus 2:1–10
Daniel	Daniel 6
Mary of Bethany	John 12:1–8
Abraham	Genesis 22:1–18

Your hero for this weekend: _____

QUESTION TIME

1. How did this weekend's hero show courage and faith in God?

2. What happened because of his or her courage and obedience?

3. What did you learn from this hero's life that will help you in your own walk with God?

DOUBLE DARE

Choose at least one of these ways to dig a little deeper into your hero's life this weekend:

1. See if you can find other Bible verses about him or her. Write the reference (or the "address" of the verses) here and also anything new that you learned.

2. Ask your parents or another Christian what they have learned from this hero's life and example.

Tell a friend or your family about your new hero!

¿Qué? Mitä? Apa?

BIBLE READING   *1 Corinthians 14:9–11*

TRUTH

When we tell others about our faith, we should speak clearly.

Do you recognize the languages in the title of today's devo? It says, "What?" in Spanish, Finnish, and Indonesian.

How many languages do you think there are in the world? Fifty? Five hundred? How many can you name? (Take a moment to try.) Actually, there are between six thousand and seven thousand spoken languages today, and hundreds of other languages are in danger of being lost because very few people still speak them. The most commonly spoken language, you might be surprised to know, is not English. It's Mandarin Chinese. About 873,000,000 people speak Mandarin!

Many people in the world speak more than one language (I speak three), but even if you speak only one, it's important to use that language in a clear and proper way, especially when you're talking about Jesus.

Today's Bible reading reminds us that it's pointless to talk about God if we use words that people don't understand. Instead of simply repeating things you hear grown-ups at church say (for example, words such as *redemption*, *sanctification*, or *perseverance*), tell your friends about what Jesus has done for you in everyday words that make sense to them.

DARE   Keep your faith story simple!

DOUBLE DARE

1. If you have a close Christian friend, practice talking about your faith in Jesus with her and help each other make sure what you say is easy to understand.

2. Are there people in your church who speak different languages? Ask them to teach you how to say "God loves you" in their language. Write it down so you'll remember!

PROMISE TO REPEAT

How did it go? What did you learn?

Spread the Good News

BIBLE READING *Matthew 28:18–20*

TRUTH

We have wonderful news to share with the world.

Coca-Cola (you might also call it Coke) was invented in 1886 by a pharmacist named John Stith Pemberton. You might be surprised to learn these facts about what started as just one simple soft drink:[2]

Coca-Cola now owns more than five hundred brands, and its products are sold in more than two hundred countries.

Over 1.6 billion servings of Coke are served each day.

Only one hundred years after Coca-Cola was created, about 94 percent of the world had heard of it and half the people had tasted it.

Please understand I'm not promoting Coke (soft drinks aren't good for you). But I listed those facts to get us thinking. I once read an interesting question: "If God had given the job of telling the world about Jesus to the Coca-Cola company, what might the results have been?" Obviously, Coca-Cola is really good at spreading the message about its product, right?

But God asked *us* to evangelize (spread the news about Jesus and salvation). He didn't ask Coca-Cola to do it. Over two thousand years have passed since Jesus's death and resurrection, but many people still don't know about Him or haven't "tasted" Him. Will you spread the good news?

DARE Tell someone about Jesus.

DOUBLE DARE

1. In today's reading, what did Jesus ask His disciples (and us) to do? Write down at least five ways you can obey Jesus's command to spread the good news.

2. What stops you from telling your friends about Jesus? Tell God about those fears or difficulties and ask Him to help you be brave and wise.

PROMISE TO REPEAT

How did it go? What did you learn?

Gentle Words

BIBLE READING *Proverbs 15:1*

TRUTH

Our words can either calm people down or make them angry.

It's time for a little science experiment! All you need is a shallow bowl or pie plate, water, black pepper, sugar, and dish soap. Ask your mom to help you with this.

Pour just enough water in the bowl or pie plate to cover the bottom (about a quarter of an inch is fine). Then sprinkle black pepper all over the water. Don't use too much or you may start sneezing! Next, add just one or two drops of dish soap to the water. What happened? If the experiment worked properly, you should have seen the black pepper flakes hurry to the edge of the plate or bowl.

Now try this: Sprinkle a little sugar into the clear center of the water. What happened this time? The pepper should have rushed back to the center.

The soap and the sugar had very different effects on the pepper, didn't they? In life, how we react to someone during a tough situation can also make a difference to what happens next. The Bible tells us that if we use harsh words, we will stir up anger in the other person, but if our words are soft and gentle, we can help them calm down.

DARE Keep your words soft.

DOUBLE DARE

1. When your parents ask you to do something you don't feel like doing, how do you answer them? Ask God to help you answer with respect and kindness so your mom or dad will not become angry.

2. If you've spoken harshly to someone lately, ask him or her for forgiveness.

PROMISE TO REPEAT

How did it go? What did you learn?

Remembering Tabitha

BIBLE READING *Acts 9:36–41*

TRUTH

God honors those who faithfully serve Him.

Count how many sentences are in the verses you read from Acts 9. There are only about ten, right? Some might say that's not many. Other people in history have many books written about them. What's the big deal about ten sentences?

Actually, the fact that God led the writers of the Bible to include Tabitha's story means her life was very important, and we can learn something from her example. We don't know much about her—for example, we don't know what she looked like or if she lived in a nice house or if she sang beautifully. What we do know is that she was "always doing good and helping the poor."

Wow! I sure would like to think that thousands of years after I die, people will read that "Ann-Margret was always doing good and helping the poor." What about you? What do you think people will remember about you after you are gone?

Tabitha's story often reminds me that how I live really matters to God. If He was going to write another book about this time in history, I would want Him to look at me and say, "Now there's a girl who has been serving Me faithfully!" I hope you feel the same way.

DARE Live a life worth remembering.

DOUBLE DARE

1. Write a list of qualities you would like people to remember about you if you were gone. Ask God to help you be someone who's "always doing good."

2. Look for good qualities in your friends and family members. Tell them today how much you appreciate them for those things.

PROMISE TO REPEAT

How did it go? What did you learn?

BIBLE READING *1 Peter 3:3–4*

TRUTH

Beauty isn't all about outward appearance.

When my birthday came around in 2012, it was a big deal because I turned forty. That might seem really old to you (your parents may be younger than I am), but I actually don't feel much different on the inside than I did when I was ten! Sure, I'm more mature now and I've learned a lot, but my personality and interests are basically the same. Sometimes I just feel like a big kid!

Two days after my birthday, though, I was thinking about how my body has gotten older. I'm not as thin as I used to be, and I've got some white hair, but I also worry less about how I look now. There's a lot more pressure on young girls to look beautiful. Now I'm more interested in the beauty of flowers, music, and art, and in creating beautiful experiences—things that others can enjoy and be blessed by.

I wrote this in my journal: *There must come a point in every girl's life when she cares less about how beautiful she is and more about the beauty she creates.*

The Bible teaches us that true beauty comes from the inside, not the outside.

DARE   Create some beauty today!

DOUBLE DARE

1. Think of some creative ways you can bring joy and beauty into someone's life. Put one of those ideas into action today, and then write about the experience.

2. Ask God to help you pay more attention to developing your inner beauty than your outer looks. Write down how you will do this.

PROMISE TO REPEAT

How did it go? What did you learn?

Karen didn't know Jesus until she was fourteen years old. The first few years of being a Christian were tough because of other things she had learned—things that don't honor God—when she was younger. But she continued to grow in her faith and obey God.

An experience Karen went through during high school taught her to be bold about her faith, trusting that God would take care of her. Check out her story:

I love drama. In school, I was a drama and music nut. I traveled in choirs and participated in the annual high school theater festival. My first year in the festival was very rewarding. I won best actress for my role as the psychologist in a play called Wolf Boy. *I had a lot of respect from my teacher and classmates ... until the following year.*

That year, we would be doing a play that was supposed to represent "our generation." It was filled with difficult topics and had some bad language in it. I was very uncomfortable being a part of the play, but it was a course I needed to graduate and I was already too far into the year to change classes. So I prayed and I got my friends praying too. The answer came in a song that's based on Joshua 1:9:

> *"Be bold, be strong, for the Lord your God is with you."*

I knew that I had to stand up for what I believed in, so I went to my teacher and told her I could not play the role of a pregnant, unmarried girl who wanted to end her pregnancy (have an abortion). She said she was disappointed in me and made my role in the play much smaller. But I was still uncomfortable with what was in the play, so I shared my concerns about the play with the school principal, who agreed that the content was not appropriate for students and asked the teacher to change the script.

I was not too popular that year, and my grade showed it. I went from a 97 percent the year before to a 75 percent. But I was glad I had stood for what I believed and the Lord was glorified. The play had been changed so much that it was too short, so my teacher gave us all the challenge of adding our own lines. At the end of the play, we were to say where we saw ourselves in ten years. I said that I believed that Jesus was the way, the truth, and the life, and in ten years I saw myself continuing to tell others of His love and salvation.

Karen was willing to take the risk of becoming unpopular with her teacher and other students because it was more important to her to obey God. What about you?

YOUR TURN

- In your journal, write about one or two things happening at school or at home that you feel don't honor God. Write out a prayer to God asking Him to help you be bold when it might be the right time to speak up.

- If you have a friend who needs courage right now to do the right thing in a tough situation, make a nice card for her with the words of Joshua 1:9 and give it to her. Offer to pray with her too, as Karen's friends did.

What are your thoughts?

Love Your Mom

BIBLE READING *Exodus 20:12*

TRUTH

God wants you to honor your mother, even when you don't feel like it.

A second-grade teacher taught her students all about magnets one day. The next day, she gave her class a quiz, and one of the questions was this riddle:

My full name has six letters. The first one is *M*. I pick up things. What am I?

When the quiz was over and the students handed in their papers, the teacher got a big surprise! Half the students wrote the correct answer (magnet), but the other half wrote something else. Can you guess what? If you said "mother," you're right!

This cute story shows that sometimes kids think of their mom only as someone who "picks up things." All of us, in some ways, have taken our moms for granted, which means we don't really appreciate them—we just expect them to do things like cook for us, buy us stuff, and wash our clothes. But our mothers aren't our servants. They're gifts from God who love us and care for us, and they have their own special purpose in God's plan.

We need to appreciate our moms all the time, not only when they "pick up things."

DARE Show your mom some love!

DOUBLE DARE

1. Draw a big heart on a piece of paper and inside the heart write all the ways your mom is wonderful. Make sure you don't just list stuff she does for you! Decorate the page and then give it to her, along with a hug.

2. Moms pray for us, but sometimes we forget to pray for them. Spend some time today praying for yours.

PROMISE TO REPEAT

How did it go? What did you learn?

Saved by a Spider!

BIBLE READING *Psalm 107:8*

TRUTH

God often works in unexpected ways.

Felix of Nola was a Christian who lived in Italy about two hundred years after Jesus. He was a kind and thoughtful person who sold everything he had so he could give money to the poor, but he was later arrested and tortured for his faith in Jesus.

Once, while he was running from his enemies, he found shelter in an abandoned building. After a while, a spider began weaving a web across the door. As the web grew, it made it look as though no one had opened that door for many months. When the men chasing Felix went by the building he was hiding in, they didn't even bother going inside because of the spiderweb they saw.

After escaping, Felix said, "Where God is, a spider's web is a wall. And where God isn't, a wall is a spider's web." He understood that it had been God who protected him.

When you find yourself in a difficult situation that doesn't make sense (for example, when you try to do something nice for someone and get mistreated instead of being appreciated), you can trust God to take care of you … even in unexpected ways!

DARE Ask God to help you when you can't help yourself.

DOUBLE DARE

1. In Psalm 107, find the sentence that is repeated in four separate verses (clue: it's today's key verse). Memorize it and thank God for specific ways He has helped you.

2. Next time you see a spider's web, tell whomever you're with the story of Felix of Nola and share today's verse with him or her.

PROMISE TO REPEAT

How did it go? What did you learn?

God Knows What You Can Carry

BIBLE READING *Psalm 103:14*

TRUTH

God made you and understands your weaknesses.

One day, a young girl was helping her mom shop for groceries. She carried the basket while her mother put different things inside. First came a can of soup, then some noodles, then a carton of eggs. As the basket started to get full, another customer noticed and worried the girl wouldn't be able to handle the weight. The lady asked the girl quietly, "Isn't that basket too heavy for you?"

The girl answered, "Oh, don't worry! My mom knows how much I can carry!"

That's a really good picture of how God takes care of us. Sure, sometimes we face problems in life. We may be tempted, someone may hurt our feelings, we may get sick, or someone we love may die. But the Bible promises that God knows how much we can handle and He'll never put more into our "basket" than we can carry. Whew! Isn't that a relief?

DARE   Don't stop trusting God when life seems too hard to handle.

DOUBLE DARE

1. Draw a large basket on a piece of paper or in your journal. On little slips of paper, write down all the things worrying you right now. "Fill" the basket by sticking the slips of paper (you might want to fold them first) onto the basket with a bit of glue. Then pray and ask God to help you carry your troubles.

2. Share today's story with a friend, along with the Bible verse.

PROMISE TO REPEAT

How did it go? What did you learn?

BIBLE READING   *Psalm 147:3*

TRUTH

God can fix whatever is broken and make it even better!

If you know what these words mean, write their definitions in the blank lines. Check the answer key at the end of the book to see if you got them right.

Origami _____

Shibori _____

Bonsai _____

Temari _____

Amigurumi _____

Today you're going to learn a bit about *kintsugi*, another cool Japanese art.

If you or I broke a valuable bowl or plate, we would likely try to fix it with glue, doing our best to hide the cracks and make the broken object look nearly as good as it did before it was broken. Of course, no matter how well we glue the pieces back together, the object will have lost a lot of its value. With *kintsugi*, the broken pieces are fixed with a special lacquer (a liquid that becomes very sticky as it dries). What's special about this lacquer is that powdered gold is sprinkled into it first. That way, it dries as gold and makes the broken object *more* valuable than before!

When we take our problems and broken hearts to God, He doesn't just fix them. With His love and power, He turns them into something even more beautiful and precious than before. Isn't He wonderful?

DARE   Trust God when life seems to be falling apart.

DOUBLE DARE

1. In your journal, write about a time when you prayed about a problem and God healed your heart. Take time today to thank Him again for His love.

2. Make a pretty card for someone who is feeling hurt right now and write today's verse on it. Memorize the verse while you work on the card.

PROMISE TO REPEAT

How did it go? What did you learn?

BIBLE READING *Mark 4:35–41*

TRUTH

When life gets stormy, we can stay calm and trust God.

The captain of a ship traveling from London, England, to New York City was happy to have his family with him for this trip. During the night, a terrible storm started to rock the ship in the middle of the ocean. The passengers woke up and felt frightened. The captain's eight-year-old daughter also woke up. She asked her mother what was going on, and her mother told her about the storm. The girl asked, "Is Daddy on deck?" Her mother said, "Yes, Daddy's on deck."

The girl went back to bed, snuggled under her covers, and fell fast asleep again. She trusted her strong father. He was an excellent captain, so she wasn't afraid.

In today's Bible story, Jesus's disciples were not that brave. They knew Jesus and had seen His miracles, but they needed more faith. Still, Jesus was gentle with them as He calmed the storm.

When we go through problems in life, we sometimes forget that our heavenly Father is "on deck" and ready to take control. When we feel afraid, we can trust God to calm the storm for us.

DARE Relax … Daddy's on deck!

DOUBLE DARE

1. How do you react when bad things happen—like the girl in the story you just read or like the disciples? Ask God to help you have more faith in His power and love.

2. Draw a picture of the story in Mark 4. Include yourself in the picture, showing how you imagine you would be reacting in the storm. Write yourself a reminder to have faith, such as, "Don't be afraid. Daddy's on deck!"

PROMISE TO REPEAT

How did it go? What did you learn?

The Civil War's Youngest Nurse

My friend Jocelyn Green has written several devotional books for military families and has also written a series of novels about the Civil War, so her brain is packed with interesting stories and facts about American war history. She recently told me about a remarkable nine-year-old girl named Sadie Bushman, who became the Civil War's youngest nurse on July 1, 1863.

Very early that morning (at 2:00 a.m.), Sadie's parents woke her up and told her to run to her grandfather's house, which was two miles out of town. They were going to follow her a little later with the younger children. Her parents knew the battle was near and they needed to get away. But before Sadie was even halfway to her grandfather's house, she heard a terrible screeching noise, and a bullet shell brushed past her skirt. Later, Sadie wrote about what happened next:

"I almost fell, when I was grasped by the arm and a man said pleasantly, 'That was a close call.'

'Come with me and hurry,' he added in a tone so commanding that I meekly followed. [That man was Dr. Benjamin F. Lyford, a surgeon in the Union army.] He led me to an army corps hospital and then he put me to work. Wounded and dying men were then being carried to the place by the score....

As I reached the hospital tent, a man with a shattered leg was carried in. 'Give him a drink of water while I cut off his leg' was the command I got. How I accomplished it I do not know but I stood there and assisted the surgeon all through the operation. I was in that field hospital all during the three days of the battle, climbing over heaps of bodies six and eight deep and always with the doctor helping him in his work. Then my father found me and took me home."

During those three days, Sadie courageously cared more for the soldiers who needed her help than for her own needs. She was little and had no experience, and she probably missed her family very much. She may have been scared and even a little horrified by all the sickness and pain around her, but she did her best and gave all her strength. But that's not all!

A little while later, a hospital was set up near the battle, and Sadie worked as a nurse there too for nearly five months. She said, "I was placed in charge of one of the wards and I was so small I had to climb up on the beds to attend to the sick and wounded men."

What a kind and brave girl! Sadie could have stayed home where it was safe and comfortable, playing with her friends and just having fun like most other children. But she wanted to help instead.

YOUR TURN

- What would you have done if you were in Sadie's place and …

  1. Your parents asked you to run two miles to your grandparents' home at 2:00 a.m.?

  2. You had a bullet shell zip by you while you were running?

  3. A strange man took you by the arm and told you to follow him?

  4. You were asked to give water to a soldier while his leg was being cut off?

  5. You were without your family for three days in an army hospital?

  6. You found out there was another hospital that needed help?

- How do you think Sadie was able to do all the things she did during those five months?

- Read 1 Timothy 4:12. In your journal, write about some ways you think God might want you to serve Him or help others even though you've been feeling too nervous or unsure to do it. How does Sadie's story encourage you?

- Ask your parents, Sunday school teacher, or pastor for ideas of ways you can make a difference for God even though you're still young. Start praying about the ideas that excite you and ask God to help you be bold and courageous.

What are your thoughts?

God Is Like a Rock

BIBLE READING *Psalm 18:2*

TRUTH

God is like a rock … only better!

Have you ever walked around with a pebble or small rock in your shoe? It's pretty uncomfortable, right? And it can be even worse if you're wearing boots that are difficult to take off.

Rocks can be a bother if they're in your shoe or if they're thrown at windows or, worse, people. But rocks can also be used for good purposes. Large rocks placed in a circle can make a safe place to have a campfire. Stones are still used to build walls and houses, just like they were used to build castles and fortresses thousands of years ago.

Today's Bible reading reminds us that God is like a strong tower or fortress built out of rock: He's solid, dependable, and safe for us to hide behind when danger comes our way. Of course, God is much better than a rock because He loves us very much.

DARE   Stay close to God, your fortress, to be safe from the enemy.

DOUBLE DARE

1. Find a nice rock with a smooth surface. Using paints or gel pens (the rock will probably absorb marker ink, so that's not your best option), write "Psalm 18:2" and keep the rock somewhere you'll see it often as a reminder that God is your "rock." Make one for a friend too!

2. Take time today to thank God for all the ways He has helped you in difficult times.

PROMISE TO REPEAT

How did it go? What did you learn?

BIBLE READING   *Isaiah 41:13 and John 3:16*

TRUTH

God will hold our hand when we're afraid.

When Nicole was a young girl, her family life was very difficult. Because she didn't have a good relationship with her father, she tried to get acceptance and love from the wrong people and by doing things that weren't healthy. Nicole got involved in activities that took her off the right path, but she had an aunt who loved Jesus and loved Nicole, and this aunt prayed often for Nicole and her family.

When Nicole was sixteen, she made a wrong choice and soon discovered that she was going to have a baby. Afraid and desperate for help, she called a pastor and said she needed to talk. She was honest about her sins and her mistakes, and the pastor helped her pray and ask God for forgiveness. Nicole started going to the pastor's church and met people who were kind and loving. She grew in her faith, and before the baby was born, she was baptized.

Although her life isn't always easy, Nicole follows Jesus—just like her aunt had prayed she would! She finds strength in staying close to the Lord, reading her Bible, and spending time with other Christians.

DARE   When life gets confusing, hang on to Jesus.

DOUBLE DARE

1. Think of someone who feels afraid because of a tough situation in her life. Write a note of encouragement and include today's Bible verses.

2. Who are some people in your life who pray for you often, like Nicole's aunt did for her? Thank God for them. Thank them too!

PROMISE TO REPEAT

How did it go? What did you learn?

Turn Fear into Faith

BIBLE READING *Jeremiah 10:5–6*

TRUTH

God gives us faith and takes away our fear.

Hannah Hurnard, the author of a beautiful book called *Hinds' Feet on High Places*, once had so much fear that she felt like it was paralyzing her and keeping her from living her life. That was until she heard a message about scarecrows that helped her have faith instead of fear.

The preacher she was listening to said that wise birds aren't afraid of scarecrows. They know:

1. The scarecrow is not a real human and can't hurt them.

2. Wherever there's a scarecrow, there's also some of the best fruits and vegetables.

Life sometimes gets scary. We face situations or even people who make us feel small and weak. We may believe we're in danger and try to run away from whatever is scaring us. But, as Hannah learned from the preacher that day, we can face those scary situations knowing that God has *good* things for us ahead. He always uses our problems to help us grow and mature.

Just like a wise bird calmly sits on the shoulder of a scarecrow, we can be calm during hard times, trusting that God is taking care of us.

DARE Sit on your "scarecrow's" shoulder!

DOUBLE DARE

1. In your journal, write about something you're feeling afraid of and why it's scaring you. Write a prayer to God asking Him to change your *fear* into *faith*. Then sit still for a few minutes as He helps you feel calmer.

2. Memorize Jeremiah 10:6.

PROMISE TO REPEAT

How did it go? What did you learn?

Spinning Around

BIBLE READING   *Matthew 6:28*

TRUTH

Focus on Jesus and He'll take care of the rest.

Have you ever been so worried or confused that you felt like your head was spinning? There are many situations that would make any of us feel concerned. But sometimes we worry about things that aren't all that serious, don't we? For example, you may wonder what you're going to wear to a special party because your parents don't have enough money to buy something new.

In today's Bible verse, Jesus was reminding His disciples that they didn't have to worry about their daily needs. If God took such good care of the beautiful flowers He created, wouldn't He also make sure His followers had whatever they needed?

That didn't mean they could be lazy and wait for God to drop stuff out of the sky. It meant that if they made following Jesus their first priority, He would take care of everything else.

Do you pay too much attention to what you *want* instead of trusting God to give you what you *need*?

DARE   Be like a lily: Just enjoy what God has blessed you with!

DOUBLE DARE

1. Take a fluffy cotton ball and pull the fibers out just a bit. Twist them tightly until you get a thin but strong thread. That's what *spinning* is. See how long you can make the thread without breaking it. As you do that, pray and thank God for all His blessings.

2. In your journal, write down some things you're worried about when you think about the future. Ask God to help you trust Him as you focus on obeying Him.

PROMISE TO REPEAT

How did it go? What did you learn?

BIBLE READING *Job 34:21–22*

TRUTH

Those who do evil can't hide from God.

Two friends were out hunting together when they suddenly came face-to-face with a bear! Terrified, they dropped their rifles and ran for cover as fast as they could. One scrambled up a tree, and the other ran into a nearby cave. The bear, who was in no hurry, settled down between the tree and the cave and smiled at his luck.

A moment later, to the surprise of the hunter in the tree, the one in the cave rushed out and almost ran into the bear lying on the ground. He paused for a second, turned around, and hurried back into the cave. Three seconds later, he was back outside! He looked at the bear and then ran back to the cave. When he came back out the third time, his friend finally yelled, "Woody! Are you crazy? Stay in the cave until he leaves!"

Woody answered, "I can't! There's a bear in there too!"

The Bible warns that those who do evil and don't follow Jesus will face the same problem one day. They will want to hide from God, but there will be nowhere for them to go. God is holy and will judge those who reject Him.

DARE   Get right with God!

DOUBLE DARE

1. Share today's devo with your family. Talk about the importance of obeying God and keeping a right relationship with Him.

2. In your journal, write down some changes you can make in your life to make sure you won't ever feel like you need to hide from God.

PROMISE TO REPEAT

How did it go? What did you learn?

White As Snow

Depending on where you live, you may never have seen snow, or you may be surrounded by it for a few months every winter. Even if you don't know what it's like to build a snowman, have a snowball fight, or make snow angels, you can still appreciate the beauty of a snowflake—one of God's most delicate little creations.

The Bible says,

> "Come now, let us settle the matter," says the LORD. "Though your sins are like scarlet, they shall be as white as snow; though they are red as crimson, they shall be like wool." (Isaiah 1:18)

> Wash me, and I will be whiter than snow. (Psalm 51:7)

The Bible is full of examples and encouraging messages about God's love and forgiveness. The verses above tell us that God not only forgives us when we confess to Him that we've sinned, but He also makes our hearts pure!

Living in a large Canadian city, I've seen snow that's mucked up with pollution or mud, and it makes me really appreciate fresh snow that's still sparkly white. What I love even more is the feeling that God has washed away the yuckiness of my sins!

FUN, FLAKY FACTS

- All snowflakes have six sides.

- In Prince Edward Island, Canada, where the soil is red clay, snowflakes often look pink because red dust from the soil is blown into the air and absorbed by the clouds.

- The largest snowflakes ever recorded fell in Montana. They were fifteen inches in diameter!

- The snow "capital" of the United States is Stampede Pass in Washington State. The average yearly snowfall there is 430 inches. That's almost thirty-six feet!

YOUR TURN

- Read Psalm 51:7 again and ask God to forgive you for each previously unconfessed sin you can think of … and then thank Him! Also, ask God to help you forgive anyone who has hurt you or done something else that's still bothering you.

- *Bonus Activity #1: Make a snowflake*

  Eight-sided paper snowflakes are easier to make than six-sided ones. Fold a square piece of paper diagonally to make a triangle, and then fold that triangle in half twice more. Now just snip out pieces of different shapes and sizes from all three sides, being careful not to cut out too much. Open it up and … surprise! You've got a pretty snowflake.

Tip: Instead of plain copier paper, try cutting snowflakes out of napkins, wax paper, tissue paper, colored paper, or even lace doilies!

- *Bonus Activity #2: Share this*

When someone asks you about your snowflake creations, that's the perfect time to tell them about God's forgiveness and what Isaiah 1:18 says.

Here's an idea: Make your own note cards (decorated with snowflakes, of course!) and write out Isaiah 1:18 on the left side. On the right side, write a fun message such as:

It's *snow* secret that God loves you!
There's *snow* one like you!
You're *snow* special!
Snow what? I love you!

BIBLE READING *Mark 9:43–48*

TRUTH

Sin will destroy us if we don't let God remove it from our lives.

Remember the story of my grandmother Osanna and how she had to have her leg cut off below the knee when she was only nine years old? Do you remember why the doctors had to cut off her leg? It was because a terrible sore was spreading higher and higher up her leg, and that sore wasn't going away. If they hadn't cut her leg off, little Osanna would have died from the disease infecting her leg.

The Bible says that when we allow sin to stay in our hearts, that sin can grow and spread and make us spiritually sick. Just as taking medicine or wrapping her leg in bandages would not have saved my grandma, things like going to church and singing worship songs are not enough to get rid of sin. We need to take more serious action.

That may mean not watching a TV show that puts bad words or thoughts in your mind or not hanging out with a girl who tempts you to disobey your parents. It also means asking God to reach into your heart and pull out that sin or cut it off. Only He has the power to do that. And that will save you!

DARE Take serious action against your sins.

DOUBLE DARE

1. In your journal, write about a temptation that keeps bugging you. Then write down what changes you will make to keep that temptation far from you.

2. Ask God to give you the courage to get rid of anything in your life that tempts you.

PROMISE TO REPEAT

How did it go? What did you learn?

Don't Give In

BIBLE READING *Proverbs 1:10–16*

TRUTH

Following those who enjoy sin will always lead you into trouble.

On the lines below, list ten things or people you sometimes feel tempted by. We've given two examples to get you started.

cheating on a test   a friend who takes money from her mom's purse

_____ _____

_____ _____

_____ _____

_____ _____

Write your name in the first blank below. Then, read the sentence slowly and, in your head, fill in the second blank with the first answer on your list above. Repeat this until you've read the sentence with all your answers.

_____, if _____ entice(s) you, do not give in (Proverbs 1:10).

Saying no to temptation can be really hard sometimes. But you don't have to fight temptation by yourself. Your heavenly Father is there to help you and to give you courage. No matter what time it is or where you are, you can pray and ask for His help. Also, remind yourself every day not to give in to temptation—before you feel tempted!

DARE When temptation comes your way, turn around and walk away.

DOUBLE DARE

1. In your journal, copy the list of temptations you wrote above. For each one, write a plan for how you will say no the next time you feel tempted. Ask God to help you.

2. Ask your parents how they overcome temptations that they face. If you feel brave, tell them about the things that tempt you and ask them to pray for you.

PROMISE TO REPEAT

How did it go? What did you learn?

Don't Let Sin Move In

BIBLE READING *Proverbs 28:13–14*

TRUTH

Not confessing sin right away is like giving it a guest room.

Many years ago, a lady noticed a few bees buzzing around in the attic of her house. They were annoying, but she didn't feel like trying to get rid of them. She figured they'd just die or find a way out. All summer, bees went in and out of the vent in her attic, but still she didn't do anything. She didn't go up into her attic, so they didn't bother her.

But there was something this lady didn't know. While she went on with her daily life, the bees in her attic were building a city! Their hive grew and grew and became so heavy with honey and bees that one day … CRASH! The floor of the attic caved in. The woman escaped in time and wasn't seriously injured, but her house could not be repaired.

All because she didn't get rid of the first few bees.

Sin is just like those bees. We may think one lie or one bad word isn't a big deal. We may think that saying a joke that hurts someone's feelings isn't so wrong. But when we let "little" sins pile up in our hearts without asking God for forgiveness, we can get ourselves into big trouble.

DARE Don't let sin hang around in your heart.

DOUBLE DARE

1. Do you have any sins "buzzing" around in your heart that you've been ignoring? Confess them to God today and ask Him to clean out your "attic."

2. Share today's story with your family and talk about the importance of confessing sin right away.

PROMISE TO REPEAT

How did it go? What did you learn?

Hold On. Pain Ends.

BIBLE READING *Psalm 33:18–22*

TRUTH

God is our helper and protector in hopeless times.

Life is full of disappointments. You look forward to hanging out with a friend and then she cancels on you or your parents say you have to finish your chores. Your family goes on vacation together and spends half the time arguing. You practice for weeks to audition for the school play and you don't get the part you wanted. Your best friend invites you to her birthday party and pays more attention to another friend.

Do you ever feel like your life is just one bad thing after another? It can feel hopeless sometimes to keep doing your best and to keep trusting and obeying God when it seems as though nothing is working out. You might wonder, *What's the point? Nothing ever goes right!*

The Bible promises that God sees every hurtful experience you go through. He may allow some bad things to happen to you, but it's not because He doesn't care. Sometimes He uses tough situations to make us stronger or to teach us things. But He's always there to hold us and give us hope—sometimes right from the start, and sometimes at the end.

I once saw someone make a cool acronym with the letters in the word *HOPE*: **H**old **O**n. **P**ain **E**nds. What a great reminder!

DARE Hold on to hope!

DOUBLE DARE

1. Make a sign with big bubble letters that says "HOPE." Inside the letters, write the words in the acronym (for example, *hold* inside the letter *H*, and so on). Decorate it and put it on your fridge.

2. Make a nice card with the words of Psalm 33:18–22 for someone who is going through a hard time.

PROMISE TO REPEAT

How did it go? What did you learn?

BIBLE READING *Romans 8:25; 12:12*

TRUTH

God's blessings are worth waiting for.

Little Katie was excited as she climbed into the backseat of the car. Her family was going to visit Grandma and Grandpa! They had to drive about 250 miles from Houston to Dallas. After about fifty miles, Katie started to get antsy and asked, "Are we almost there?" Her dad answered, "No, sweetie, we're still pretty far."

After another fifty miles, Katie asked again, "Are we there yet?" This time her mom said, "No, not yet, dear." Katie tried to sit still, but she was too excited. Fifty miles later she asked, "Now are we almost there?" Her dad said, "No, we still have about a hundred miles to go." Katie thought for a moment and then asked, "Daddy, am I still going to be four years old when we get there?"

Have you ever felt like Katie? Isn't it hard to be patient when we're waiting for something exciting to happen? Or when we can't wait for something to finish? For example, if you're not good at geography, you may sit in class thinking, *When is this going to end?* Or maybe you have a broken arm and can't wait to get your cast off so you can go swimming again.

The Bible reminds us that it's good to be patient.

DARE Don't be in a hurry.

DOUBLE DARE

1. What is something you're having trouble waiting for? Ask God to help you focus on other things you can be thankful for while you wait.

2. Make a pretty bookmark with the words of Romans 12:12 and give it to someone who needs some encouragement.

PROMISE TO REPEAT

How did it go? What did you learn?

HERO LIST

Choose ONE of these heroes to learn about this weekend:

Name	Bible Verses
Esther	Esther 3:1–11; 4:4–17; 5:1–8; 7:1–10; 8:1–11
Stephen	Acts 6–7
Ruth	Ruth 1–4
David	1 Samuel 17
Abigail	1 Samuel 25:1–42
Gideon	Judges 6–7
The Bleeding Woman	Mark 5:25–34
Joseph	Genesis 37; 39–41
The Widow of Zarephath	1 Kings 17:8–24; Luke 4:25–26
Noah	Genesis 6–8
Miriam	Exodus 2:1–10
Daniel	Daniel 6
Mary of Bethany	John 12:1–8
Abraham	Genesis 22:1–18

Your hero for this weekend: _____

QUESTION TIME

1. How did this weekend's hero show courage and faith in God?

2. What happened because of his or her courage and obedience?

3. What did you learn from this hero's life that will help you in your own walk with God?

DOUBLE DARE

Choose at least one of these ways to dig a little deeper into your hero's life this weekend:

1. See if you can find other Bible verses about him or her. Write the reference (or the "address" of the verses) here and also anything new that you learned.

2. Ask your parents or another Christian what they have learned from this hero's life and example.

Tell a friend or your family about your new hero!

What are your thoughts?

The Importance of Rest

BIBLE READING *Lamentations 3:25*

TRUTH

Moments of rest can help us be our best.

If you take music lessons, you might recognize these symbols:

Each of these symbols represents a rest—a moment during a song when there's no sound at all, or, in other words, a pause. The symbol that looks like an upside-down hat is the longest rest, and the one that looks like a funny 7 is the shortest.

A rest may not seem like an important part of a song since no one is playing an instrument or singing at that moment. But rests add something special to songs because they make the audience listen for the next note, and they allow a song to breathe, just like we need to take deep breaths sometimes or pause while we're working on something to keep up our energy.

Our lives are like songs. Sometimes God allows things to happen that force us to stop what we're doing or to change our plans, such as sickness, moving, or a parent losing his or her job. It could be that He wants us to rest for a moment and trust Him while we wait for the next notes of our life's song.

DARE   Take time to be quiet now and then.

DOUBLE DARE

1. Do you usually try to cram your day with activities and fun? Make an effort to take five-minute pauses a few times today to rest your mind while you talk to God.

2. The next time you're sick in bed, think of it as a chance to rest and give your body a break. Use the time to pray for others or to read your Bible.

PROMISE TO REPEAT

How did it go? What did you learn?

Counting Sheep

BIBLE READING *Psalm 4:8*

TRUTH

We sleep better when we have peace with God.

I don't know about you, but I have trouble falling asleep quickly. I can lie there thinking about things for a really long time, which keeps my brain going instead of letting it relax. Some people say that counting sheep (for example, imagining them jumping over a fence one by one) can help you fall asleep because it's such a boring thing to do.

Actually, scientists who have done research on sleeping say this doesn't work. The problem is that it's so boring that most people get tired of it and stop counting before they've fallen asleep! Experts say that the best thing to do is to imagine a relaxing scene, such as a gentle stream or falling rain. This works because it keeps the brain from thinking about whatever might have been worrying the person during the day.

The Bible gives even better advice. In today's verse, we see how David—a shepherd who could have really counted sheep!—knew he could sleep peacefully because God was taking care of Him. We can have that kind of peace too when we trust in the Lord.

DARE Talk to the Lord when you have trouble sleeping.

DOUBLE DARE

1. Before going to bed tonight, write in your journal or on this page at least ten things you can thank God for. After thanking Him in prayer, think about those things as you go to sleep.

2. Do you have a friend who finds it hard to fall asleep? Share today's devo with her and help each other memorize the Bible verse.

PROMISE TO REPEAT

How did it go? What did you learn?

Courage to Do the Right Thing

BIBLE READING *Philippians 4:13*

TRUTH

There's nothing we can't do when God gives us the strength we need.

Thirteen-year-old Brielle's mom is very proud of her. Brielle has a younger sister and also a younger brother who has autism; she has been a great role model to them and also a big help to her mom. Brielle really loves Jesus and was baptized when she was twelve.

But Brielle is also a normal girl, and one day she and her mom got into a big fight. They didn't talk to each other for the rest of the day, and what started as a misunderstanding just got worse and worse the longer they ignored each other. Brielle didn't deal with it right away. She didn't want to talk about it, so she just kept ignoring her mom, thinking her mom didn't understand her. But then she realized that not talking to her mom was going to hurt her in the long run.

Remembering Philippians 4:13, Brielle got her courage up and finally went to her mom to talk. And, to her surprise, it actually wasn't as hard as she thought it was going to be! Because Brielle was willing to do what she knew in her heart was right, God gave her the strength she needed, and everything worked out.

DARE Do hard things for God.

DOUBLE DARE

1. What is something you really don't want to do right now because you don't think you *can* do it? Ask God for strength and start taking the first step toward getting it done.

2. Memorize Philippians 4:13. Write it on five sticky notes and put them in obvious places where you'll see them often.

PROMISE TO REPEAT

How did it go? What did you learn?

An Extra Mile

BIBLE READING *Matthew 5:41*

TRUTH

God wants us to be generous when we help others.

A couple of years ago, I had to fly from Montreal to Toronto (one hour by plane) for a meeting the next day. When the plane got close to Toronto, instead of hearing that we were getting ready to land, the passengers were told that there was too much fog and no planes could land at the Toronto airport.

The pilot had to make a quick decision, so he flew a bit farther to Hamilton, a smaller city about an hour's drive from Toronto, and landed there. I panicked. How was I going to get from Hamilton to Toronto late at night?

Finally, I called the lady who was supposed to pick me up in Toronto, and she called our friend Joanne, who lives in Hamilton and was planning to drive to the meeting the next day. Joanne picked me up from the airport, drove me (and three strangers from the plane) all the way to Toronto, and then turned around and drove all the way back. The next morning, she had to make the same trip!

I will never forget how Joanne gave up a few hours of her time to rescue us. She obeyed this verse and drove an extra ninety miles!

DARE Do more than you're expected to do.

DOUBLE DARE

1. Does a friend or a family member need your help? Think of a way you can make her day by doing *more* than what she asked you for.

2. Did someone impress you by helping you out like my friend Joanne did? Be sure to show how thankful you are.

PROMISE TO REPEAT

How did it go? What did you learn?

Remember Those Who Serve

BIBLE READING *Philippians 2:3–4*

TRUTH

As Christians, we must treat others with great respect.

Long ago, when an ice cream cone cost only ten cents, a little boy went into a coffee shop and sat at a table. A waitress came to take his order. The boy asked how much an ice cream sundae cost. The waitress said, "Fifty cents." The boy counted his coins. "How much is a plain bowl of ice cream?" The waitress started to feel impatient but answered, "Thirty-five cents." The boy looked at his coins again and then said, "I'll have the plain ice cream."

The waitress brought his ice cream, put the bill on the table, and quickly walked away. After the boy finished his ice cream, he paid the cashier and quietly left. Later, when the waitress went to wipe the table, she began to cry. Next to the empty bowl, the boy had left two nickels and five pennies.

Even though he had fifty cents, the boy didn't order a sundae because he knew he wouldn't have enough left over for a tip.

The Bible tells us to think of others—just like this boy did—and not only ourselves.

DARE   Be a blessing to someone today!

DOUBLE DARE

1. Is there anyone that you're tempted to make fun of or think badly of? Confess this to God and ask Him to help you have a more humble attitude toward this person. Then think of a way to be kind the next time you see him or her.

2. Memorize today's Bible reading. Look up any words you're not sure about.

PROMISE TO REPEAT

How did it go? What did you learn?

The Remarkable, Powerful Pinkie

How much do you know about your pinkie finger? (Some people also call the pinkie *piggy*, after the nursery rhyme "This Little Piggy.")

Do you think it's a very strong part of the body? Let's test it out:

Try lifting a pen using *only* your pinkie. Impossible, right?

Now try writing by holding the pen with your thumb and your pinkie. Write your name here:

How did that go? Not very well, I would guess.

Try buttoning your shirt using your pinkie and your thumb. Probably not too bad, but a bit more awkward than using your index finger, right?

The pinkie, because it's the finger at the end, is less protected, and people fracture that finger twice as often as any other finger. But, believe it or not, the pinkie is quite powerful. If you lost your pinkie, you would also lose 50 percent, or half, of the strength in your hand!

There are other parts of our bodies that might seem small or weak or even weird—like the little hanging thing at the back of your throat. (That's called the uvula, by the way.) But God designed each little bitty part of you for a special purpose.

The body of Christ—the people all over the world who have accepted Jesus as their Savior and follow Him—works the same way. We're all different (inside and out)— some are strong, some are shy, some are bold, some are gentle, some are leaders, some are followers—but we're all valuable to God and valuable to one another. We should never feel that we're not useful or important in God's plans. And we should never feel that way about anyone else either!

YOUR TURN

- Read 1 Corinthians 12:12–27. In your journal, write what you learned from this weekend's Bible reading and devo.

- Get your family or a group of Christian friends together and make a list of all your names. Next to each name, write down a couple of ways that person is special and how he or she can serve God and bless others. Try to identify one another's strengths and encourage one another to use them.

- Are there people in your church who don't seem to get noticed much? If you know their names, write them in your prayer journal and pray for them this weekend. The next time you see them, why not share a smile with them? You might make their day!

What are your thoughts?

BIBLE READING   *Lamentations 3:18, 21–23*

TRUTH

God is faithful every single day.

WHEN WE FEEL HOPELESS, WE CAN FIND STRENGTH IN GOD.
21   5   29   20   32 7 31   26 35   10 27 13

HIS LOVE FOR US IS FAITHFUL AND NEVER FAILS.
22 9   15   23 6   30   2   33   4 19

NO MATTER WHAT HAPPENS TO US,
11 36 16   17   34 28 3   14   24

WE CAN TRUST HIM TO TAKE CARE OF US.
25   1   8   12   18

Fill in the blank spaces below with the letters from the paragraph above that match the numbers. This will reveal a verse you may remember from last week.

"___ ___ ___ ___ ___ ___ ___ ___ ___ · ___ ___ ___ ___ ___ ___ ___ ___ ___ ___ ___ ___ ___ ___ ___
1 2 3   4 5 6 7   8 9 · 10 11 12 13   14 15   16 17 18 19 20   21 22 23 24 25

___ ___ ___ ___ ___ ___ ___ ___ ___ ___ ___."
26 27 28 29   30 31   32 33   34 35 36

Tweens may not have the same kinds of pressures and problems as grown-ups, but that doesn't mean they don't have bad days. Kids get sick. Kids suffer when their parents get divorced or die. Kids get bullied and picked on. You've probably had days when you just wanted to stay in bed and cry.

God is there for you, even in the worst situations. Put your hope in Him!

DARE   Trust God, no matter what.

DOUBLE DARE

1. In your journal, write about a day when you felt hopeless or sad and how God helped you get through it.

2. Memorize Lamentations 3:22–23.

PROMISE TO REPEAT

How did it go? What did you learn?

Camel Knees

BIBLE READING *Psalm 95:6–7*

TRUTH

God is our Maker and Master.

What do you think is the funniest-looking part of the human body? I've always thought that knees were kind of strange. Some are big and round, others are crooked and bony, some are smooth, and some are rough. But there's an animal that has even funnier-looking knees than humans do: the camel!

Camels have thick calluses (layers of hardened skin) on their front knees because they always drop their front legs down to let riders climb onto their backs. With their knees hitting the ground so often, they get roughed up and hardened.

When someone is known for spending a lot of time praying to God, we sometimes say he or she has "camel knees," because the Bible talks about kneeling when we pray. It seems that Christians these days don't kneel very much when they pray, but it's a good habit to develop, at least when praying alone. Of course, you can pray without kneeling (especially since you can pray anywhere, such as on the bus, at school, while walking down the street, and so on). But when we get down on our knees to talk to God, it is a way of showing that we respect Him as our Maker and that we want to be humble.

DARE Give yourself "camel knees"!

DOUBLE DARE

1. Think about how much time you spend praying each day. What's your posture when you pray? Try praying on your knees today, and then write about the experience in your journal.

2. When you're praying at church, make sure your posture and attention are respectful, even if you're not kneeling. Remember that you're talking to God, your Maker.

PROMISE TO REPEAT

How did it go? What did you learn?

Care for Creation

BIBLE READING *Psalm 104:10–14*

TRUTH

God takes care of the earth, and we should too.

Have you heard the story of Peanut the turtle? In 1993, someone found a strangely shaped turtle with a plastic ring from a six-pack of drinks tightly stuck around her middle. She was taken to a zoo in St. Louis, Missouri, where the plastic was removed—but it was too late to fix the damage done to her shell. Peanut's shell, instead of being round, looks a bit like the number eight or the shape of a violin—narrower in the middle. She had gotten stuck in the plastic ring when she was still little, and as her shell grew, there was no way for her to get free.

Although she lived, there was damage done to some of her internal organs too. Sadly, there are many cases of animals who get injured or sick—or even die—because they eat or get stuck inside plastic garbage that people litter on beaches, in parks, or along the highway.

Our heavenly Father created an incredibly beautiful earth with a vast array of beautiful plants, animals, mountains, and lakes. It shows disrespect to God and it harms nature when we are careless about littering and wasting.

DARE Treat creation with respect.

DOUBLE DARE

1. Ask your parents or a teacher to help you find more information about Peanut or other animals harmed by littering. Then remind your friends about the importance of caring for God's creation.

2. Take time today to thank God for all the wonderful things He has created, naming them one by one.

PROMISE TO REPEAT

How did it go? What did you learn?

Let's Applaud for God

BIBLE READING *Psalm 29:2*

TRUTH

God deserves the biggest applause.

Can you think of a few different examples of times when people applaud (clap)? For example, you might clap when a player on your favorite basketball team scores a point. When else?

It's hard to know where or when the custom of clapping started, but several Bible verses mention clapping, so people thousands of years ago were doing it too! It's something we seem to do naturally when we're happy or excited about something or when we want to cheer for someone who has done a great job. Have you ever noticed that even little babies clap their hands together when they're happy?

It's great to encourage our friends by clapping, and it feels nice when people applaud for us. Now think about how awesome God is and all the incredible things He has done since the beginning of time. Does anyone deserve more praise and applause than He does? Of course not. But, sadly, God is often forgotten because most of us are too busy thinking about ourselves or our friends and family. Maybe that's why we have a reminder in the Bible!

DARE Applaud for God.

DOUBLE DARE

1. In your journal, list ten or fifteen things that God deserves praise and applause for. Every time you write one, give God a little cheer. If you're feeling shy because you're not alone, do it silently in your mind.

2. Whenever you hear clapping, silently thank God for the talent or ability He gave the person being applauded (especially if it's you!).

PROMISE TO REPEAT

How did it go? What did you learn?

He's All You Need

BIBLE READING *Psalm 16:1–5*

TRUTH

When God is all you have, you have everything you need.

What would be the best thing to have in these situations? (Write your answers on the lines.)

The tip of your pencil breaks: _____

You get pudding on your chin: _____

You're thirsty: _____

It's raining: _____

You get a splinter in your finger: _____

You start going to a new school where you don't know anyone: _____

Your answers may have been different from mine, which were *a pencil sharpener, a napkin, water, an umbrella, tweezers,* and *a friend.*

Many things in the world can help us with small problems, like those in the list, or even with big ones. For most of the problems we have, there is a solution. But sometimes we get stuck. Some kids don't have loving parents, or their parents don't have enough money. Some people don't have a place to live or food to eat. Others are very sick or struggle with addictions.

The Bible says that God is the ultimate solution to *all* our needs. When there doesn't seem to be any hope, God gives us what we need. He may not take away the problem, but He will give us strength or courage or wisdom or peace—whatever we need to make it through. We simply have to trust Him.

DARE Depend on God more than anything else.

DOUBLE DARE

1. Ask a friend what her answers would be to the question in this devo. Then talk about how God is the only One who can solve all our problems.

2. What are some problems you have trouble trusting God with? Talk to Him about it today.

PROMISE TO REPEAT

How did it go? What did you learn?

Soul Surfer

If you've seen the movie *Soul Surfer*, you already know who Bethany Hamilton is. But some of you may not, so I'm going to tell you a little bit about her exciting (and at times scary!) story.

Bethany, who was born in Hawaii into a family who loved to surf, was only eight years old when she entered her first surf competition and participated in two categories (short and long board). She won both times! After that, she became really excited about surfing competitively.

When Bethany was thirteen, she was surfing on the North Shore of Kauai. Suddenly, a shark that was fourteen feet long (about half the length of a bus) attacked her. Thankfully, Bethany survived the attack, but she came out of it missing her left arm. She lost over half the blood in her body and had to have many surgeries, but she made it! She kept a positive attitude and started to get better.

A lot of people would have given up surfing at that point. They might be too afraid to go into the ocean again, or they might think they couldn't surf with only one arm. But Bethany was determined, and just one month after the shark attack, she was back on her board. Not only that, but she continued to train and became a professional surfer. In 2005, when she was only fifteen, Bethany won first place in a national competition.

Where did Bethany find the courage to survive the shark attack and the difficult time in the hospital, to cope with the loss of her arm, and to continue surfing? She found that courage in her relationship with Jesus. Bethany asked Jesus to be her Savior when she was five years old, and her faith in Him helped her be strong and hopeful. She says it was Jesus who gave her peace when the shark attacked her.

Today, Bethany is a young woman who helps and encourages others, and her life story points people to Jesus because she's not shy to honor and praise Him. Bethany says, "When people ask me what my faith in Christ means to me, I usually answer in just one word: everything! This was true before the shark attack as well as after.... It helps to know that even when you don't have a clue why something has happened in your life, the head honcho up there has a master plan and is watching over you. It's a tremendous relief to be able to put your trust in God and take the burden off your shoulders."

YOUR TURN

- Read Philippians 4:6–8. How does this passage relate to Bethany's story?

- Think of a time when you went through a difficult or scary situation and God helped you. Have you shared your story with others? Ask God to show you how you can encourage others who are struggling by telling them about a miracle God has done in your life. Write out your ideas here.

- If you haven't seen it yet, ask your parents if you can watch *Soul Surfer* together. Afterward, talk about how trusting in God can give you courage, strength, peace, and hope. You can also read more about Bethany online at www.bethanyhamilton.com.

What are your thoughts?

Turning a Bully into a Friend

BIBLE READING *Matthew 5:44–45*

TRUTH

God's children love their enemies.

What's your favorite part of the day when you're at school? A lot of kids would say they look forward to recess most of all. Unless there's a bully around. Nobody wants to hang around bullies, right? Not quite nobody. Here's a story about a girl in Oregon named Anna.

One autumn day, when Anna was in third grade, she went outside with the rest of the students to play at recess. A bully from fifth grade started coming toward her. Instead of running away or trying to pick a fight with him, she told him to follow her over to the fence surrounding the play area. In a quiet voice, Anna asked him, "What's bothering you?" The boy was surprised at first, but then he started to share his story with her. Afterward, Anna asked him how he felt. He said he felt better! Then he added, "In fact, I think I'm going to go and make a couple of friends."

Just like that, the worst bully at Verne A. Duncan Elementary School stopped picking on other kids, just because a daring eight-year-old girl was willing to show him kindness.

DARE Reach out to someone who is difficult to love.

DOUBLE DARE

1. Is there someone in your life who is difficult to get along with or is always mean to others? Ask God to show you a way to show compassion to this person, like Anna did to the bully.

2. Share Anna's story—and today's Bible verses—with your friends and encourage them to love their enemies too.

PROMISE TO REPEAT

How did it go? What did you learn?

BIBLE READING *John 8:12*

TRUTH

When you follow Jesus, you can walk safely through life.

Have you ever played a game where you had to be blindfolded with a scarf or cloth tied around your head so that you couldn't see anything? It might have been for a piñata or Pin the Tail on the Donkey, for example. How easy is it to walk around or know what you're doing when you can't see? It might make you nervous if you know there is a lot of furniture in the room that you could trip over or if there are people you could bump into. But it's still fun because you know there's no real danger.

Now imagine you were blindfolded (or blind) and had to walk from one end of your house to the other. Would that be more difficult? What if you had to walk to your neighbor's house blindfolded? It's getting more dangerous, isn't it?

Going through life without Jesus to light your way is like going through life with a blindfold on. You won't know where you're going or be able to avoid the dangers along the way. But when you walk with Jesus, you walk in the light instead of darkness.

DARE   Walk in the light of Jesus.

DOUBLE DARE

1. Ask someone in your family to blindfold you, and then try to walk through your house (while they watch out for you). In your journal write how that made you feel about following Jesus.

2. If you have a friend who doesn't think it makes a difference to follow Jesus, share today's Bible verse with her.

PROMISE TO REPEAT

How did it go? What did you learn?

Spread Some Sunshine

BIBLE READING *Matthew 5:14–16*

TRUTH

God's light shining through you will help others find Jesus.

Don't you just love sunshine? I live in Montreal, Canada, where it doesn't get really hot until July, but I don't mind cold weather or snow. Even if it's freezing cold, a sunny blue sky can cheer me up. But a cloudy gray day can make me feel a bit blah.

When it's sunny, I feel energetic, happy, and creative. And when I'm cheerful, it's easier to be nice to and more patient with others. I can't control the weather, though, and I can't use it as an excuse for not being nice on cloudy days. Even when the weather is blah, I need to stay positive. Do you know how I do that?

I remember John 8:12 (yesterday's Bible verse) and how Jesus said that He is the light. I don't need sunshine to have light in my life—I can just go to Jesus! When I stay close to Him, His light brightens my day, shows me the way to go, and gives me joy and comfort. Then I can share that light with others, just like today's reading says.

How sunny is your heart? Can others see the joy that Jesus gives you? Don't hide your light—spread it around!

DARE Let others see Jesus's light in you.

DOUBLE DARE

1. When you see someone who looks sad today, share a warm smile with her. If it's a friend, remind her that God loves her.

2. Make a sun out of yellow paper, write "You are the light of the world" in the middle, and stick it up on your bedroom window or mirror.

PROMISE TO REPEAT

How did it go? What did you learn?

BIBLE READING *Philippians 1:21*

TRUTH

For a Christian, death just means moving to a better place.

One day, a bank in New York called a flower shop and asked them to send a bouquet of flowers to another bank that had just moved into a new building. There must have been a mix-up at the shop because the little card attached to the flowers said, "With our deepest sympathy." (Sympathy is the sadness you feel when someone is going through a difficult time.)

When the florist found out about the mistake, she was terribly embarrassed and apologized to the bank. But she was even more embarrassed later that day when she found out the card that should have gone to the bank had been attached to flowers sent to a funeral. That card said, "Congratulations on your new location!"

There's something pretty cool about this funny story. Although the people at the funeral probably thought it was rude to send such a message to someone who had died, it actually would make sense if that person was a Christian! The Bible promises that when we believe in Jesus and ask Him to save us, He gives us eternal life in heaven. That means that when we die, we will go to a great new location, so death isn't a bad thing for us.

DARE   Get ready for your new home.

DOUBLE DARE

1. None of us knows at what age we'll die. If you're not sure you'll go to heaven when you die, take a look at page 426 and ask Jesus to be your Lord and Savior.

2. Share today's story with your family, as well as what you learned about going to heaven.

PROMISE TO REPEAT

How did it go? What did you learn?

BIBLE READING *Matthew 21:28–32*

TRUTH

You can't get to heaven by being religious on the outside.

My dad used to joke that I reminded him of the story Jesus told about two brothers. When I was younger, sometimes he would ask me to do something and I would complain or argue at first, but later, thinking about it and knowing that I was wrong, I would obey him.

But Jesus wasn't just telling His disciples a story about two brothers and their father. He was describing two kinds of people:

1. Those who don't seem very religious on the outside and are judged by others but who later believe in God and change their ways. They are like the first son. They will go to heaven.

2. Those who are outwardly religious and say all the right things but don't obey God in their hearts or follow Him. They are like the second son. They won't go to heaven.

This is a good reminder that:

1. We shouldn't judge people by how good or bad they look on the outside. We can never know what changes God is making in their hearts.

2. We should obey God not just with our actions but also with our hearts.

DARE Say yes to God and then follow through.

DOUBLE DARE

1. Is there someone you've judged as being a bad person? Today, take time to pray for him or her, asking God to help this person believe in Him.

2. Which of the two brothers are you more like? Make an effort to be someone who always says yes and obeys right away.

PROMISE TO REPEAT

How did it go? What did you learn?

Obeying When It Doesn't Make Sense

Read 2 Kings 5:1–15.

Who are the main characters in this story?

The man who had leprosy:

The kings of two countries:

The prophet:

Did you notice another character in this story? There was a young girl whose name we don't know, but she did something so important that it's written in the Bible! She was a servant in the army commander's family and had been captured from Israel, so she wouldn't have been considered important. Still, she was brave and wise and caring enough to tell her mistress about the prophet who could heal her master. Isn't that cool?

What did Elisha tell Naaman to do to be healed of his leprosy?

How did Naaman react?

How do you think you would have reacted?

What do you think Naaman might have been expecting Elisha to do or tell him to do?

What happened when Naaman finally obeyed?

In several other stories in the Bible, God asked His children to do things that didn't make sense to them. During the weekend, read at least *two* of these stories and then answer the questions.

John 11:30–44: Lazarus's family

What did Jesus ask Lazarus's family to do in verse 39 that surprised them?

What happened at the end because they obeyed?

Joshua 6:1–20: Joshua

What did God ask Joshua to do that might have seemed strange?

What happened at the end because he and his army obeyed?

Luke 1:26–38: Mary

What did God ask Mary to do that probably frightened her?

What happened because she obeyed? (The answer isn't in these verses, but you can probably figure it out!)

Judges 7:1–21: Gideon

What did God ask Gideon to do that might have seemed strange?

What happened at the end because he and his army obeyed?

YOUR TURN

- Read Romans 12:19–20 and Matthew 5:39. What does God ask us to do in these verses that wouldn't make sense to the rest of the world?

- Read Proverbs 14:12. Why shouldn't we trust our own wisdom about whether or not God's commands make sense?

- Read 1 John 5:3. When we obey God, what does it show?

What are your thoughts?

The Dreaded Roller Coaster

BIBLE READING *Matthew 10:28*

TRUTH

Sometimes we are afraid of the wrong things!

One summer, I went with some friends from church to an amusement park in Montreal, Canada, where I live. I'm not fond of rides, so I said I would sit on a bench and enjoy the view while they rode the roller coasters. After teasing me a little, they finally convinced me to try one.

Those were the scariest, most awful thirty seconds of my life! Thinking back on that day, I know I wasn't in any danger, but it sure felt like I was when we were a bajillion feet over the ground racing down at light speed!

Most people don't know that the chance of dying in a car crash is forty thousand times higher than dying in a roller coaster accident. So why do we scream on roller coasters and not in cars? It's because we are more afraid of what looks like danger right in front of us than dangers we can't see (such as sleepy truck drivers).

Today's Bible verse teaches us not to be afraid of things that hurt only our bodies or our feelings. What we should be concerned about is the danger our soul is in if we don't trust Jesus as our Savior and Lord.

DARE Give your life to Jesus today!

DOUBLE DARE

1. If you're not sure about going to heaven after you die, pray today and ask Jesus to forgive you for your sins and to give you eternal life. Talk to your parents or pastor if you have questions.

2. Write down five things you're afraid of. Ask God to help you with those fears.

PROMISE TO REPEAT

How did it go? What did you learn?

Is Church a Chore?

BIBLE READING *Psalm 122:1*

TRUTH

Going to church is an important part of our Christian growth.

Use the chart below to solve this puzzle and see what Hebrews 10:24–25 says about going to church.

	©	★	¢	∂	¶
1	A	B	C	D	E
2	F	G	H	I	J
3	K	L	M	N	O
4	P	Q	R	S	T
5	U	V	W	X	Y

"
_____ _____

3★ 1¶ 4¶   5© 4∂   3∂ 3¶ 4¶   2★ 2∂ 5★ 1¶   5© 4©   3¢ 1¶ 1¶ 4¶ 2∂ 3∂ 2★

_____ _____ _____ _____ _____ _____ _____ _____
."
4¶ 3¶ 2★ 1¶ 4¶ 2¢ 1¶ 4¢

Some people think it's not important to go to church. They say, "I can worship God at home. I can read my Bible, pray, and even sing a few songs." That's true, of course, but there's more to church than that (or at least there should be!). The word *church* is *ekklisia* in Greek, and that means a gathering of people. Even in Bible times, followers of Jesus knew it was important for them to meet regularly. They could study the Bible together, pray together, and encourage one another.

It doesn't matter if a church has thirty-five people or thirty-five hundred people. What matters is that they worship and serve God together.

DARE Don't give up on church.

DOUBLE DARE

1. If your family doesn't go to church, ask your parents if they would like to go or if you could go. There may be another family that would be happy to pick you up.

2. If your family does go to church, ask God to help you pay attention during worship and teaching times and to give you the courage to participate. Maybe you could invite a friend to go with you too.

PROMISE TO REPEAT

How did it go? What did you learn?

Don't Delay!

BIBLE READING *Psalm 119:59–60*

TRUTH

We have to obey God today, not wait until tomorrow.

Amanda had a bad habit. She always postponed doing things until later. Another word for this is *procrastination*.

When she got home from school, she would play first and do her homework later. Sometimes she didn't have enough time to finish her lesson before she had to go to bed. When her dad asked her to take out the trash, she wouldn't do it right away and then she'd get in trouble.

One Friday, Amanda found out she had won a prize in a singing competition at school. She was told to pick up her prize from the principal's office before going home that day. But Amanda wasn't in a hurry to get it, so she didn't pick up her prize until the following Monday. That's when she discovered that her prize was a ticket to the circus on the Saturday that had just passed. Her prize was useless now.

Amanda learned her lesson and made sure she didn't postpone things anymore.

Sometimes, like Amanda, we delay in obeying God. This doesn't please Him, and it shows we don't truly honor Him. If we love God, we should follow Him today.

DARE Don't delay in obeying God.

DOUBLE DARE

1. Write down the things that you sometimes postpone even though you know you should do them right away. Ask God to help you stop procrastinating.

2. In what ways do you think God is asking you to obey Him today? Make a promise to follow Him, even if it's difficult.

PROMISE TO REPEAT

How did it go? What did you learn?

Thursday

How to Get to Heaven

BIBLE READING *Ephesians 2:8–9*

TRUTH

Being good isn't enough to get you into heaven.

One day, a Sunday school teacher asked her students, "If I sold my house and car and had a garage sale and then gave all that money to the church, would that get me into heaven?" The children yelled, "No!" Then she asked, "What if I cleaned the church every day, mowed the grass, and visited all the sick people?" Again the children said, "No!"

The teacher asked, "So how can I get into heaven?" One little boy answered, "I know! You gotta be dead!"

You have to admit that his answer makes sense! But that's obviously not the answer the teacher was hoping for. Still, the children were right: Doing good and being helpful are great, but those things don't get us into heaven. Ephesians 2:8 says it is God's grace that saves us. Grace is a gift we don't deserve. It's also something we could never pay for.

God knew we could never be good enough to get to heaven on our own. That's why He sent His Son, Jesus, to earth to die on the cross in our place. When we believe in Him and ask for His forgiveness, He gives us eternal life. Being good is just our way of saying, "Thank You, God!"

DARE Say yes to God's grace!

DOUBLE DARE

1. If you're not sure whether you're going to heaven, read page 426. Talk to your parents, pastor, or youth leader if you still have questions.

2. Do you have a friend who isn't sure how to get to heaven? Share with her what you've learned.

PROMISE TO REPEAT

How did it go? What did you learn?

BIBLE READING   *Colossians 3:8*

TRUTH

When we don't feed ourselves spiritually, it affects other people too.

My friend Delina was born in France and moved to Canada when she was already grown up, so she still has her lovely French accent (which is a little different from a French Canadian accent, just like British English sounds different from American English). It's fun to go out for dinner with Delina because she really enjoys eating. She makes an effort to appreciate her food and to enjoy every bite instead of rushing through the meal.

Delina was once telling me that if she hasn't eaten for a while, she can get so hungry that she gets nervous and easily irritated. She said, "I get really angry!" If you've never heard French people speak English, you may not know that they sometimes put an *h* before a word that starts with a vowel and drop the *h* from the front of other words. So I asked her, "Do you mean hungry or angry?" She laughed and said, "I guess I get hangry!"

That reminds me of the importance of eating spiritual food (reading the Bible, praying, and going to church). When we let ourselves get spiritually hungry, we can become angry and start behaving in ways that don't show we love Jesus.

DARE   Don't let yourself get "hangry"!

DOUBLE DARE

1. Do you get angry easily? Maybe you're not spending enough time with God and in His Word. Pray about this and try to give more time to your devos each day.

2. On a sticky note, write, "Don't get HANGRY!" Put this in your lunch bag as a reminder to eat spiritual food too.

PROMISE TO REPEAT

How did it go? What did you learn?

HERO LIST

Choose ONE of these heroes to learn about this weekend:

Name	Bible Verses
Esther	Esther 3:1–11; 4:4–17; 5:1–8; 7:1–10; 8:1–11
Stephen	Acts 6–7
Ruth	Ruth 1–4
David	1 Samuel 17
Abigail	1 Samuel 25:1–42
Gideon	Judges 6–7
The Bleeding Woman	Mark 5:25–34
Joseph	Genesis 37; 39–41
The Widow of Zarephath	1 Kings 17:8–24; Luke 4:25–26
Noah	Genesis 6–8
Miriam	Exodus 2:1–10
Daniel	Daniel 6
Mary of Bethany	John 12:1–8
Abraham	Genesis 22:1–18

Your hero for this weekend: _____

QUESTION TIME

1. How did this weekend's hero show courage and faith in God?

2. What happened because of his or her courage and obedience?

3. What did you learn from this hero's life that will help you in your own walk with God?

DOUBLE DARE

Choose at least one of these ways to dig a little deeper into your hero's life this weekend:

1. See if you can find other Bible verses about him or her. Write the reference (or the "address" of the verses) here and also anything new that you learned.

2. Ask your parents or another Christian what they have learned from this hero's life and example.

Tell a friend or your family about your new hero!

What are your thoughts?

BIBLE READING *Psalm 119:36*

TRUTH

A follower of Jesus shouldn't be selfish.

Have you heard the "Ten Property Laws of Toddlers"? It basically describes how little children feel about "stuff" …

1. If I like it, it's mine.
2. If it's in my hand, it's mine.
3. If I can take it from you, it's mine.
4. If I had it a little while ago, it's mine.
5. If it's mine, it must never appear to be yours in any way.
6. If I'm doing or building something, all the pieces are mine.
7. If it looks just like mine, it's mine.
8. If I saw it first, it's mine.
9. If you are playing with it and you put it down, it becomes mine.
10. If it's broken, it's yours.

While this is meant to be funny, it's not too far from the truth of how many people—and not just small kids—behave. The world around us teaches us to be selfish and to go after what makes *us* feel good. People forget how to think of others, and they focus mostly on getting more and more and more for themselves.

King David asked God to help him focus on the Lord and not on his own wants. We can do that too.

DARE   Make God your biggest "want."

DOUBLE DARE

1. Write a list of ten things you really want or wish for. Then ask yourself if you want to know God and His Word more than those things. If not, ask God to help you have the same attitude as King David.

2. Memorize today's verse and repeat it silently during the day as a prayer to God.

PROMISE TO REPEAT

How did it go? What did you learn?

Learning to Pray

BIBLE READING *Luke 11:1*

TRUTH

Prayer is better when we're humble.

There's a joke about a woman who drove by a bakery and saw some yummy-looking cookies in the store window. They looked very tempting, but she was trying to lose some weight and knew it would be better if she didn't buy any cookies. So she prayed, "Dear Lord, if You want me to have some of those cookies, please let me find a parking spot in front of the bakery." The story ends like this: After driving around the block eight times, she finally saw an empty parking spot in front of the store!

This is how people pray sometimes. They ask God for answers, but they don't accept His answers. This woman drove around eight times until she finally got what she wanted. Do you think she really wanted to obey God? No. She just tried to change the situation until it looked like she was obeying Him. This woman's prayer was not a real prayer. She wasn't really asking God what He wanted her to do. Instead, she was telling Him what she wanted, and she wasn't even honest about it.

We should be more like Jesus's disciples, who humbly asked Him to teach them how to pray.

DARE Let God teach you how to pray.

DOUBLE DARE

1. Spend a few minutes asking Jesus to teach you how to pray. Tell Him about any doubts or questions you have about prayer.

2. Read Luke 11:1–13. In your journal, write what you learned about prayer.

PROMISE TO REPEAT

How did it go? What did you learn?

BIBLE READING   *Isaiah 45:9*

TRUTH

It's foolish to tell God what to do!

My father owns a little radio shop in Montreal where you can buy radios (obviously), CD players, and lots of other electronics and supplies. He has many antique and vintage items too, which kind of makes you feel like you're in a museum! But the main reason people go to his shop is to get their old radios repaired. He's been fixing radios since he was a young boy and he's over seventy years old now, so he knows everything there is to know about them. In fact, there's no one else in our great big city who repairs old radios, so he's an expert that even people from far away come to.

Do you know what surprises my dad sometimes? When people bring him a radio that's not working and tell him how to fix it. Hmm ... Doesn't that make you wonder why they brought it to him if they could do it themselves? But we humans sometimes think we're smarter than we actually are!

Sometimes we complain to God about our problems and tell Him what we want Him to do to fix them. Instead, we should trust Him with those problems and humbly ask Him to help us.

DARE   When you go to God with a problem, leave it there.

DOUBLE DARE

1. In your journal, write about a time when someone asked you for help and then told you how to help them. How did you feel? Ask God for forgiveness if you've ever done that to Him.

2. Do you know someone who is having trouble trusting God? Tell her about what you learned today.

PROMISE TO REPEAT

How did it go? What did you learn?

The Wise Old Owl

BIBLE READING *James 1:19*

TRUTH

We should listen more than we talk.

> A wise old owl lived in an oak;
> The more he saw, the less he spoke;
> The less he spoke, the more he heard.
> Why aren't we all more like this bird?

A couple of years ago, I copied this poem into my art journal and decorated it with a little drawing of an owl. It reminded me of today's Bible verse and the importance of listening.

Part of being wise is taking time to look around and listen to what's going on before opening our mouths. Sometimes we're too quick to blurt out whatever is on our minds, and that can get us in trouble, hurt someone, make the situation worse, or make us look foolish if what we said was wrong.

The Bible tells us to slow down when it comes to talking and to be quicker to listen, just like the wise old owl!

DARE Think before you speak.

DOUBLE DARE

1. Make a poster or bookmark of the poem above, decorate it, and write "James 1:19" (or the whole verse if you have space) somewhere on your design. Put it on your fridge or in your locker at school.

2. Make an effort today to listen to your friends when they talk, without interrupting them. Then think about what you're going to say before you say it. Ask God for help if you're having trouble.

PROMISE TO REPEAT

How did it go? What did you learn?

BIBLE READING *James 3:5–6*

TRUTH

Thoughtless words can cause great damage.

In May 2012, I got to visit Colorado Springs for the first time. It was awe-inspiring to see Pikes Peak, which is part of the Rocky Mountains, in the distance wherever I went. Surrounding this mountain is more than a million acres of forest.

Less than two months after I returned home to Canada, I started to hear news reports that Pike National Forest was on fire! For the next few weeks, brave firefighters worked day and night to control the terrible wildfires that were spreading.

Every year, millions of acres of forests in the United States, Canada, and other countries are destroyed by fire. Nearly 90 percent of the time, these fires are started by humans, either because of carelessness (for example, not watching a campfire or putting it out properly, dropping cigarettes that are still burning, or burning garbage without being careful) or on purpose. The rest of the time, lightning or lava cause the fires.[3] Once a fire starts in a forest, it quickly spreads and gets out of control.

The Bible warns that our tongues (the words we say) can be as dangerous as the spark that starts a wildfire. We can't take back words that hurt others, so we must watch what we say!

DARE Watch your tongue!

DOUBLE DARE

1. Have you ever said something that hurt someone or started a fight? Were you able to fix the situation? Write about it in your journal and ask God to help you have better control of your tongue.

2. How well do you know fire safety rules? Go over them with your family this week.

PROMISE TO REPEAT

How did it go? What did you learn?

Pop Quiz #1

This is a two-part devo. You'll do most of the reading on Saturday. Then there's a pop quiz to do on Sunday to see how much you remember.

WISE SAYINGS

For some of the devotions in this book, you've had to read verses from the book of Proverbs, so you already know the word *proverb* … But do you know what it means? A proverb is a wise saying that gives good advice. Since King Solomon was the wisest man who ever lived, he had a lot of good advice to give—enough to write a whole book in the Bible! Not all proverbs are from the Bible, though. Other people's wise sayings have been passed down through the years and have become well known.

Sometimes teachers have fun with these sayings by asking their students to finish the second part of famous proverbs. The answers are usually funny!

Here are some examples I've found. For each proverb, first you'll see the answers of children in first and third grades. Then you'll be able to complete the saying yourself. The *real* endings can be found in the answer key on page 429. See how many you get right.

Rome wasn't built <u>in my neighborhood</u>.
Rome wasn't built

If you can't stand the heat <u>take a cold bath tonight</u>.
If you can't stand the heat

People who live in glass houses <u>get seen undressing</u>.
People who live in glass houses

Ask me no questions <u>and stay in your seat</u>.
Ask me no questions

Life is just a bowl of <u>cereal</u>.
Life is just a bowl of

You can't teach an old dog <u>to meet me on the porch</u>.
You can't teach an old dog <u>math</u>.
You can't teach an old dog

If at first you don't succeed, <u>get new batteries</u>.
If at first you don't succeed

Don't bite the hand that <u>looks dirty</u>.
Don't bite the hand that

Out of the mouths of babes <u>comes spit</u>.
Out of the mouths of babes

Out of the nine proverbs, how many did you get right? If you didn't get any right, or just a few, don't worry about it. These are interesting proverbs, but you can get through life just fine without knowing them. But the Bible is different.

THE WISEST WORDS OF ALL

Read John 6:63 and John 6:68.

Jesus and Simon Peter both said that only Jesus's words (which includes the Bible) give life, not only here on earth but also forever in heaven. We need to study the Bible carefully and learn how to live it out. Doing your devos each day is part of that, but it isn't enough. You need to really absorb God's Word, just like a sponge absorbs water.

Now we get to the *real* pop quiz for the weekend. Here's the challenge: Today (Saturday), read the verses below. You may already know a few (or all) of them. Read them a few times to make them "stick" in your memory. Tomorrow, come back and try to finish the verses in the quiz without looking them up in your Bible. (Don't fill in the blanks today.)

Psalm 23:1	Hebrews 13:8	Colossians 3:2	Matthew 22:39
Psalm 119:105	Romans 3:23	James 4:7	Colossians 3:20
Philippians 4:13	Psalm 119:11		

SUNDAY POP QUIZ

Psalm 23:1—The LORD is my shepherd,

Colossians 3:2—Set your minds on things above, not

Psalm 119:105—Your word is a lamp for my feet, a

James 4:7—Submit yourselves, then, to God. Resist the devil, and

Philippians 4:13—I can do all this through him who

Hebrews 13:8—Jesus Christ is the same

Matthew 22:39—Love your neighbor

Romans 3:23—For all have sinned and

Colossians 3:20—Children, obey your parents in everything, for

Psalm 119:11—I have hidden your word in my heart that

Out of the ten verses, how many did you get right? If you missed some, put a bookmark at this page and try again later.

What are your thoughts?

Watch Out for Fake Friends

BIBLE READING *Proverbs 12:26*

TRUTH

Wicked friends can lead us far from God.

In the box, draw a picture of a girl.

Now add a shadow behind her. Where would you have to draw the sun to match where the shadow is?

A shadow is created when the sun, or another source of light, shines on an object and that object blocks the light from the floor or wall behind it. You can't have shadows if there isn't any light. Someone once said:

> "Fake friends are no different than shadows. They stick around during your brightest moments but disappear during your darkest hours."

Think about this. Have you ever noticed that some people want to be your friend when you're popular, when you have a new toy, or when you're planning a party, but they're never around when you're hurt or needing help or in trouble? Those are fake friends. The Bible warns us to be careful to choose friends who are true. Fake friends don't care about you, so it might be dangerous to follow them.

DARE   Choose your friends wisely.

DOUBLE DARE

1. In your journal, write about a time when a friend disappointed you by not being there for you when you needed her. Ask God to help you forgive her but also to help you choose future friends wisely.

2. What kind of friend are you? Write down some ways you can be a better friend to those you love and not just a "shadow" friend.

PROMISE TO REPEAT

How did it go? What did you learn?

Keeping Promises

BIBLE READING *Leviticus 5:4–5 and Matthew 5:36–37*

TRUTH

Breaking a promise is a sin.

Have you ever had a friend make a promise that she didn't keep? How did you feel? What about you—did you ever make a promise you didn't keep? What happened?

It's astonishing how often people break promises. Usually it's because:

1. We foolishly promise something that's impossible for us to do, so we have to break the promise.
2. We unkindly promise something we already know we're not going to do. That's lying.
3. We carelessly promise something without really thinking about it, and then we forget.
4. We honestly promise something but then change our mind about it. That's wrong too.

The Bible tells us that when we say we're going to do something, we must do it. And if we promise not to do something, then we must not do it. People should be able to trust our words, just like we want to be able to trust theirs.

Did you know that God has kept every single promise He's ever made? Since He's God and can do whatever He wants, how does it make you feel to know that He keeps His promises? What a great example He has set for us!

DARE Make promises carefully. Then keep them.

DOUBLE DARE

1. In your journal, write about any promises you know you've made and broken. If there are any you can still keep, make a plan to do it soon. Don't forget to apologize to the person you made the promise to.

2. Thank God for keeping His promises and ask Him to help you be more careful about keeping yours.

PROMISE TO REPEAT

How did it go? What did you learn?

Smooth Talkers

BIBLE READING *Romans 16:17–19*

TRUTH

Good words don't always come from a good heart.

Aesop, who lived about six hundred years before Jesus was born, wrote may fables (short stories that have lessons). In one of them, a crow found a nice chunk of cheese and flew off with it to a nearby tree. As she settled down on a high branch to eat her snack, a fox down below saw her and thought, *That cheese is for me because I am Mister Fox!*

"Good day, Miss Crow," he said in his sweetest voice. "How nice you look today! Your feathers are glossy and your eyes are bright. I am sure your voice is as beautiful as your looks and that you sing more beautifully than all the other birds. Please let me hear you sing just one song so that I can honor you as Queen of Birds."

Miss Crow happily lifted her head and began to caw. But the moment she opened her mouth, her cheese fell to the ground and was snapped up by Mister Fox.

"That's enough," said the fox. "That was all I wanted. In exchange for your cheese, I will give you some advice for the future: Do not trust flatterers."

The Bible also warns us about flatterers (people who say nice things about others just to get something from them). They can deceive you and lead you away from God.

DARE Don't be fooled by flattery.

DOUBLE DARE

1. In your journal, write about a time when someone was nice to you without really meaning it. What happened? Have you ever flattered someone to get something? Ask God to forgive you.

2. Share today's devo with a friend who is easily influenced by people who say nice things to her.

PROMISE TO REPEAT

How did it go? What did you learn?

It's for Your Own Good

BIBLE READING *Romans 8:28–29*

TRUTH

Sometimes, unpleasant things end up being good for us.

Many years ago, a man was visiting a friend in England who had excellent riding horses. Looking around one morning, he saw a beautiful horse feeding in the pasture. It had some difficulty walking because there was a heavy weight attached to one of its legs. The man asked his friend why he had put the uncomfortable weight on such a nice horse.

The friend explained that this horse liked to run and jump over fences. "He could really hurt himself if he wasn't controlled," he said. Even though it seemed unfair that the horse couldn't run around freely, it was because his owner was wise and wanted to protect the animal.

Sometimes our Christian life is like that too. We may wonder why God doesn't allow us to do something or why a situation is so difficult. But that's because we're not as wise as our Maker and Master, who knows exactly what we need and what's good for us.

DARE Be thankful for difficulties, even when you don't understand them.

DOUBLE DARE

1. Write down three things you know a Christian shouldn't do but might be tempted to. Then write down why you think it's for our good that God has given us the "weight" of rules to follow. Ask Him to help you trust Him in tough situations.

2. Ask your parents or another experienced Christian to tell you about a time when God turned a difficulty in their life into something good.

PROMISE TO REPEAT

How did it go? What did you learn?

Jesus Honors Children

BIBLE READING *Mark 10:14*

TRUTH

Jesus loves you even when others make you feel unloved.

In the list below, circle the person you think is the most respected by other people:

school principal	police officer	cleaning lady
president of a country	third grader	pastor
airplane pilot	homeless person	truck driver
college student	fashion designer	doctor

Now look at the list again and draw a star next to the person you think God respects the most.

The more you study the Bible, the more you'll see that Jesus loved everyone equally. Sometimes He got angry with the religious leaders for being hypocrites (pretending to be holy on the outside but not really loving God on the inside). But He still loved them and wanted to save them. We also see that Jesus honored children. When the disciples were telling the kids to be quiet and go away, Jesus told the disciples to stop. He wanted the children to be near Him.

If you don't have a star next to each person on the list above, go back and add one. And remember that Jesus wants you to spend time with Him and learn from Him just as much as He wants grown-ups to. Don't let the way others treat you make you forget how much Jesus loves you.

DARE Hang out with Jesus!

DOUBLE DARE

1. Read Mark 10:13–16. In your journal, write how these verses make you feel about your relationship with Jesus.

2. If you usually forget to have quiet time with God, write yourself a note in your planner or on your calendar. Then take a moment to thank God for wanting to spend time with you.

PROMISE TO REPEAT

How did it go? What did you learn?

Double Dare— Your Way!

We're halfway through the year—and you're halfway through *Truth, Dare, Double Dare*! If you've been doing your devos every day and completing the dares, great job! I'm sure you've already seen changes in your life and in your relationship with God.

As a reward for your good work, you get a bit of a break this weekend. You can choose one (or more!) of these activities to complete this weekend.

1. Encourage someone

Think of someone you want to encourage. It could be a friend, someone in your family, your pastor, your Sunday school teacher, a neighbor, or the school secretary. If you're not sure whom to choose, pray for guidance first.

Get a blank journal from the dollar store. If it's plain, decorate it.

On random pages, write encouraging Bible verses or notes. Flip through this book for reminders of verses that encourage people.

Write a personal message on the inside of the cover.

Wrap the journal and give it to the person you made it for the next time you see him or her.

2. Write your own devo

Using the ones you've already done in this book as examples, see if you can create a brand-new devo.

Choose a Bible verse of your own (or use one we've already done if you can't find a new one).

Look for the "truth" in the Bible verse.

Think of a story that explains the verse or just explain it in your own words. Think about your own experiences for ideas.

Look for the "dare" in the Bible verse.

Come up with two "double dares" that can help someone practice what your devo is about.

Show your devo to your parents or pastor and ask for their feedback. Work on any changes they suggest.

Type your devo on the computer or write it neatly by hand.

When it's ready, share your devo with a friend.

3. Hang out with God

Choose one or two of your regular activities to skip this weekend so that you can have some extra quiet time with God.

Find a quiet place to "hang out" with Him. It could be your bedroom, your backyard, the front porch, or anywhere you can be alone for a while.

Take along your Bible, your journal, and some colored pens or markers.

If you have a music player with worship songs on it, take that along too.

Start by just sitting quietly for a few minutes, resting your mind while you focus on God. Ask Him to calm your heart and your thoughts and to be with you.

Then do whatever seems to come naturally. Here are some ideas:

Read a portion from your Bible (for example, a psalm).

Listen to a worship song and really pay attention to the words. Quietly sing it back to God as a prayer.

Write whatever you're feeling or thinking in your journal.

Write down things you're thankful for.

Confess your sins to God.

Doodle your thoughts or prayer or the words to a worship song.

Take your time and don't be in a rush to finish. Imagine Jesus is sitting with you (He is!) and just enjoy knowing that He loves you and loves it when you spend time with Him. Try being silent and listening to see if He's speaking to your heart.

When you feel like you're done, thank Him for the special quiet time.

At the end of the weekend, write about the activity you chose and how it went. Remember, you can do the activities on this page again and again during the year! Put a bookmark right here so you'll be able to find this Double Dare again.

BIBLE READING   *Colossians 3:12*

TRUTH

God's children should be patient.

We live in a fast-paced world where people can instantly get almost anything they want. We have email, digital cameras, the Internet, photocopiers, bank machines, vending machines, and so much more! While the convenience is nice, the problem is that some people have forgotten how to wait. Many of us have become greedy with our time and feel like we're wasting it if we have to wait for someone else.

Do you ever feel frustrated when you're waiting in line somewhere? How about when the person in front of you is walking kind of slowly? Or when your sister takes too long in the bathroom? Do you get antsy during the last hour of school or a few days before your birthday?

The Bible tells us that as followers of Jesus, we need to develop special qualities, such as compassion, kindness, humility, and gentleness. Another quality—one that a lot of people have difficulty with—is patience.

Patience isn't only about waiting for something to happen. It can also be about controlling our anger when someone is annoying us. With God's help, you can do both!

DARE   Don't be in such a hurry.

DOUBLE DARE

1. Write down a few examples of times when you feel impatient and get tired of waiting. Ask God to help you stay calm during those times. Also, think of positive things you can do while you wait.

2. Ask your mom, pastor, or youth leader to help you find other Bible verses about patience. Choose one to memorize and practice it during the next few days.

PROMISE TO REPEAT

How did it go? What did you learn?

What Money Can't Buy

BIBLE READING   *1 Timothy 6:10 and Ecclesiastes 5:10*

TRUTH

Money can buy things, but not the things that really matter.

In North America, not too many people worship statues, which is what we usually think of when we see the word *idol* in the Bible. We may think that because we don't bow down to and pray to objects, we're not guilty of worshipping other gods. But we forget about one of the most popular "idols" that people all over the world worship: money.

Money is not a bad thing. We need it to buy food and clothes, pay for electricity, go to school, and so on. The Bible doesn't tell us not to have money, but it does warn that loving money can lead us into many sins, such as greed, jealousy, stealing, lying—and more.

I read something once that explains really well why we shouldn't make money an idol:

> Money will buy a bed but not sleep; books but not brains; food but not appetite; finery but not beauty; a house but not a home; medicine but not health; luxuries but not culture; amusements but not happiness; religion but not salvation; a passport to everywhere but heaven.

DARE   Don't let money become your idol.

DOUBLE DARE

1. Write the last paragraph of the devo in your own words, or come up with your own examples of what money can buy and what it can't.

2. Do you ever wish you had more money—or more things—than what you have? Ask God to help you be more thankful for what you do have.

PROMISE TO REPEAT

How did it go? What did you learn?

Mind Your Own Business

BIBLE READING *1 Thessalonians 4:11–12*

TRUTH

Christians shouldn't be busybodies.

Are you surprised to see the phrase "Mind your own business" in the Bible? When we hear other people say it, they usually aren't being very nice. It is a half-polite way of saying, "Leave me alone!" or "Get out of here!" or "Stop bothering me!" You may even hear people say, "Mind your own beeswax!" which means pretty much the same thing and is just as rude.

Of course, there are times when you might need a reminder to mind your own business. For example, if you're in class working on a project or taking a test and you start looking at your friend's paper, your teacher may say, "Keep your eyes on your own work!" She's not being rude. She's just warning you about cheating.

In John 21:22, Jesus said to one of His disciples, "What is that to you?" He was gently reminding Peter to mind his own business instead of wondering about what would happen to another disciple.

In today's Bible reading, we are given good advice on how to live as Christians: to lead quiet lives (not drawing too much attention to ourselves), minding our own business, and doing our best in whatever we do for God.

DARE Mind your own business.

DOUBLE DARE

1. Do you ever complain because you think someone else is getting better treatment than you are? Ask God to help you focus on your own life and to be thankful for your blessings.

2. Do you know a Christian who serves God quietly, without trying to get attention? Thank him or her for being a good example to you.

PROMISE TO REPEAT

How did it go? What did you learn?

The Lion's Head

BIBLE READING *1 Samuel 2:3*

TRUTH

God sees everything, so we shouldn't feel too proud.

There's a story about a man who once went up to his friends and said, "Look! I cut off a man-eating lion's tail with my pocket knife!" His friends were amazed, and then one of them asked, "Why didn't you cut off its head?"

The man shrugged and said, "Someone had already done that."

It's tempting sometimes, isn't it, to brag about little things we've done just to make people think we're smart or good or strong. We may even exaggerate the truth to make our story a little more exciting. For example, if a well-known Christian basketball player came to speak at your church and shook hands with you afterward, you might be tempted to make it sound like you hung out with the basketball player and that you know him or her personally.

God warns us about talking proudly and being boastful. God knows the truth behind everything we say, and He will judge us for every lie or exaggeration that comes out of our mouths. Have you ever played with a rubber band and stretched it just a little too far so that it snapped and hit your hand really hard? Boastfully stretching the truth can also get us into trouble!

DARE Don't stretch the truth.

DOUBLE DARE

1. Think of a time when you exaggerated the truth to impress someone. Did it make you feel better in your heart? Ask God to help you speak only honest words.

2. Make a bookmark that looks like a lion's tail and write "1 Samuel 2:3" on it. Keep it in your planner as a reminder not to boast.

PROMISE TO REPEAT

How did it go? What did you learn?

BIBLE READING *Proverbs 14:7*

TRUTH

Hanging around with foolish friends can make you foolish too.

Once upon a time, ten friends were standing on the side of the road crying. The girls thought that one of them had been lost along the way because each girl counted how many were with her, and each girl kept counting only nine friends.

A lady walking by asked, "What's the matter, girls? Why are you crying?"

The girls answered, "We were ten when we started out this morning, but now we are only nine!"

The lady saw right away what silly girls they were. Each of them had forgotten to count herself! So she told each of them to take off one shoe and place it on the ground. The girls each did this, and they counted ten shoes! So they felt better knowing that they were all there, but they couldn't figure out how this was possible.

This isn't a true story; it's an old fable that I updated to make a point. While it's important to be good and loving toward everyone, we need to be wise in choosing the people we spend most of our time with. If they are silly or foolish, they will influence us and keep us from growing wise, which is what God wants for us.

DARE Look for friends who are wise.

DOUBLE DARE

1. Do your friends spend most of their time telling jokes, talking about celebrities, or worrying about how they look? Ask God to show you whether it might be time to find a couple of more mature friends.

2. Tell your family today's story and see what they think the lesson is.

PROMISE TO REPEAT

How did it go? What did you learn?

Read 2 Corinthians 2:5–11.

The apostle Paul visited many cities in Europe to tell people about Jesus. Afterward, he wrote letters to the Christians in those cities to encourage them and give them advice. He was like a caring father talking to his children, and he tried to help them grow in their faith and love one another as they served God. This weekend's reading is part of the second letter he wrote to the Christians in Corinth, a city in Greece.

Paul wanted to talk to them about a man in their church who had done something wrong. We don't know the man's name and we don't know what his sin was, but it sounds like it was pretty bad. It hurt Paul more than anyone else. But Paul didn't focus on that in his letter. What he really cared about was the attitude of the other Christians. He knew that they had already punished the man (again, we don't know how). Now he wanted them to forgive.

It's hard to forgive someone when he or she does something that really hurts us or the people we love. Imagine how you would feel if …

1. Your best friend told all your secrets to another girl, who then told everyone in your class.

2. Your mom and your aunt had a big fight and stopped talking to each other and you were not allowed to see your cousins anymore.

3. Your teacher made fun of you in front of the whole class because you believe in God.

4. Someone you trusted at church was caught stealing money at his job.

When we feel angry, embarrassed, scared, or confused, we might feel as though we can never forgive someone for the way he or she hurt us. But the Bible tells us we must forgive. In fact, Jesus said, "If you do not forgive others their sins, your Father will not forgive your sins" (Matthew 6:15).

YOUR TURN

- When you're not willing to forgive someone, how does that hurt them?

- When you're not willing to forgive someone, how does that hurt *you*?

- Look again at the four examples of hurtful situations. For each one, write what you think would happen if the people who were hurt chose to forgive.

  1.

  2.

  3.

  4.

- Think of someone you've been having trouble forgiving. Write about it in your journal.

- Spend some time praying and asking God to help you forgive this person. Make a list of all the good things that could happen if you forgave him or her.

- When you're ready to forgive, find a way to reach out to this person and show that you've let go of the hurt.

- Don't forget to go back to your journal and write about the experience of forgiving someone.

What are your thoughts?

Don't Be Quick to Judge

BIBLE READING *John 7:24*

TRUTH

When we judge too quickly, we usually judge wrongly.

The Colgate company once created some funny advertisements to encourage people to brush their teeth. In these ads, they showed a man and woman standing together, both with big smiles. The first thing you notice in each ad is that the man has food stuck in his teeth. What you don't notice right away is that one of the people in each ad has another, much bigger problem.

In one ad, the man has only one ear. In another ad, the woman has two arms in front of her and one around the man's shoulder. In the third ad, the woman has six fingers on one of her hands!

The point of the ads is that nothing can be worse than having food stuck in your teeth since it's the first thing everyone notices.

These ads, without really meaning to, also show us how quick people are to judge others about little things instead of looking at the whole situation. When a classmate gets in trouble for not completing her homework, you might be tempted to think she's lazy or stupid. But there may be problems at home that make it hard for her to study. The boy who can't run in gym class because he's heavy may have a sickness that causes weight gain.

As Christians, we shouldn't judge someone until we know the whole story.

DARE Think before you judge.

DOUBLE DARE

1. Think of a time when someone wrongly judged you and how it made you feel. Ask God to help you not make that mistake with others.

2. Think of someone you've judged lately. Pray for him or her while you brush your teeth today!

PROMISE TO REPEAT

How did it go? What did you learn?

Listen Carefully

BIBLE READING *Isaiah 55:3*

TRUTH

We can't hear God if we're listening to other voices.

Have you ever tried to watch two TV shows at the same time? What about listening to two songs at the same time? Can you read two books at the same time, listen to two phone calls at the same time, or write two letters at the same time? Even if you could do these things, how well do you think you would do them? Probably not well at all!

As Christians, we know we're supposed to listen to God to know what He wants for us (and from us), and today's verse reminds us of that. God invites us to listen to Him because He knows that it's only through Him that we can have life. But how well do we listen to Him?

When you read your Bible in the morning, do you start thinking about what you're going to wear? Your eyes see the words, but your brain isn't getting the message. In church, do you really listen to the words being sung or what the teacher or pastor is saying? Often, we're too distracted by other things going on around us or by our own thoughts to really listen to God.

Do you know who misses out when we do that? We do.

DARE   Listen to God's voice carefully.

DOUBLE DARE

1. If you can't concentrate when you pray, try writing your prayers like letters to God. Take a notebook to church to write down things you learn. That will help you pay more attention.

2. The next time someone starts talking to you, stop whatever you're doing and really listen.

PROMISE TO REPEAT

How did it go? What did you learn?

Digging Holes

BIBLE READING *Psalm 7:15*

TRUTH

Sin always gets us into some kind of trouble.

In the summer of 2012, I went on my first mission trip to a small village in northern Quebec called Mistissini. It was a beautiful place, and we enjoyed talking about Jesus and the Bible with the ladies and young girls who came to our meetings at a Bible camp.

I quickly became friends with Makayla, an energetic and funny five-year-old whose grandfather was the pastor at the camp. One day, we were playing together and she started digging in the sand with her bare hands. She was quite strong, so pretty soon she had made a large hole in the ground. When she was happy with how big it was, she turned around and—plop—sat in the hole! I have a photo of her, with her legs and arms sticking out of the hole and a big smile on her face.

Makayla's hole wasn't dangerous, but the Bible warns about other kinds of holes we dig. Foolish actions can make us fall into trouble. Hitting your sister is wrong. Lying about it is like digging your hole a little deeper. If you get in trouble and then talk back to your parents, your hole gets even bigger. Get the picture?

DARE   Stop digging sin-holes!

DOUBLE DARE

1. In your journal, write about a time when you did something wrong and then made it worse instead of making it right. Ask God to help you be wiser next time.

2. Draw a picture of someone holding a shovel and falling into a hole. Add today's verse and put the picture on your fridge as a reminder.

PROMISE TO REPEAT

How did it go? What did you learn?

BIBLE READING *Psalm 90:12*

TRUTH

It matters how we spend each moment.

Did you know this? For the average human being, in a twenty-four-hour period (one complete day) …

Our heart beats 103,689 times.
Our blood travels 168,000,000 miles.
We breathe in 23,040 times.
We eat 3.25 pounds of food.
We drink 2.9 quarts of liquid.
We speak 4,800 words.
We move 750 muscles.
Our nails grow .000046 inch.
Our hair grows .01714 inch.
We exercise 7,000,000 brain cells.[4]

These are cool facts about *quantity* (numbers we can measure), but they don't tell us anything about the *quality* of the things we do in a typical day. How much time do we spend praying? How much kindness do we show? How much money do we waste? How many people do we ignore? How many lies do we tell? How many smiles do we give?

Every second of your life is a precious gift from God. Think carefully about how you're using the time He's given you.

DARE   Honor God with each of your twenty-four hours.

DOUBLE DARE

1. Try to keep a detailed list of everything you do today (but pay attention in class!). At the end of the day write your thoughts about how you spent your time.

2. Write some ways you can add *quality* to each day of your life. Ask God to help you do your best to honor Him.

PROMISE TO REPEAT

How did it go? What did you learn?

BIBLE READING   *Psalm 84:11 and Job 36:5*

TRUTH

God is mighty, but He's also good.

What's your favorite book? My absolute favorite (after the Bible, of course!) is *The Chronicles of Narnia* by C. S. Lewis. (I know … that's seven books, but they're all part of the same story!) ☺

And my favorite character in all the Narnia books is Aslan the Lion. When C. S. Lewis wrote these books, he meant for Aslan to be a picture of Jesus Christ. Many of the things that happen to Aslan or that he does are similar to the life of Jesus. After Aslan dies to save the land of Narnia, he comes back to life, proving that God's goodness and love is more powerful than evil.

Early in the story, Susan and Lucy are about to meet Aslan and are talking to Mr. and Mrs. Beaver about him. Susan, surprised to learn that Aslan is a lion and not a man, asks, "Is he quite safe? I shall feel rather nervous about meeting a lion."

Mr. Beaver answers, "Who said anything about safe? Of course he isn't safe. But he's good. He's the king, I tell you!"

Our heavenly Father is powerful, and those who do evil should fear Him, but He is also very, very good!

DARE   Be good, just as God is good.

DOUBLE DARE

1. Divide your journal page in half by drawing a line down the center. On one side, write some ways God is mighty or "dangerous," and on the other side write the ways He's good. Then thank Him for *all* His qualities.

2. How good are you? Ask God to help you live in a way that pleases Him.

PROMISE TO REPEAT

How did it go? What did you learn?

HERO LIST

Choose ONE of these heroes to learn about this weekend:

Name	Bible Verses
Esther	Esther 3:1–11; 4:4–17; 5:1–8; 7:1–10; 8:1–11
Stephen	Acts 6–7
Ruth	Ruth 1–4
David	1 Samuel 17
Abigail	1 Samuel 25:1–42
Gideon	Judges 6–7
The Bleeding Woman	Mark 5:25–34
Joseph	Genesis 37; 39–41
The Widow of Zarephath	1 Kings 17:8–24; Luke 4:25–26
Noah	Genesis 6–8
Miriam	Exodus 2:1–10
Daniel	Daniel 6
Mary of Bethany	John 12:1–8
Abraham	Genesis 22:1–18

Your hero for this weekend: _____

QUESTION TIME

1. How did this weekend's hero show courage and faith in God?

2. What happened because of his or her courage and obedience?

3. What did you learn from this hero's life that will help you in your own walk with God?

DOUBLE DARE

Choose at least one of these ways to dig a little deeper into your hero's life this weekend:

1. See if you can find other Bible verses about him or her. Write the reference (or the "address" of the verses) here and also anything new that you learned.

2. Ask your parents or another Christian what they have learned from this hero's life and example.

Tell a friend or your family about your new hero!

What are your thoughts?

BIBLE READING   *Romans 12:10 and John 13:34–35*

TRUTH

God's love in us helps us to think of others before ourselves.

Elsa Green is the six-year-old daughter of my friend Jocelyn. She is a happy, loving, and funny little girl. One day, her first-grade teacher asked the students to write about anything that was on their minds. So Elsa wrote this:

Title: Snow Storm!

Theres a snow storm!!! **MY MOM!** My mom. She is out in the freezing cold! But ... she is in the groshre store!!! I hope she gets home in time!!!!!!!!!!!!!!!!!!!!!!!!!

Elsa may be only six, but she is already obeying God's commands to love one another and to think of others before ourselves. She was worried about her mom being out in the cold during a snowstorm. The Greens live in Iowa and it was the end of February, so it probably was very cold! Elsa wasn't thinking about her own problems at that moment. Her thoughts were only on her mom. When her mom read her note later, it made her smile. And I'm sure that made Elsa smile!

When we remember how much God loves us, we can start to share that love with others and put them first. And that doesn't only make them feel good ... it makes us happy too!

DARE   Love others as God has loved you.

DOUBLE DARE

1. Write five different ways you can show your love by putting others first. For example, let your little sister watch her TV show even though yours is on at the same time.

2. Do you have a hard time thinking of others before yourself? Talk to God about it and ask Him to help you be more loving.

PROMISE TO REPEAT

How did it go? What did you learn?

Grasshopper Greatness

BIBLE READING *Proverbs 30:24–28*

TRUTH

When we work together, we can accomplish great things!

Have you ever seen a grasshopper? Although some types can grow to about four inches long, many of them are much smaller, not even an inch long.

How much damage do you think one grasshopper could cause? Even if it ate as much as it could while hopping around a field of vegetables, it wouldn't be a big problem. But grasshoppers become incredibly powerful when they team up and swarm over a field as one large group. They can wipe it out completely in a short time!

In today's Bible reading, we learn about four different creatures that are small but mighty. This is a good reminder that as Christians, we can do great things for God— even when we feel small and insignificant—as long as we are humble enough to work with others and share our talents as best we can.

You may be surprised to discover how God can use you if you're willing to offer your time and abilities!

DARE Be ready to work with others to serve God.

DOUBLE DARE

1. Ask your parents to help you list a few ways you can use your talents to serve God and bless others. Make a plan to volunteer at your church or to start your own project!

2. Draw a picture of a grasshopper in your journal and write today's verse next to it. Then take time to pray, asking God to show you ways you can be part of His great work.

PROMISE TO REPEAT

How did it go? What did you learn?

Praying with Friends

BIBLE READING *Matthew 18:20*

TRUTH

When we pray with other Christians, we get closer to them and to God.

My friend Jill was born in Kingston, Ontario, so she often goes there to visit her family. A couple of years ago she invited me to go with her, and we got to hang out for about four days. One afternoon, Jill and I were sitting with her mom in the living room, and we decided to use our free time to pray together. We each mentioned things we wanted to pray about, and then we prayed together for about twenty minutes. We all felt really good afterward!

Later that evening, Jill said she was so happy we had prayed together. She felt that it had brought the three of us closer together. Then her mom said something I'll never forget: "It brought us closer without making us pile on top of each other." She meant we hadn't revealed too many personal things that made us uncomfortable later. Sometimes girls tell each other everything they're thinking or feeling—and that's not always wise.

Praying together with Christian friends can encourage us and help us get stronger in our faith. But we have to make sure we're doing it to pray to God and not just to spill out everything in our hearts to each other.

DARE Make time to pray with friends.

DOUBLE DARE

1. The next time a Christian friend comes over, ask her if she'd like to pray with you for a few minutes. Later, write about the experience in your journal.

2. If you don't have a Christian friend, ask God to help you meet one.

PROMISE TO REPEAT

How did it go? What did you learn?

Do Geese See God?

BIBLE READING *Matthew 5:8*

TRUTH

If our hearts are pure, we will see God.

The title of today's devo is quite silly, I will admit. But there's something kind of cool about it too. Look at it carefully. Do you notice anything? No? Look at it again, maybe in a different way.

"Do geese see God?" is a palindrome, one of my favorite ways to play with words. A palindrome is when you can read a word or phrase forward or backward exactly the same. Other examples are "lonely Tylenol," "Dennis sinned," "Go, dog!" and "No, tie it on." Some people have come up with really long sentences that are palindromes, but they're too complicated for me!

So back to our question. I don't know whether geese see God, but it's much more important for us to ask whether we see God. Sometimes people are so busy with schoolwork, friends, TV, sports, fashion, music, and other activities that there's very little room left for God. And if there's no room for God in our hearts, then we can't receive the forgiveness for our sins that makes our hearts pure and gives us eternal life in heaven.

Do *you* see God?

DARE Ask God to clean out your heart.

DOUBLE DARE

1. Take time today to see if there's anything in your heart that you need to confess to God. Ask Him to forgive your sins and to make your heart pure.

2. With your best friend or someone in your family, try to come up with your own palindromes. Then show your partner "Do geese see God?" and talk about what you learned in today's devo.

PROMISE TO REPEAT

How did it go? What did you learn?

BIBLE READING *Joshua 24:15*

TRUTH

You have to make a choice to follow God.

There's a strange expression that says "You can't have your cake and eat it too." My mother shakes her head whenever she hears someone say that because it just doesn't make sense to her. She sometimes wonders out loud, "If I have a cake, why can't I eat it?" When one of us tries to explain the saying, we all usually end up laughing because she still thinks it's weird!

Okay, let's try it with you. Once you've eaten your cake, it's gone, right? So you don't have it anymore. In other words, you have to choose to either have a cake (that you can look at) or eat a cake. You can't eat it if you want to keep it! Got it? Great!

The point is, you can't always have everything you want. Sometimes you have to choose between two things you really like by deciding which one is more important to you or which one is right. In today's Bible verse, Joshua told the Israelites they had to choose between idols and God. They couldn't have both.

DARE Choose God!

DOUBLE DARE

1. Ask a friend what she thinks "You can't have your cake and eat it too" means. Then share today's devo with her.

2. Think of a time when you had to choose between something wrong and something that honored God. What did you do? What did you learn from that situation? Write about it here or in your journal.

PROMISE TO REPEAT

How did it go? What did you learn?

Playing It Safe?

Read Matthew 25:14–30.

On a hot summer day, a farmer in Georgia stood barefoot on the steps of his old house. It looked like it was about to tumble down. A stranger who was walking by stopped and asked for a glass of water. While he drank, he looked at the farm around him. He asked the farmer, "How is your cotton coming along?" The farmer said, "Ain't got none!" When the man asked him why, he answered, "I didn't plant any 'cause I'm 'fraid of boll weevils."

Then the man asked, "Well, how is your corn?" The farmer answered, "Didn't plant none. 'Fraid it weren't gonna rain."

The man tried again and asked, "What about your potatoes?" The farmer said, "Ain't got none. Scairt of potato bugs."

"So, what *did* you plant?" asked the man. The farmer shrugged and said, "Nothin'! I just played it safe."

YOUR TURN

- How is this story similar to the one you read in Matthew 25?

- What do you think Jesus was trying to teach His disciples by telling the story about the talents (or bags of gold)?

- God has given each one of us a special set of talents and abilities that we can use to serve Him, encourage others, and just make the world around us a little more joyful and beautiful. When you use your talents with a humble attitude (not to make yourself look good), people will be able to see God's beauty and creativity and love in you. But if you decide to "play it safe" and hide your talents because you're afraid of failing or being laughed at, God won't bless those talents. It will be like you're telling Him you're not grateful for those special gifts He's given you. What do you think your talents are? Remember, talents aren't only abilities to use in art, music, or sports. Being good at teaching, organizing, and getting along with people are also talents. Write yours here:

- Thank God for giving you talents and ask Him to show you how you can use them instead of hiding them.

- This weekend, plan to use at least one of your talents in a way that would honor God and encourage others. Here are a few ideas to get your creative juices flowing …

  - If you're good at poetry, write a poem about someone you appreciate and give it to him or her in a pretty card.

  - If you're good at sports, offer to play with a younger child who likes the same sports. Encourage that child when he or she does well.

  - If you're good at math, offer to help a friend or sibling who is struggling with math homework.

  - If you're good at art, draw or paint a picture of your favorite Bible story and give it to your Sunday school teacher or pastor.

- What will you do?

What are your thoughts?

The Way of Wisdom

BIBLE READING   *Hosea 14:9*

TRUTH

When we follow Jesus, we won't stumble.

Many years ago, a poor widow who lived in Scotland got a visitor. A gentleman who knew about her problems wanted to see how she was doing. The old lady complained that while she was suffering, her rich son in Australia was doing nothing to help her. The man was surprised, so he asked, "Doesn't he help you in any way?" The woman said, "No. All he does is send me a letter once a month, along with a little picture."

The man asked if he could see the pictures. When the widow showed them to him, he discovered that each one was actually a draft (similar to a bank check) for about fifteen dollars!

We are sometimes like this woman who didn't realize her son had been helping her all along. God may answer our prayers in a way that's different from what we hoped for, so we think He hasn't answered. The biggest gift from God that many people miss out on is the gift of eternal life. It's free, but they don't pay attention to it or accept it.

When we open our spiritual eyes, we can see that God's way is the wisest way.

DARE   Walk in wisdom.

DOUBLE DARE

1. Think of at least two ways God has helped you that you didn't recognize at first. Write about them in your journal, and then thank God for His help.

2. Share today's story with your family. Talk about why it's important to ask God for wisdom and understanding.

PROMISE TO REPEAT

How did it go? What did you learn?

Just Like a Bride

BIBLE READING *Isaiah 61:10*

TRUTH

When we trust in God, He gives us beautiful spiritual "clothes."

There are many things in a tween girl's life that she may look forward to with excitement, such as summer camp, her thirteenth birthday, the arrival of a baby sister, or getting a new bicycle. But there's one day, especially, that many girls imagine will be the most wonderful day of their lives: their wedding day. Some dream of looking like a princess on that special day, wearing a beautiful white gown that is fancier than anything they'll ever wear again, sparkly jewelry, and maybe even a tiara.

In today's Bible reading, the prophet Isaiah compared the salvation and righteousness that God gives to the pretty clothes that a bride wears when she gets married. Not only does God make our spirits (our inside) beautiful, but He also gives us a breathtaking sense of joy, just like the excitement a bride feels as she gets ready for her wedding.

Even though you're still too young to be married, you can be just as beautiful and happy as a bride by trusting and rejoicing in God.

DARE Get excited about God!

DOUBLE DARE

1. In your journal, write about a day that was very special for you. Why is being a child of God even more wonderful? Write your thoughts down, and then thank God for what He's done for you.

2. Write a list of your ten favorite activities. If spending time with God isn't on your list, ask Him to help you be more excited about your relationship with Him.

PROMISE TO REPEAT

How did it go? What did you learn?

BIBLE READING *2 Corinthians 4:7*

TRUTH

It's what's inside that matters.

Companies spend a lot of money to design attractive packaging for their products. Whether it's cookies, music, shoes, games, or shampoo, they want you to look at the container and think, *Wow! That's really nice! I've got to have one.*

But do you keep the packaging on something once you've opened it up to get to what's inside? Do you just put the wrapper on your shelf and admire it … or do you use the product it contains? Little kids sometimes will play with the box or wrapping paper their Christmas gift came in (instead of the toy itself!), but that's because they don't know any better. When we grow up, we understand that the packaging is just a temporary way to hold the really good stuff.

The verse above says we're like containers that God pours His goodness into so that we can share it with others. It doesn't matter if we're big or small, colorful or plain … It's what God does through our lives that really counts!

DARE   Share the treasure inside you!

DOUBLE DARE

1. Write today's verse on a small piece of paper, decorate it, and then put it inside a container that you open often, such as your jewelry box. Whenever you see it, thank God for the treasure inside you: His Spirit!

2. Pray that God would give you the courage to tell others about Jesus and that, even without using words, your life would show that you know Him.

PROMISE TO REPEAT

How did it go? What did you learn?

BIBLE READING *Proverbs 19:20*

TRUTH

Listening to good advice makes you wise.

Do you collect anything? I have several collections: dark blue bottles, giraffes (not real ones, of course!), foreign coins, antique tins, and craft supplies. Lots of craft supplies! Most of my collections don't do anyone any good, except the craft supplies when I make a gift or card for someone. But I collect the other stuff just because I find them nice to look at; they cheer me up.

There's one other thing I like to collect. Whenever I read something that teaches me a lesson that will help me, or when someone gives me good advice that I know I should follow, I write it down in a notebook or at least try to store it safely in my brain so that I'll remember it.

It's not always easy to take someone's advice or to be humble when our parents and teachers discipline us, but as we become more mature, we realize more and more it's for our own good to "collect" wisdom. Of course, just like it would be pointless for me to collect markers and keep them in a box until they dry up, it's pointless to keep good advice in a notebook and not follow it.

DARE Collect (and use) wisdom.

DOUBLE DARE

1. Write down important lessons you learn and want to remember in your journal, in a separate notebook, or on little slips of paper that you keep in a jar. Read through them every so often as a reminder.

2. Has someone given you good advice that helped you in a difficult situation? Make sure you thank that person so he or she will be encouraged too.

PROMISE TO REPEAT

How did it go? What did you learn?

Weak and Worried?

BIBLE READING *Psalm 31:9–14*

TRUTH

God is there for you when you feel weak.

There's a funny story about a man who, after having an operation, said, "Boy, am I glad that's over with!" The patient in the bed next to him said, "Don't be so sure. The surgeon left a little sponge in me and they had to cut me open again." Another patient in the room said, "That's nothing! I heard about a lady who had to have her stitches removed so they could take out a tool they'd accidentally left inside her."

The man who had just had surgery started to feel nervous. Just at that moment, the surgeon who had operated on him came into the room and asked, "Has anyone seen my hat?" The patient fainted!

The truth is, we all feel a little nervous when we're sick or if we need to go to the hospital for tests or an operation. Maybe you've been to a hospital only to visit a grandparent or friend. It's good to remember that they might be feeling anxious too.

What's great is that we can put our hope in God and say, like King David did, "You are my God."

DARE Don't let worry get you down.

DOUBLE DARE

1. Read all of Psalm 31. Read it slowly and imagine that you are praying the words to God. Afterward, write your thoughts about the prayer in your journal or on this page.

2. Is someone at your church sick? Write him or her a cheery get-well note with a reminder that God cares. Ask your parents or your pastor to help you get the card to this person.

PROMISE TO REPEAT

How did it go? What did you learn?

Are You a Factory or a Garden?

Read Ephesians 2:8–10 and Galatians 5:22–23.

Factories are buildings where different products (such as shoelaces, bicycles, staplers, or computers) are made. They usually contain many large and complicated machines that are controlled by humans.

Gardens are areas of land where seeds are planted into the soil and different plants, vegetables, or fruits are grown. They may be taken care of by humans, but they depend more on natural influences to grow.

Thinking about the differences between factories and gardens can help us understand the difference between "works" and "fruit"—two things the Bible says we should have as Christians.

Works are good deeds *we* choose to do. For example, giving money to poor people, going to church every week, or helping in the church nursery. Fruits are qualities *God* produces in our hearts through His power. For example, being patient, loving your enemy, or controlling your anger.

We can sometimes do good works without thinking because they've become a habit or we don't have a choice, such as when we go to church with our family every Sunday. That's like a factory machine that automatically does what it's programmed to do.

Spiritual fruits, on the other hand, grow in our hearts naturally when the Holy Spirit is in us. But they do not grow easily, just as a plant has to struggle out of its seed and up out of the soil to start growing and stretching. Plants and fruits aren't made by sticking parts of them together. They have to grow from almost nothing.

The "works" that come out of a factory all look exactly the same, like photocopies. Also, they have no life; they're only objects. The works we do with our own strength may be useful, but only to a limit. The fruit and flowers that grow in gardens are all unique and special in their own way. And they're living, growing things that continue to give life to other plants through their seeds and pollen. Likewise, the fruit God produces in us can grow and be passed on to others.

We don't become Christians by doing good works, but we should do good works because we're Christians. Do you see the difference? Works and fruit are both important. Many Bible verses tell us our faith should produce good works. But works are what we do on our own effort, and fruit is what God produces in us. We need both!

YOUR TURN

Look at the following list and try to figure out if the action is a good work or a spiritual fruit. Remember, if it's something you can do on your own, it's a work; if it's a quality that God has to grow in you, it's a fruit. Check off the correct box.

FRUIT   WORK

❑   praying for your mom when she's having a bad day   ❑
❑   stacking chairs at church after a meeting   ❑
❑   not giving in to the temptation to cheat on a test   ❑
❑   visiting a sick person in the hospital or at her home   ❑
❑   donating clothing and toys to a charity   ❑
❑   not arguing with a friend even though you're right   ❑
❑   answering respectfully when your dad gets angry with you   ❑
❑   raking the leaves on your elderly neighbor's lawn   ❑

As you can see, good works and spiritual fruit are both good. What's important to remember is this: If you are only doing good works but don't have the fruit of the Spirit listed in Galatians, your faith is more like a factory than a garden. Ask God to help you develop spiritual fruit as you spend more and more time with Him. That will give you the strength and energy you need to also produce good works.

You Can't Cover Up Sin

BIBLE READING *Psalm 32:1–5*

TRUTH

Hidden sin will eat us up on the inside.

What's the worst smell you can imagine? Moldy cheese? A dead rat? Bad breath? A dirty toilet? In my experience, the worst smell is sulfur, a yellow chemical that is common around volcanoes but is also found in some foods and even our bodies (just a tiny amount). Sulfur is what you smell when you crack open a rotten egg.

Many years ago, I carefully dyed an egg with a fancy design and put it on a shelf. Over time, the inside of the egg would dry up and the shell would be hollow. But a few months later, before the egg was dried up, I accidentally dropped it and it broke. The smell made me feel awfully sick! But I covered my nose and mouth and quickly cleaned it up.

Why didn't I just spray air freshener or hide the mess under a towel? The problem with stinky things is that if you don't get rid of them, they just get worse and worse.

That's how sin is. If we don't ask Jesus right away to forgive us and make our hearts clean, that sin sits there and rots, spoiling our relationship with God and making it easier to sin again.

DARE Confess your sins right away.

DOUBLE DARE

1. Are there any sins in your life that you've been trying to hide from God? Be sure to confess them today so that you can receive His forgiveness.

2. What are some ways people try to cover up their sins when they do wrong? What happens when we do that?

PROMISE TO REPEAT

How did it go? What did you learn?

Travel Light

BIBLE READING *1 Peter 2:11*

TRUTH

As Christians, we're just travelers in this sinful world.

There's an old tale about some Christians who were traveling in a faraway land when they heard about a wise old believer who lived in that area. They went out of their way to find this man so they could talk to him. When they found his hut, they were surprised to see that all he owned was a cot, a chair, a table, and an old stove for heat and cooking. One of them curiously asked, "Where is your furniture?"

The old man responded by asking, "Where's yours?" The visitor said, "Well, at home, of course! I am not carrying it with me. I'm traveling!"

"So am I," said the old man. "So am I."

You see, this wise old Christian understood that we're here on earth only for a while, so it's more important to focus on obeying God than collecting material possessions that won't last forever. Today's verse reminds us that we're "foreigners" in this world, so we need to resist temptation.

DARE Let go of your earthly wants so that you can "travel light."

DOUBLE DARE

1. Think about where you keep your "furniture"—or the things you own. If your heart is crowded with earthly things you think are important, ask God to help you clean it out to make room for Him.

2. Write down five temptations you struggle with. For each one, plan how you will fight the temptation the next time it comes around.

PROMISE TO REPEAT

How did it go? What did you learn?

Thanks for the Fleas!

BIBLE READING   *1 Thessalonians 5:18*

TRUTH

God deserves our thanks for everything—even what we see as problems.

Corrie and Betsie ten Boom were two sisters in Holland during World War II. For two years, their family helped Jews escape from the German army by letting them hide in a secret room in their house. But then they got caught and the whole family was arrested. Corrie and Betsie were sent to a terrible place called a concentration camp.

Their barracks (a building that soldiers usually sleep in) was overcrowded and full of fleas. Betsie, who was older, reminded Corrie that they had read 1 Thessalonians 5:18 just that morning. She said they needed to thank God for everything about their new place to live. At first Corrie refused to thank God for the fleas, but finally she listened to Betsie.

In the months after they arrived at the camp, they were surprised that they were able to study the Bible and pray openly without the guards bothering them. It wasn't until much later that they found out the guards didn't want to go into their barracks because of the fleas!

God used what looked like a problem to protect the women in the barracks. Betsie was right. They could give thanks for everything!

DARE   Thank God for the "fleas" in your life.

DOUBLE DARE

1. In your journal, write about something that's difficult to thank God for. Then write a prayer of thanks anyway, trusting that God knows what He's doing.

2. Memorize today's verse while you make a bookmark with the words written on it. Share today's devo and the bookmark with a friend.

PROMISE TO REPEAT

How did it go? What did you learn?

God As Your GPS

BIBLE READING *Psalm 5:8 and Psalm 27:11*

TRUTH

Only Jesus can lead us perfectly on the right path.

Do you know what a GPS is? Your parents might have one in their car. The letters GPS stand for global positioning system, which means that, with the help of a satellite, a car can be tracked on a computer somewhere. With that information, a GPS can guide you to wherever you want to go. When you enter your destination into the GPS, it begins to give directions, such as "Turn left at the next light" or "Continue for two miles."

If you take a different direction than what the GPS suggests, it will give you new instructions to get you back on the road you should be following.

When you become a Christian, God's Holy Spirit lives in you and helps you find the right path to follow, one that will keep you away from danger and sin. When you start to get lost, He is right there to remind you to follow Him.

DARE Follow God's driving instructions!

DOUBLE DARE

1. On a piece of paper, draw a GPS (ask your parents to help you find a picture of one if you're not sure what they look like). In the middle of the screen, write "Lead me, Lord!" Put the picture somewhere you'll see it often.

2. Memorize Psalm 5:8.

PROMISE TO REPEAT

How did it go? What did you learn?

Our Father Is Wiser

BIBLE READING *1 Corinthians 3:18–20*

TRUTH

Our wisdom is like foolishness compared to God's.

D. L. Moody, a well-known evangelist in the 1800s, had three children, including a daughter named Emma.

When Emma was little, she asked her mother for a muff (a furry accessory shaped like a tube that you stick your hands into to keep them warm). When her mother brought one home one day, Emma was so excited that she wanted to try it out right away, even though there was a bad storm. Emma's dad agreed to walk with her, but he said, "I want you to hold my hand." Emma didn't want to hold her dad's hand. She wanted to try her new muff with both hands.

After a little while, Emma slipped on some ice and fell. After her father helped her get up, she said, "Papa, let me just hold your little finger." She was okay for a little while holding on to his pinkie, but then she slipped again and down she went. This time she hurt herself. When she got up, she said, "Papa, I'll hold your hand now." So Mr. Moody held her hand in his strong hand, and she was able to walk without falling.

God is our wise Father in heaven. He knows the dangers ahead of us and gives us warnings. If we obey Him instead of trusting our own wisdom, we will be safe!

DARE   Hold God's hand!

DOUBLE DARE

1. Think of a time when you trusted your own wisdom instead of God's. Write about it in your journal and ask God to help you trust *Him* next time.

2. Share today's devo with a friend who has trouble trusting God.

PROMISE TO REPEAT

How did it go? What did you learn?

When God Says No

In the summer of 2012, Abbie, a teenager who lives in Kansas, applied to participate in an international exchange program. Through the program, she would learn about leadership and working with people from other countries. Abbie was studying European history and looked forward to visiting a foreign country one day, so when she found out the program wouldn't cost her a dollar, it seemed like a dream come true!

Abbie remembers how she wanted so much to be a part of this program that she convinced herself that's what God wanted for her too. She believed He had a plan for her, so she tried to focus on that while she waited for an answer. Understandably, she was heartbroken when she got the email that told her she hadn't been chosen and that instead she would be hosting a student visiting from Europe for two weeks. Even though that would be a fascinating experience, it didn't make up for the fact that she couldn't join the four students from Kansas who got to go to Europe.

She cried at home. She cried at youth group. As she met the other teens who would be going to Europe, she continued to feel the pain. Abbie said, "It was awkward for me to meet the kids who were going because I kept thinking, *'Oh, you got in and I didn't. You are going to have the time of your life and I'm going to be stuck at home.'*"

But this story doesn't have a sad ending. Abbie was able to learn that when God allows challenges in our lives, we can draw closer to Him. After everything was finished with the exchange program, Abbie felt much closer to God and more experienced and mature. It was a strange feeling to fail at something, but whenever she really felt hurt, it was as if God was saying to her, "Okay, I know you wanted this, but this isn't for you. I've got other plans for you. Focus on Me. I've got it."

So Abbie kept repeating to herself, "God's got it. I'm going to be okay."

YOUR TURN

Abbie has two verses to share with you about this experience:

1. **Matthew 7:7**—Abbie says, "I was asking, but I wasn't getting. Then I realized this: I *was* getting, but it was what God wanted, not what I wanted. It's tough to admit, but that is so, so, so much better." Abbie also discovered that when we learn to want what God wants, we always get what we want!

2. **Psalm 40:17**—Abbie wrote this verse on an index card and stuck it on her wall. Whenever she felt stressed or thought, *Augh! I can't take this anymore!* this verse helped her connect with God. She says, "He is always there for me and loves me like no other, no matter what."

- This weekend, take some time to work on the following project:
  - Turn to the next side-by-side blank pages in your journal.
  - On the left page, divide your page into four sections. In each section write about something you have felt disappointed by, such as hoping for something that didn't happen.
  - Divide the right page into four sections also. In each corresponding section, write why you think God let you be disappointed and how His plan for you was better.
  - You don't have to work on this all at once. You can keep coming back to it throughout the weekend.
- Thank God that His plans for you are perfect and good. Just like Abbie did, write Psalm 40:17 on a card and put it somewhere you'll see it often.

What are your thoughts?

266

BIBLE READING *1 Kings 11:38*

TRUTH

God blesses us when we obey Him.

Do you know what happens if you put a sewing needle into a glass of water? It sinks to the bottom. But if you cut a small square out of tissue paper, float that on top of the water in your glass, and then put your needle on top of that, the needle will float. Even after the tissue paper sinks to the bottom, the needle will keep floating for a while because the molecules at the top of the water sort of pull toward each other and create what's called surface tension, like an invisible skin. But the weight of the needle will eventually break the "skin" and drop. It has to obey the law of gravity, which says that if you drop something, it will go down toward the ground.

You don't need to do experiments to know that if you throw a rock in the air, it will drop. So will a sock. So will a grape. So will a pillow. Anything you toss up will obey the law of gravity and drop down.

Just as we know what the results of natural laws are, we also know that when we obey God's laws and do what's right, He is with us and blesses us.

DARE Do what is right in God's eyes.

DOUBLE DARE

1. Ask your mom for a needle, tissue paper, and a glass of water and try the experiment with your family. Then share today's verse with them.

2. Write out a prayer to God asking Him to help you obey Him and to show you the right way to live.

PROMISE TO REPEAT

How did it go? What did you learn?

The Rocky Road

BIBLE READING *James 1:2–4*

TRUTH

Sometimes our problems turn into blessings.

Long, long ago in a land far away, there was a king who had a boulder (a huge rock) placed in the middle of a road. Then he hid behind a tree to see if anyone would try to remove the rock. Some of the wealthy and important people in his kingdom came down the road and simply walked around the boulder. Many people complained loudly that the king was doing a bad job of keeping the roads clear. Everyone grumbled, but no one tried to move the rock.

Finally, a poor worker came down the road. When he saw the boulder, he tried to move it. It was very heavy, but he pushed as hard as he could and finally got the rock to the side of the road. When he turned around, he noticed a small sack where the rock had been. It was full of gold coins! There was also a note from the king saying that the money was a reward to whoever moved the boulder.

That wise man was the only one who learned that obstacles sometimes create opportunities that are good for us.

DARE   Find the good in every difficulty.

DOUBLE DARE

1. In your journal, write about a difficulty you or your family is facing that seems awful. Then, as you pray for God's help, write down one or two *good* things that might come out of this situation.

2. On a piece of paper, draw a big rock and write the words of James 1:2 inside it. Post this on your fridge and share today's devo with your family.

PROMISE TO REPEAT

How did it go? What did you learn?

One Pebble at a Time

BIBLE READING *James 5:7–11*

TRUTH

God blesses us when we're patient.

Another fable by Aesop is called "The Crow and the Pitcher." It's about a crow that was nearly dying of thirst when she found a water pitcher on the ground. She saw that there was just a little bit of water left in the pitcher, yet she couldn't get her head in far enough for her beak to reach the water. What a disappointment!

But after thinking for a moment, the crow came up with an idea. She dropped a pebble into the pitcher, and then another one, and then another, and another, and another … Pretty soon, all the pebbles in the pitcher made the water rise up to the top and the crow was able to drink it!

Sometimes we feel discouraged when we don't see a solution to a problem we're facing. We might think there's no hope. But the Bible teaches us to patiently trust in God. He cares, and He will help us in His own special way.

DARE   Don't panic when hard times come.

DOUBLE DARE

1. In your journal, write about a situation you're facing that's making you feel impatient. Ask God to help you find the right solution and to be patient while you wait for it.

2. Fill a cup about halfway with water. Then start putting pebbles (or marbles) into it slowly until the water reaches the top. While you do this, talk with God about anything bothering you.

PROMISE TO REPEAT

How did it go? What did you learn?

The Lazy Crow

BIBLE READING *Proverbs 28:19*

TRUTH

Laziness can end in disaster.

Remember the story you read yesterday about the patient crow that slowly filled a pitcher with pebbles until it could drink the water in it? Well, there once was another thirsty crow that remembered the story too.

When this crow found a pitcher with a little bit of water at the bottom, she thought, *Hmm, I don't feel like looking for a whole lot of pebbles to drop into the pitcher one by one.* So she found a big rock instead and, after struggling to lift it, dropped it into the pitcher.

CRASH!

The pitcher broke and all the water spilled out and went into the ground. The lazy crow ended up with no water to drink and flew home feeling ashamed.

When we're too lazy to do small jobs carefully and patiently, we often have to rush at the end and, like this crow, find ourselves in trouble. The Bible warns us that unless we're willing to work, we cannot enjoy the blessings God has for us.

DARE Get moving!

DOUBLE DARE

1. If you often get in trouble for being lazy, ask your mom to help you make a weekly schedule you can follow to get all your chores done on time. Ask God to help you stick to it!

2. Draw an empty pitcher in your journal. Whenever you complete a difficult task, draw a pebble in the pitcher. When the pitcher is full, find a fun way to celebrate with your family.

PROMISE TO REPEAT

How did it go? What did you learn?

BIBLE READING *Philippians 3:13*

TRUTH

The best direction to face in life is forward.

Have your parents or a teacher ever told you that "God gave you two ears and one mouth so that you can listen twice as much as you speak"? (I'm sure I heard that a few times when I was a young girl!)

People also joke that mothers have eyes in the back of their heads and that's why they always know when you're up to no good! Of course, they don't really have eyes there. That would look pretty strange, wouldn't it? And how would they see through their hair anyway?

Those are silly questions, but it's worth thinking about the fact that our eyes are in the front of our heads and not in the back. It's as if God wants to remind us of what it says in Philippians 3:13. We're told to forget what is behind us and to strain (make a strong effort) toward what is ahead of us.

Some people are so busy feeling bad about things in their past or remembering how great things used to be in their lives that they miss out on what's happening right now. God has big plans for us, but we'll never get to them if we're stuck in the past!

DARE Don't look back!

DOUBLE DARE

1. Are you still upset about something a friend did to you in the past? Ask God to help you let it go so that you can move forward with peace in your heart.

2. Walk through your house backward for five minutes. Afterward, write about it in your journal. What did you learn that can help you in your Christian walk?

PROMISE TO REPEAT

How did it go? What did you learn?

HERO LIST

Choose ONE of these heroes to learn about this weekend:

Name	Bible Verses
Esther	Esther 3:1–11; 4:4–17; 5:1–8; 7:1–10; 8:1–11
Stephen	Acts 6–7
Ruth	Ruth 1–4
David	1 Samuel 17
Abigail	1 Samuel 25:1–42
Gideon	Judges 6–7
The Bleeding Woman	Mark 5:25–34
Joseph	Genesis 37; 39–41
The Widow of Zarephath	1 Kings 17:8–24; Luke 4:25–26
Noah	Genesis 6–8
Miriam	Exodus 2:1–10
Daniel	Daniel 6
Mary of Bethany	John 12:1–8
Abraham	Genesis 22:1–18

Your hero for this weekend: _____

QUESTION TIME

1. How did this weekend's hero show courage and faith in God?

2. What happened because of his or her courage and obedience?

3. What did you learn from this hero's life that will help you in your own walk with God?

DOUBLE DARE

Choose at least one of these ways to dig a little deeper into your hero's life this weekend:

1. See if you can find other Bible verses about him or her. Write the reference (or the "address" of the verses) here and also anything new that you learned.

2. Ask your parents or another Christian what they have learned from this hero's life and example.

Tell a friend or your family about your new hero!

"I Want to See"

BIBLE READING Mark 10:46–52

TRUTH

Jesus cares about your needs.

Use the telephone keypad to crack the code of the secret message below. For each blank, the first number tells you which button to look at and the second number tells you the position of the letter on the button. The answer is a phrase from Psalm 146:8 (don't look it up until you try the puzzle).

"
___ ___ ___   ___ ___ ___ ___   ___ ___ ___ ___ ___
8-1 4-2 3-2   5-3 6-3 7-3 3-1   4-1 4-3 8-3 3-2 7-4

___ ___ ___ ___ ___   ___ ___   ___ ___ ___   ___ ___ ___ ___ ___ "
7-4 4-3 4-1 4-2 8-1   8-1 6-3   8-1 4-2 3-2   2-2 5-3 4-3 6-2 3-1

I love this story about the blind man named Bartimaeus because he is a great example of someone trusting in Jesus and His power. We also see how kind and loving Jesus is. Bartimaeus was not only blind; he was also poor, and he was always begging in the streets. When he heard that Jesus was coming his way, he started calling out to Him. People tried to quiet him, but he just yelled louder. Finally, Jesus asked him, "What do you want me to do for you?"

Bartimaeus didn't ask for money or food. He knew that Jesus could do more for him, so he said, "Rabbi, I want to see." And Jesus rewarded his faith by giving him sight! Jesus can also take away our spiritual blindness and help us see the right path to follow. Imagine Jesus is asking you today, "(Your name), what do you want Me to do for you?" How will you answer?

DARE Ask Jesus to give you spiritual "sight."

DOUBLE DARE

1. In your journal, write a story about what would happen if you met Jesus while walking down the street. What would the conversation be like?

2. Read Psalm 146. Copy into your journal any phrases that encourage you.

PROMISE TO REPEAT

How did it go? What did you learn?

BIBLE READING *Romans 12:16*

TRUTH

In God's eyes, we're all equal.

If you play an instrument or sing in a choir, you probably know about melody and harmony. No, this isn't the story of two friends, although both those words are used as girls' names!

A melody is a musical tune. When you sing a song alone or play an instrument that can make only one sound at a time, you're usually singing or playing the melody. Harmony occurs when different voices, instruments, or notes are sung or played together. The different notes blend together to create a new sound. Each note or voice is important and adds something special to the music. Some of those notes or voices may be very high and some may be very low or deep.

That's a lot like people. We're all different—some are rich, while others are poor; some have high positions, while others do simple jobs; some are popular, while others are not. The Bible tells us that, especially as Christians, we must never look down on anyone, even if others disrespect them.

God wants you to love and respect your school janitor, the pizza deliveryman, the person at church who doesn't speak English well, and the girl at school who doesn't wear stylish clothes. If you don't, you're being conceited, and that's a sin.

DARE Don't look down on anyone.

DOUBLE DARE

1. Is there someone you're tempted to look down on or disrespect? Ask God to help you not to be conceited but to start caring for that person.

2. Imagine how it feels to be someone in a low position who is usually ignored. Write about it in your journal.

PROMISE TO REPEAT

How did it go? What did you learn?

BIBLE READING *Romans 12:15*

TRUTH

Christian love means sharing in each other's joy and pain.

Empathy is a little different from sympathy. We use the word *sympathy* when we're talking about feeling sorry for someone who is suffering or sad. To have empathy is being able to understand how others are feeling and feel the same emotions they're experiencing. It's when you can say "I know how you feel" and really mean it.

In each situation below, see if you can figure out if it's an example of empathy or sympathy. Write your answers in the blank spaces, then check page 429.

1. When your cousin gets a new puppy, you feel really happy for her because you know she's patiently waited for one for a long time.

2. When your friend's father dies, you write her a nice card, hug her, and pray for her.

3. When one of your teachers trips on the steps at school in front of a lot of students, you get an awful feeling in your tummy because you can imagine how embarrassed she is.

4. When you don't get invited to a birthday party that most of your friends are going to, your older sister says, "Don't worry. There will be other birthday parties."

Romans 12:15 tells us that as Christians, we should have empathy for others.

DARE Go further than sympathy.

DOUBLE DARE

1. Think of someone who is either really happy or really sad about something today. Find a way to show this person that you know—and care about—how he or she feels.

2. Quiz a friend on the difference between empathy and sympathy. Talk about the importance of being empathetic.

PROMISE TO REPEAT

How did it go? What did you learn?

In a Nutshell

BIBLE READING *Romans 13:9*

TRUTH

When we love one another, we obey all the commandments.

Do you know why people use the expression "in a nutshell"? It's a way to say that you're going to take a long story or thought and shrink it down to a few words. Nutshells are very small, so what's inside has to be small enough to fit.

Today's Bible verse explains all of God's commandments "in a nutshell"—and that is that we must love our neighbor as ourselves. Besides the Ten Commandments in Exodus 20, did you know that 613 other commandments were given to the Jewish people? Can you imagine trying to remember 623 rules every day? God knew that none of us could ever possibly keep all those laws. That's why "being good" isn't the way we get to heaven. And that's why God gave us one easy commandment to remember. If you loved everyone around you as much as you love yourself, would you …

> be jealous when your friend gets to go on a school trip but you're not allowed?
> talk back to your mom?
> daydream in school?
> borrow your brother's book without asking him?

Every sin starts from not loving God and not loving others. But God's love in our hearts helps us obey all His commandments.

DARE Learn to love.

DOUBLE DARE

1. In your journal, write about someone you have trouble loving. Ask God to change your heart and help you love this person the way God wants you to.

2. Find a way to show love to someone who needs it today.

PROMISE TO REPEAT

How did it go? What did you learn?

You Can't Mix Those!

BIBLE READING *2 Corinthians 6:14–15*

TRUTH

Believers and unbelievers don't mix well.

Can you think of things that you can't mix together? Here are a couple of examples:

    oil and water (they will separate from each other)

    kiwi fruit in Jell-O (the Jell-O won't harden)

Some things in this world were never meant to be put together, and it's useless (even foolish) to try. Other things work together beautifully (like root beer and vanilla ice cream!). The Bible says Christians and those who reject God don't fit together. That doesn't mean unbelievers are our enemies or that we should stay away from them. In fact, we should love them and help them learn about Jesus. But we can't get involved in the things they do that don't honor God.

The best example of this is getting married to an unbeliever. It's against God's will for us because He knows if two people don't have the same faith, they can't successfully walk through life together. But two believers can encourage each other, serve God together, and teach their children about Jesus.

Make the decision now to always trust God and obey this verse.

DARE Don't "yoke" yourself with unbelievers.

DOUBLE DARE

1. If most of your friends are not Christians, ask God to help you be careful about being influenced by them, and ask Him to send you a Christian friend for encouragement.

2. Ask your parents if they can think of other examples of things that don't mix well. If they ask you why, tell them what you learned in today's devo.

PROMISE TO REPEAT

How did it go? What did you learn?

Best Is Better Than Good

Read Luke 10:38–42.

Read the situations below and put an X next to the answer you think is *wrong*.

Your friend is feeling a bit blue. You …

a. ignore her. She'll get over it.
b. invite her to your house to play her favorite game.
c. give her a hug and ask her if she wants to talk about it.

Your favorite author comes to your school to talk to the students. You …

a. sit in the back and whisper with your friends.
b. volunteer to help with the snacks that will be given out after the talk.
c. sit in the front quietly and listen. You even write down some things you want to remember.

Your parents say you can sign up for a Saturday activity at church. You …

a. don't sign up for anything. You'd rather watch cartoons.
b. sign up for the music and drama team.
c. sign up to visit hospitals and seniors' homes.

If you chose *a* as the *wrong* answer for each question, you were right! Now go back and put a star next to the *right* answer. Is that a bit tougher? In each situation, answers *b* and *c* are both good. Neither of them is wrong. But what if I told you to look at them again and choose the *best* answer? In each situation, answer *c* means you're willing to give your time for someone else, to listen to them, and to learn from them. It shows you care about others more than yourself. Again, the *b* answers aren't *wrong*. They're just not the *best*.

In the story of Mary and Martha, we see two sisters who are both doing good things. One is serving Jesus, and the other one is listening to Him. What Martha did was not *wrong*. She was being kind and good. But Jesus said that Mary's choice to sit near Him and listen was *better*.

YOUR TURN

- How do you think Jesus would have felt if Martha had sat and listened to Him and there was no meal prepared?

- All Martha had to do to spend time with Jesus was walk into the room and sit down with the others. What would you have to do to spend time with Jesus?

- Imagine Jesus is at your house, sitting across from you in the living room. What would you say to Him or ask Him?

- What do you think He would say to you?

DOUBLE DARE

This weekend find three ways to spend more time with Jesus and get to know Him. Write your ideas here (or in your journal), and then come back to write about how it went.

What are your thoughts?

Make Every Effort

BIBLE READING *2 Peter 3:14*

TRUTH

God deserves our best efforts.

One day, a man was walking along the beach in the morning while it was still quiet and peaceful, and he noticed a boy up ahead. He saw that the boy kept bending down, picking up a starfish, and throwing it as far as he could into the sea. When the man caught up to him, he asked the boy, "What are you doing?" The boy said if the starfish were left on the sand, they would die as the sun rose higher and got hotter.

The man noticed that there were thousands of starfish all along the shore, which went on for miles. He said to the boy, "You'll never be able to get all of them back in the ocean. How can your effort make any difference?" The boy picked up another starfish, said, "It makes a difference to this one," and then threw it into the sea.

You may think the things you do for God don't really matter or that He doesn't notice. But He does! Every time you are kind to someone, every time you forgive someone, every time you obey your parents, God is pleased. He sees each little effort you make, and He will bless you for it.

DARE   Keep up all your good efforts!

DOUBLE DARE

1. In your journal, write about good things you've done that you feel no one noticed or cared about. Ask God to help you trust that He sees what you do and is pleased.

2. Write down five things you can do today to make a positive difference in someone's life. Try to do them all.

PROMISE TO REPEAT

How did it go? What did you learn?

What Are You Waiting For?

BIBLE READING *Ecclesiastes 11:4–6*

TRUTH

If you wait for perfect conditions, you'll never get anything done.

In an earlier devotional, we talked about the problem of procrastination (not starting something right away). It's something I have struggled with for most of my life and have had to ask God to help me with over and over again.

For example, when I had to write this book, there were so many days when I thought, *Well, I should clean up my desk first and answers those emails and tidy my bookshelves first. I'll start tomorrow … or next week …* I nervously waited until it felt like the right time. But the right time is always now, not later. We may not be able to do it later, and then we'll regret waiting.

If farmers waited for perfect weather before they planted seeds, or if bus drivers waited until there were no cars on the street before driving, they'd never do anything.

Sometimes we wait until it feels right before we tell someone about Jesus. But the Bible says not to wait. We don't know how God will use our efforts. We should just move forward, even if we feel unsure. If we do nothing, nothing happens!

DARE Stop procrastinating!

DOUBLE DARE

1. Do you have a friend who needs to hear about Jesus but you've been procrastinating talking to her? Ask God to help you not to wait and to do it while you can.

2. Write a list of things you've been "waiting" to do. Make it your priority this week to get started on the most important ones.

PROMISE TO REPEAT

How did it go? What did you learn?

Be Happy Where You Are

BIBLE READING *Philippians 4:11*

TRUTH

Having unrealistic goals won't make you happy.

There's an old story about a little watch that was unhappy about its size. It thought that by simply sitting on a lady's wrist, it didn't have much influence in the world. The watch compared itself to Big Ben, the large, beautiful clock at the top of Elizabeth Tower, part of the Palace of Westminster in London, England.

One day, as the owner of the watch was walking by the clock tower, the little watch cried out, "Oh, I wish I could go up there! Then I could tell the time to thousands of people instead of to just one!"

The little watch got its wish and was transported to the very top of the tower. What do you think happened next? The little watch completely disappeared from view! It was too high up for anyone to see.

We also have to be careful not to wish for "big" jobs that we might not be made for. God has a special job for each of us, and we need to be content to serve Him where we are.

DARE Be content with what you have, wherever you are.

DOUBLE DARE

1. Tell a friend today's story, and then memorize Philippians 4:11 together.

2. Write down some ways you might be like the little watch, wishing that God had given you a different life. Then ask God to help you be thankful for what He's given you and to use you wherever you are.

PROMISE TO REPEAT

How did it go? What did you learn?

Old-Fashioned Goodness

BIBLE READING *Ecclesiastes 1:9–10*

TRUTH

New doesn't always mean better.

One winter a woman in Michigan who was about to have a baby was being rushed to the hospital in an ambulance. Suddenly, the worst thing you can imagine happened. The ambulance slipped on ice and went into a ditch at the side of the road! A large truck was passing by and stopped to help, but the driver couldn't get the ambulance out because his truck's wheels were spinning on the ice too.

A moment later, an Amish man who was driving a team of two horses stopped. He said his horses' shoes had been sharpened to dig into the ice. He hooked up the ambulance to the horses, and they were able to walk forward, pulling the ambulance out.

In our world of large-screen TVs, fast cars, and smartphones, we might be tempted to laugh at old-fashioned ways of living, such as traveling by horse and carriage. But this story is a great example that what's old-fashioned can sometimes be better than what's new.

Modern things sometimes look or work differently than old things, but the Bible says there's nothing really new in the world. That's why we should respect our elders and listen to them. They may be older, but they have a lot to offer!

DARE Give what's "old" a chance.

DOUBLE DARE

1. Ask your grandparents about things they miss from the "old days" and listen patiently as they tell you about them.

2. Before you ask for or buy something new, pray. If it won't make your life better or fill a real need, why not save your money?

PROMISE TO REPEAT

How did it go? What did you learn?

BIBLE READING *Psalm 71:20*

TRUTH

Sometimes pain is good for us.

Match the problems or challenges on the left with their appropriate solutions on the right.

Problem	Solution
You have a cavity.	Stre-e-e-etch those muscles.
There's gum firmly stuck in your hair.	Read, study, memorize, read ...
You have a bad cough.	Drill and fill.
You have a big test coming up.	Take gross-tasting medicine.
You're trying out for the soccer team.	Snip, snip, snip!

WHAT WOULD HAPPEN IF ...

You didn't get your tooth fixed?
You didn't snip the gum out of your hair?
You didn't take medicine?
You didn't study for your test?
You didn't exercise?

Sometimes God allows pain in our lives to help us grow or learn or to solve a bigger problem. For example, moving to another city may be hard, but He may have special new friends or a special purpose for you there. Other times, we never find out why He let us go through a hard time, but we can trust that, one day, all our pain will be over. There's no pain in heaven!

DARE   Trust God when life is painful.

DOUBLE DARE

1   Are you going through something hurtful or difficult right now? Talk to God about the situation and how you feel. Ask Him to comfort you and help you trust Him.

2.   Do you know someone else who is going through a hard time? Pray for her and make her a card with the words of Psalm 71:20.

PROMISE TO REPEAT

How did it go? What did you learn?

Modeling Modesty

Elyana, who lives in Grand Prairie, Texas, is passionate about competitive cheerleading. She finds it fun and challenging but, as she discovered when she was ten years old, some things about cheering are more challenging than others. Read her story below and see how knowing God's Word helped her make a daring choice.

One day, while I was watching TV, my mom called me into her room. She looked very concerned and told me to sit down near her, so I did. "I have some news," she said. "Your cheer coach just sent me the uniform for the cheer competition. It is very revealing."

My belly filled with butterflies. I knew this was a very serious problem. I knew that as a Christian girl there were some fashion trends I could not wear. Mom said, "Let's have a conversation with the coach." I knew then that I would have to choose. My mom said choosing could mean I would have to walk away. I was willing to walk away, but my heart broke. Tears ran down my face. Without cheerleading, I would feel like a zebra without stripes, like a plant without leaves.

Mom and I sat there for what seemed like forever. It was one of the worst feelings I have ever had. It was hard, but my mom was right. Those uniforms dishonored God. I decided then that if this was the only uniform option, I would no longer cheer. I remembered 1 Timothy 2:9, which says, "I also want the women to dress modestly, with decency and propriety, adorning themselves, not with elaborate hairstyles or gold or pearls or expensive clothes."

The days after this were long and dreadful. Cheerleading practice was hard too. Everyone was surprised that I couldn't wear the uniform. They all could wear it. It was as if the girls' questions and comments were a dark shadow following me day and night.

When the fitting day came, I was very nervous. My heart sank and my legs shook. My mom and I prayed before we went in. When I tried on the uniform, it was awkward putting it on, and I felt very uncomfortable. When we finished putting it on, we went to my coach so she could adjust it. My mom asked if she could do anything to make it less revealing since my belly was showing. It turned out that I was able to wear a bodysuit under the uniform.

I was so relieved! God had honored me for making the right choice, and He let me stay in cheerleading. So now I know that God will honor anyone anywhere anytime who honors Him. There was definitely a reward.

YOUR TURN

- Read Hebrews 13:6 to discover another verse that Elyana was able to understand better because of this situation.

- In the space below, write about one or two situations in which Christian girls might be tempted to go along with what others are doing instead of being different and honoring the Lord. Write a prayer to God asking Him to give you the courage to make the right choices, even if that means you might have to give up something you like.

- Ask your mom or another Christian lady to tell you about a time when she made the difficult decision to obey God instead of choosing what would have been easier. What was the result?

What are your thoughts?

BIBLE READING   *Proverbs 20:13 and Hebrews 6:12*

TRUTH

Laziness won't get you anywhere in life.

- Jenny looks for the dollar she lost in her messy room. She gives up after five minutes.
- If Sarah can't reach the remote control, she just watches the same channel, even if she doesn't like what's on.
- On Saturday mornings, Emma prefers to wake up late instead of having fresh pancakes with her sisters.
- They're giving out activity books in the gym during lunchtime, but Annie doesn't feel like waiting in the long line.
- Mia drops a piece of ice on the kitchen floor. Instead of picking it up, she kicks it under the fridge.

What do these girls have in common?

The Bible has many warnings about being lazy. It reminds us that we can't expect to do well in school, get good jobs, earn the money we need to live, and so on if we're not willing to work. Besides that, people won't respect us if we don't do our share.

We also shouldn't be lazy in our Christian life. We can't expect God to bless us if we don't read the Bible, pray, go to church, or obey Him in other ways. We have to wake up spiritually and get going!

DARE   Be an active Christian.

DOUBLE DARE

1. Are you a lazy Christian or an active one? Ask God to help you be excited about following and serving Him. You'll be amazed by how He blesses you!

2. In your journal, write five ways you can "wake up" as a Christian. Choose one to do today.

PROMISE TO REPEAT

How did it go? What did you learn?

Safety in Numbers? Not Always!

BIBLE READING *Matthew 7:13–14*

TRUTH

Following the crowd can get us into trouble.

There's an expression that says there's safety in numbers; in other words, if you are alone in a place you don't know, it's better to stay close to a crowd of people than to be off by yourself. When it comes to our physical safety, this can certainly be true. But there are situations in life when following the crowd is not good for us. We're going to learn a lesson about this from the example of the alligator.

One type of alligator is laaaaazy and doesn't bother hunting for its food. It just lies near the riverbank, opens its mouth wide, and pretends it's dead. Soon flies start landing on its tongue, as well as other insects. That attracts lizards who want to eat the bugs. Pretty soon, frogs are joining the party and even other small animals. All of a sudden …

WHAM! The alligator snaps its jaws shut and enjoys a nice big meal.

The lesson we can learn from this is to be careful about following big groups. The Bible tells us that God's children must walk along a narrow path to reach Him. It may not be crowded or popular, but it's safe!

DARE Take the right path, not the popular one.

DOUBLE DARE

1. What are some activities kids your age feel pressured to participate in but aren't right or safe? Ask God to give you the courage to say no to those things, even if you're the only one.

2. In a gentle way, share today's devo with a friend who seems easily influenced by "the crowd."

PROMISE TO REPEAT

How did it go? What did you learn?

Be Careful About Judging

BIBLE READING *Matthew 7:3*

TRUTH

We're no better than the people we're tempted to judge.

There once was an old couple who had been happily married for many years, but they were starting to have trouble talking to each other. The husband thought, *I think my wife is going deaf. I'm going to do a test to prove it.*

So one evening the man sat across the living room from his wife. When she had her back turned to him, he whispered, "Can you hear me?" She didn't answer, so he got up and moved closer. He softly asked again, "Can you hear me?" Again, he got no answer. He took a few more steps toward her and whispered, "Can you hear me?" She still wasn't answering. Finally, he moved so he was right behind her and whispered again, "Can you hear me now?"

To his surprise, she said loudly, "For the fourth time, yes!"

You can imagine how ashamed he felt when he realized he was the one who had trouble hearing. Sometimes we convince ourselves that someone else is bad because of what we see and hear. But we don't realize that the problem may be with us. Judging someone harshly makes us guilty too.

DARE Think twice before judging someone else.

DOUBLE DARE

1. Think of someone you judged in your heart lately. Do you know the whole story? Do you think you're less guilty in God's eyes? Ask Him to forgive you for being judgmental.

2. How do you feel when someone judges you? Try to remember that the next time you're tempted to judge and ask God to help you be kind instead.

PROMISE TO REPEAT

How did it go? What did you learn?

The Same on the Inside

BIBLE READING *Acts 10:34–35*

TRUTH

In God's eyes, the color of our skin makes no difference.

We're all tempted at times to treat people who are similar to us better than people who seem different. If a student at your school speaks a different language, has different color skin, eats food you've never seen before, or dresses differently, some kids might make fun of him or her. How do you think God feels about that?

Here's something to think about: What color are eggs? Well, there are white eggs and brown eggs, right? The shells look a little different from each other. But what happens when you crack those eggs open? Do they look different on the inside? Nope. Do they taste different when you cook them? Again, no.

People might look different on the outside, but our bodies—our skin, hair, eyes, body shape, and so on—are just "shells" like the ones eggs have. When you get to what's inside a person, we're made just the same way. And I'm not talking about our bones, muscles, and organs. I mean our souls.

The Bible says that we are all equal in God's eyes. Let's treat each other that way.

DARE Don't judge people by their outer shells.

DOUBLE DARE

1. If your family usually buys white eggs, ask your mom if you can buy brown ones next time (or the opposite). When she asks why, tell her about today's devo.

2. Have you been ignoring a girl because she's different from you? Ask God to help you show love to her the next time you see her.

PROMISE TO REPEAT

How did it go? What did you learn?

BIBLE READING *Ecclesiastes 3:11*

TRUTH

God made you beautiful, whether or not you can see that.

Who doesn't love butterflies? I live in the city where we don't have many butterflies, so I'm always excited when I see one.

Scientists have figured out that there are between fifteen thousand and twenty thousand different types of butterflies in the world. Just imagine how many total butterflies there are if you were to count all the butterflies of each type! Some of these butterflies have magnificent patterns and colors on their wings, which often have interesting shapes themselves.

But did you ever think about the fact that a butterfly can't see its own beauty? Butterflies don't look into mirrors and see the pretty colors of their wings. It's our human eyes that admire the butterflies and enjoy their beauty.

In the same way, sometimes we can't see our own beauty. Even when you look in the mirror, you might see only the things you don't like. You might wonder if anyone thinks you're special.

The Bible reassures you that God made you very special and beautiful! You may not see it, but others can.

DARE Thank God for making you just the way you are.

DOUBLE DARE

1. Write today's verse on some nice paper and decorate around it with butterflies (stickers, cut-out pictures, or your own drawings). Ask your mom if you can stick this on the bathroom mirror to remind everyone in your family how beautiful God made them.

2. Do you have a friend who feels down about herself? Share today's devo with her, and then tell her why she's special to you.

PROMISE TO REPEAT

How did it go? What did you learn?

Everyone Needs a Friend

Remember Anna, the girl who turned a bully into a friend (see page 195)? A couple of years later, she had another opportunity to be a courageous friend and show God's love.

After her first day of fifth grade, Anna's dad asked how her day went. "Well, I have a lot of work to do," she answered. Her dad was surprised and said, "You have homework after your first day of school?" Anna said that it wasn't a school assignment she had to work on. She went on to explain: "There's a special girl in our class. She's new to our school and her name is Krestin. She is autistic and the other kids pick on her. So I'm going to take my biggest stuffed animal, wrap it up in a large gift bag, decorate the bag with ribbons, and make a special card to give her first thing tomorrow morning."

"Wow, Anna, that's very kind of you," her dad said. "But you do know what will happen, don't you?"

"Yes, the other kids will start picking on me," Anna replied. "But that's okay because Krestin has to have a friend." Anna told her dad about how Krestin had asked to go to the bathroom only an hour after school started. "I thought about why she did that, so a minute later I asked to go to the bathroom too. Sure enough, I found her crying, so I comforted her."

Anna's dad was really touched by what his daughter had told her, and he prayed for Anna. The next day after school, her teacher asked her to stay behind. "Anna, do you know why the other kids were picking on you today?" she asked. "Yes, but that's okay. Krestin has to have a friend."

At the end of the week, Anna's dad asked her what the highlight of her first week in fifth grade was. "That's easy, Dad. Krestin has other friends now." A few months later, after the Christmas holidays, Anna gave all the girls in her class invitations to her eleventh birthday party. Krestin's mother called that evening to ask about the invitation. "We sure hope she can come," said Anna's dad. Krestin's mom seemed worried because her daughter had never been to a birthday party before and wouldn't know how to behave, but Anna's dad said they would make sure Krestin had a wonderful time.

And that's exactly what happened. Krestin had a great time, and so did Anna!

YOUR TURN

- Read Matthew 5:15–16. How did Anna live out this Bible verse?

  - Krestin has autism. If you're not sure what that is, ask your parents to help you look it up in an encyclopedia or on the Internet.

  - Do you know any kids who are picked on because they're different? Maybe you're that kid. How does it feel, or how do you think it feels? How will you change the way you treat others after doing today's devo?

- Think of someone who gets picked on a lot. Come up with a plan, either alone, with your family, or with a friend, to do something extraspecial for this person to "let your light shine."

What are your thoughts?

Don't Forget to Graduate!

BIBLE READING *Hebrews 6:1*

TRUTH

We can't stay in spiritual "elementary school" forever.

I'm not sure how old you are, but you're probably either in elementary school now or you were a few years ago, right? It's been a lo-o-o-o-o-ong time since I was in elementary school, but I have great memories of friends, teachers, and interesting activities. Whether you're homeschooled or you go to a big school with hundreds of kids, elementary school is really important. That's where you learn basic skills such as reading, writing, math, and other subjects that will help you when you're older.

You can't skip elementary school. It wouldn't make sense to send a small child to middle school or high school before she learned the basic subjects. But you also can't stay in elementary school forever. At the end of every school year, you should know more than you did at the start. That makes you ready for the next grade.

The Bible says we have to "graduate" in our spiritual lives too. When we're young or still new in our faith, we have to learn the basic facts about Jesus and the Bible. But as time goes on, we have to study the Bible more so that we can understand it better. If we don't, we'll stay in "elementary school" and be immature in our faith.

DARE Keep on learning and growing!

DOUBLE DARE

1. Think back to when you started this book. In your journal, write about five things you've learned since that time.

2. Do you sit with the grown-ups during church? If not, try it. Even if you don't understand everything, you will still learn about God!

PROMISE TO REPEAT

How did it go? What did you learn?

What's Inside?

BIBLE READING *1 Samuel 16:7*

TRUTH

When we look only at someone's outside, we miss the treasure inside.

One day, a man exploring some caves near the ocean found a bag full of small, rolled-up clay balls. They didn't look useful, but he took the bag with him anyway.

Walking along the beach, he started to throw the clay balls into the ocean, one by one, as far as he could. He did this for a while without thinking about it, until he dropped a ball. It hit a rock and cracked open. Looking closer, the man saw a beautiful jewel! There were about twenty balls left in the bag, so he broke them open and found treasure in each one, all together worth thousands of dollars.

He remembered all the balls he had thrown into the ocean—about fifty of them— each with its hidden treasure now lost on the ocean floor. He had thrown away thousands of dollars' worth of jewels!

Sometimes if we look at people and they don't seem to "sparkle"—if they're not beautiful or smart or funny or rich—we think they're not worth our attention. But God has hidden treasure inside each person, and if we ask Him, He'll help us find the jewels and see people the way He sees them.

DARE Look for the treasure in people.

DOUBLE DARE

1. Is there someone you've ignored because you don't like how she looks? Ask God to help you discover her *inner* qualities.

2. Do you ever feel like a dull clay ball? Thank God for making you special just the way you are!

PROMISE TO REPEAT

How did it go? What did you learn?

BIBLE READING   *1 Thessalonians 5:11*

TRUTH

Our words can either lift someone up or knock her down.

Five friendly frogs fearlessly hopped through the forest one fine Friday in February.

Suddenly, two of the frogs fell into a deep pit. The other frogs came close to see what had happened to their friends. When they saw how deep the pit was, they told their friends there was no way they would get out. They were doomed to die down there.

The two frogs in the pit ignored their friends and tried to jump out. Their friends told them to stop, but the frogs kept trying, harder and harder. The three frogs up above waved their little arms and shouted, telling their friends to just give up.

Finally, one of the frogs listened to his friends, fell down, and died. But the other one kept jumping as high as he could. He couldn't hear what his friends were saying because he was deaf, so he thought they were cheering him on, and that gave him courage to keep trying. He jumped so high that he made it out.

The Bible says we can have either a positive or a negative influence on people when we talk, so we must make sure we always use our words to encourage one another.

DARE   Encourage someone today.

DOUBLE DARE

1. In your journal, write about a time when someone's words discouraged you. Then write about a time when someone encouraged you. Ask God to help you be an encourager.

2. Do you know someone who feels like giving up? Find a special way to encourage her with your words (and actions) today.

PROMISE TO REPEAT

How did it go? What did you learn?

People Pleasers

BIBLE READING *Galatians 1:10*

TRUTH

We can't get approval from God if we're trying to get it from other people.

When I graduated from high school, I added a little quote to what was written next to my photo in the yearbook. It said, "There is no reward from God to those who seek it from men."

Many people waste a lot of energy always trying to make other people happy. There's nothing wrong with making people happy if you're doing it because you love them and want to see them happy. But there is something wrong if you're doing it only because you want them to like you. I used to worry that if I didn't do what people wanted, they would stop liking me. That's called being a people pleaser, and it's not a very good way to go through life.

Today's Bible verse reminds us that when we serve God, it should be to please Him and not to get the attention and praise of people around us. We shouldn't give money just so people will say, "Wow, look how generous she is!" And we shouldn't volunteer to help with a project just so people will think nice things about us. Instead, we should do these things simply because we love God and want to serve Him.

DARE Serve God for His glory, not yours.

DOUBLE DARE

1. Are you a people pleaser more than a God pleaser? Ask God to help you love Him more than you love the approval of others.

2. In your journal, write about one situation where you will change your goal from pleasing others to pleasing God. How will you do it?

PROMISE TO REPEAT

How did it go? What did you learn?

BIBLE READING *Ephesians 4:2*

TRUTH

Relationships take work.

Someone once said, "A relationship is like a house. When a lightbulb burns out, you do not go and buy a new house. You change the lightbulb."

That sure makes sense! You could look at it another way: When your bicycle gets a flat tire, you don't buy a new bike. You put air in the tire or replace it. Or like this: When a button falls off your shirt, you don't throw out your shirt. You sew a new button on (or ask your mom to do it for you!).

In the same way, when your sister hurts your feelings or when a friend lies to you, you don't get a new sister or a new friend. You work out the problem with her—with humbleness, gentleness, patience, and love.

DARE Work on that difficult relationship instead of giving up.

DOUBLE DARE

1. Think of someone you are having a hard time loving or getting along with. Ask God to show you how you can fix that relationship and to give you the strength to do your part.

2. With a friend, think of five other examples that fit today's lesson, and then memorize Ephesians 4:2.

PROMISE TO REPEAT

How did it go? What did you learn?

H.O.W. (Hero Observation Weekend) #9

HERO LIST

Choose ONE of these heroes to learn about this weekend:

Name	Bible Verses
Esther	Esther 3:1–11; 4:4–17; 5:1–8; 7:1–10; 8:1–11
Stephen	Acts 6–7
Ruth	Ruth 1–4
David	1 Samuel 17
Abigail	1 Samuel 25:1–42
Gideon	Judges 6–7
The Bleeding Woman	Mark 5:25–34
Joseph	Genesis 37; 39–41
The Widow of Zarephath	1 Kings 17:8–24; Luke 4:25–26
Noah	Genesis 6–8
Miriam	Exodus 2:1–10
Daniel	Daniel 6
Mary of Bethany	John 12:1–8
Abraham	Genesis 22:1–18

Your hero for this weekend: _____

QUESTION TIME

1. How did this weekend's hero show courage and faith in God?

2. What happened because of his or her courage and obedience?

3. What did you learn from this hero's life that will help you in your own walk with God?

DOUBLE DARE

Choose at least one of these ways to dig a little deeper into your hero's life this weekend:

1. See if you can find other Bible verses about him or her. Write the reference (or the "address" of the verses) here and also anything new that you learned.

2. Ask your parents or another Christian what they have learned from this hero's life and example.

Tell a friend or your family about your new hero!

Chicken Pie Charity

BIBLE READING *Proverbs 25:21–22*

TRUTH

The best way to get rid of an enemy is to turn her into a friend.

It can be really tough to be nice to people who are mean to us instead of hating them, but with God's help, it's not impossible. Here's an example of how God wants us to treat our enemies.

A Christian lady who owned two prize chickens had a neighbor who was always grumpy. One day, her chickens got loose and were roaming around in the garden next door. When the man saw this, he caught the chickens, broke their necks, and threw them back over the fence. Of course, the woman was upset to see her chickens dead, but instead of screaming at the man, she did something else.

She took the dead hens inside, prepared them, and cooked two chicken pies. When they were still warm, she took one to her neighbor and said she was sorry that her chickens had gone into his yard. The man felt very ashamed when he heard her apology and saw the gift of the chicken pie. This lady wasn't trying to make her neighbor feel bad. She just wanted to show him true Christian love. By doing this, she may have helped him change his heart!

DARE Pay back meanness with God's love.

DOUBLE DARE

1. Think of a time when someone really hurt you and made you upset. How did you react? After reading today's devo, how would you act differently if it happened again? Write your thoughts in your journal.

2. Who are you having trouble loving? Ask God to help you show her love this week.

PROMISE TO REPEAT

How did it go? What did you learn?

Scattered Words

BIBLE READING *Proverbs 16:28 and Proverbs 26:20*

TRUTH

Gossip can ruin friendship.

A fun game to play with a big group of friends is Broken Telephone. One person starts by whispering a word or sentence into the ear of the person next to her. Then that person whispers it to the next friend and so on until the secret message has gone all the way around the circle to the last person. That person then says what she heard. Sometimes the final message is so different from the original one that everyone bursts out laughing!

Gossip is spread when people pass along stories or comments that they overhear about others. Even if what's being said is true, the goal is usually to make someone look bad, so the story ends up being twisted around.

Another way to look at how gossip is spread is to imagine a pillow full of down feathers being torn and shaken on the roof of a tall building. When those feathers start drifting away, do you think anyone would be able to collect them again? Nope! In the same way, we can't take back words we say, so we must be careful to say only things that are true and kind.

DARE Stop gossip before it starts.

DOUBLE DARE

1. When a friend starts telling you a story about someone that you know is none of your business, ask her to stop. It may be tempting to listen, but God can use you to break the gossip chain.

2. Play Broken Telephone with a group of friends, and then talk about how harmful gossip can be.

PROMISE TO REPEAT

How did it go? What did you learn?

Leave That Dog Alone!

BIBLE READING *Proverbs 26:17*

TRUTH

Getting involved in other people's arguments can get you "bitten"!

Some verses in the book of Proverbs create interesting mental pictures, don't they? I remember smiling the first time I read today's verse. I have never owned a dog, so I thought, *That's funny! What's wrong with grabbing a dog's ears?*

The fact is, once you've grabbed a dog's ears, there's no easy way to let go of them without having the dog bite you. I guess dogs don't like it when people do that. (You know, I don't think humans would like being grabbed by the ears either!)

In one of the folktales about Hodja, two people were fighting in the street below his house. Hoping to stop the fight, Hodja wrapped a quilt around himself and went outside. In an instant, one of the men grabbed his quilt and ran away, and the other one ran in the opposite direction. When he went back in, Hodja's wife asked what the fight had been about. "I don't know," he said, "but my quilt is gone and the fight is over!"

Like Hodja, we sometimes meddle in other people's quarrels and end up being the biggest loser. The Bible tells us to mind our own business.

DARE   Stay away from trouble that isn't yours.

DOUBLE DARE

1. When you see people arguing, do you ever feel like you should try to help them stop? Ask God to give you wisdom to know when you should just leave them alone.

2. Do you know anyone who owns a dog? Ask about what happens if you grab a dog's ears. Why not share today's devo with him or her?

PROMISE TO REPEAT

How did it go? What did you learn?

Beauty and the Beast

BIBLE READING *Romans 3:10–18*

TRUTH

Beauty is only skin deep.

What do you think most girls and even older women want more than anything else? It's something they will spend a lot of time and money on. Some girls want it so badly that they'll even try to change themselves to get it. You guessed it: it's beauty.

List six things females do to try to look more beautiful. We've given a few examples.

wear makeup   dye their hair   buy expensive clothes

_____   _____   _____

_____   _____   _____

Have you ever noticed that some girls who try hard to look good on the outside are not very nice on the inside? It's like taking a rotten banana and piling ice cream and chocolate syrup on top of it to hide the icky stuff.

The Bible says that sin makes *all of us* ugly beasts on the inside. Does it really matter how beautiful we are on the outside if we're ugly inside? Nope. God cares more about our hearts (as do the people who really matter in our lives), and He makes our hearts beautiful when we ask Him to forgive our sins.

DARE   Let God make you beautiful inside!

DOUBLE DARE

1. Read Isaiah 53:2, which describes Jesus's physical appearance. In your journal, write about how important outward beauty is to God.

2. Read Proverbs 31:30. If you pay more attention to how you look on the outside than on your inner beauty, ask God to forgive you and to make you beautiful inside.

PROMISE TO REPEAT

How did it go? What did you learn?

BIBLE READING *Romans 12:2*

TRUTH

When we follow God instead of the crowd, we can discover His special plan for us.

Do you like fish? My family eats salmon or trout three times a week because fish is really good for you.

Did you know that salmon swim upstream? Most fish naturally swim downstream because it's easier. The water's current pushes them along and they don't have to expend a lot of energy. But fish like salmon and trout swim against the current, which takes extra work. They do this because they like to lay their eggs in cool, fast-flowing freshwater. They usually live in the river for two years before going down to the sea. When they've grown, they swim upstream back to the river they were born in (smart fish!) to have their babies.

Swimming upstream is like running uphill. It's much harder than running downhill. It's also harder to stand up for what you know is right than to do what everyone else is doing. But the Bible tells us to follow Jesus instead of the world. If you dare to obey God's Word no matter what people around you say, God will bless you.

DARE   Follow God, not the crowd.

DOUBLE DARE

1. In your journal, draw a picture of a fish swimming upstream in the opposite direction of other fish. While you draw, work on memorizing Romans 12:2.

2. Think of one or two ways you might feel tempted to follow the crowd instead of doing what God would want you to do. Talk to God about it and ask Him to give you the confidence and wisdom to stick to what's right.

PROMISE TO REPEAT

How did it go? What did you learn?

Have you ever seen those cute little wooden dolls that "nest" inside each other? In Russia, they're known as *matryoshka* dolls. The smallest doll is usually painted to look like a baby and is made of one piece of wood. The other larger dolls are made of two pieces that fit together like the plastic eggs you get treats or toys in. The shapes of these dolls are quite simple and smooth, but the painted designs can be strikingly detailed and beautiful. I love the ones with bright colors!

Other types of toys nest or fit one inside the other, and you'll often see babies or toddlers playing with these. For example, they may be different colored cups or square blocks with one side that's open. The child has to figure out how to put the pieces inside each other in the right order of size. If you try to fit a big piece into a smaller piece, it just doesn't work. You have to go in order.

Can you think of other things in life that have to be done in a certain order? For example, when you get dressed, you start with your underclothes, then your top and bottom, and last of all your jacket and shoes. You can't wear a dress over a coat or tights over sneakers, right?

Or think about making scrambled eggs. Do you first put the whole eggs (with the shells) in the frying pan, cook them, and then break them? No, that would be a disaster! First you have to break the eggs, then scramble them up, and then cook them in the frying pan.

What are some other examples? Write them here:

YOUR TURN

- Read 2 Peter 1:1–11. The Bible explains what we need to do to grow as Christians, and it gives us a list of qualities to "add" on top of each other, in order. List the seven qualities that today's reading says Christians should develop. We start with faith and then add:

    1.

    2.

    3.

    4.

    5.

    6.

    7.

What these verses tell us is that it's not enough to just have faith in, or to believe in, God. Our faith should motivate us to do good deeds and behave well. Our good deeds show that we know and understand God's Word. And our knowledge helps us to have self-control. Then, self-control helps us to stick to our faith and keep going on hard days, or to persevere. The longer we persevere, the more godly (or holy) we become, and that helps us to be kind to one another. And, finally, as we learn to be kind and unselfish, our love for one another grows. Do you see how the order makes sense?

When we do our best to develop these qualities, God helps us to grow in our faith and become stronger Christians.

DOUBLE DARE

1. When you look at the list of seven qualities in these verses, which ones do you think you need God's help with?

2. What are some things you can do to make that quality grow in your life?

On a piece of paper or in your journal, draw a set of eight *matryoshka* dolls lined up, starting with a baby and ending with the largest one. Underneath each one, write the eight qualities we learned today in order, starting with faith (the baby) and ending with love (the largest doll). Write "2 Peter 1:1–11" somewhere on the page as a reminder of today's devo.

What are your thoughts?

Are You God's Mirror?

BIBLE READING *John 1:6–9*

TRUTH

As Christians, we should reflect God's light to the world around us.

In the story of Snow White, the wicked queen asked her mirror the same question repeatedly: "Mirror, mirror, on the wall, who is the fairest of them all?" When we look into a mirror, most of us hope to see a pretty face looking back at us, don't we? It's natural to want to feel confident about our beauty, but spending too much time in front of a mirror can be a bad thing. We either start feeling bad about how we look, or we become very proud of our looks.

Believers in Jesus should focus more of their attention on being a mirror instead of looking in a mirror. What does this mean? John the Baptist is a good example for us. John was a humble believer who did his best to tell people about Jesus. His life "reflected" the light of Jesus.

When you hold a mirror at just the right angle, it catches the light from the sun or from a lightbulb and reflects it into the room. The mirror should face the light but also face the direction that needs the light.

When we stay close to Jesus and obey Him, people will see His love and truth reflected in our lives.

DARE Be a mirror for Jesus.

DOUBLE DARE

1. When people meet you, can they see that you love Jesus? In your journal, write down a few ways you can be a better mirror of God's light.

2. Write "I am God's mirror" on a sticky note and put it up on your bedroom mirror.

PROMISE TO REPEAT

How did it go? What did you learn?

Every Part Is Important

BIBLE READING *1 Corinthians 12:27*

TRUTH

Every part of God's family is important.

Put a check mark next to the following things that you can do:

Scratch your ear with your elbow.
Sit down without using your knees.
Open a drawer with your nose.
Pick up a book with your shoulder.
Walk around your room on your head.
Button your shirt with your teeth.

How did you do? Not very well? That's because every part of your body was made for a special purpose, and each part is important. Of course, some people are born without certain parts or have accidents or sicknesses that make some parts stop working. But the parts of their bodies they do have will always have a special purpose. For example, you can't hear with your nose, smell with your eyes, or taste with your hair.

In the "body" of Christ (the family of Christians around the world), each person has a special purpose. We can't say that someone else isn't important or that we're not important. God wants to use preachers, singers, cleaners, cooks, teachers, encouragers, writers, artists, builders, and drivers to do His work. He wants people who pray, people who shovel snow or cut grass, people who give hugs, and people who listen. And He can use you too!

DARE Do your part in the body of Christ.

DOUBLE DARE

1. What do you think your purpose might be in God's family? Write your ideas in your journal and pray that God will show you what you can do.

2. Say thank you to someone who joyfully serves God in his or her special way.

PROMISE TO REPEAT

How did it go? What did you learn?

Aim for Perfection

BIBLE READING   *2 Corinthians 7:1*

TRUTH

Christians should aim for the best instead of just good enough.

Have you ever gone bowling? It's a fun game but not as easy as it looks!

The goal in bowling is to roll a heavy ball down the center of a long lane and make the ten white pins at the other end, which are arranged in a triangle, fall down. The wood floor of the lane is polished and very slippery, so if you don't throw properly, the ball often spins toward the sides, where there are gutters. If your ball goes into the gutter, it won't hit any pins, and you get a score of zero for that turn.

Do you think you could win a bowling game if you concentrated only on not getting your ball in the gutter? No, you have to do your best to hit the pins!

Another example to explain today's verse is how you study for school. Your goal shouldn't be just to pass but to get the highest possible grade you can.

In the same way, Christians shouldn't feel satisfied simply by not committing "big" sins. Instead, our goal should be to be our very best for God. We should try to be pure because we love Him, not just because we don't want Him to punish us.

DARE   Aim for perfection!

DOUBLE DARE

1. Besides bowling and homework, think of a few other examples of ways we should aim for perfection. Ask God to help you always do your best instead of just good enough.

2. Do you have friends or family members who like bowling? Share this devo with them!

PROMISE TO REPEAT

How did it go? What did you learn?

Keep On Praying

BIBLE READING Ephesians 6:18

TRUTH

God's children must "keep on praying."

List seven things you do (or should do) at least one time every day. We've listed a few examples to get you started.

brush your teeth   eat   make your bed   _____

_____   _____   _____

_____   _____   _____

Why is it important to do all those things every day? Some of the things on your list are probably habits that keep you healthy.

Did you write *pray* on your list? If you did, good job! If not, I hope this devo will encourage you to pay more attention to making prayer a special part of each day's routine. Just as brushing your teeth keeps them from built-up plaque and decaying, praying and talking to God can keep your heart from getting dirty and sick.

DARE Make prayer an important part of your daily routine.

DOUBLE DARE

1. Do you forget to pray on some days? Write or doodle the word *pray* on ten sticky notes and put them in places where you'll see them often, such as in your planner or on your mirror.

2. Instead of waiting until bedtime to pray, try to do it as soon as you wake up. That will probably help you remember to pray during the day also.

PROMISE TO REPEAT

How did it go? What did you learn?

BIBLE READING   *Exodus 17:8–13*

TRUTH

Our spiritual leaders and teachers need our support.

Who do you think are the most important people in your church? The senior pastor? The youth leader? The Bible class teachers? Our leaders and teachers are very important and deserve our respect and honor. But did you know that church leaders couldn't do what they do if there weren't people like you praying for them and encouraging them?

My dad is a pastor, and he often says that one of the most valuable people in our church is a little old lady who has been praying for him and for the church every single day for many years. Some people don't even know her name or have never talked to her, but she is faithful in her prayers and that's a big boost for my dad. It's just like the story we read today in Exodus. This lady is like one of the men who held up Moses's arms when he got tired.

You may not be old enough or experienced enough to teach, go on mission trips, or do "big" things in the church, but that doesn't mean you're not important and useful! You can support and encourage the people who do the things you can't do, just as Aaron and Hur supported Moses. God can use you to help those people stay strong when their jobs are tough.

DARE   Be an encourager!

DOUBLE DARE

1. Make a pretty card for someone in your church who works hard and might need some encouragement. On the card, write a note saying how much you appreciate him or her.

2. Don't forget your parents! Find a way to "hold up their arms" today.

PROMISE TO REPEAT

How did it go? What did you learn?

A Robe of Righteousness

Anastasia Isch has been serving God for many years as a missionary, traveling to different countries, especially in Africa, to encourage and help other women and to tell them about Jesus and His love.

Soula, which is the nickname Anastasia uses most of the time, was born in Greece but now lives in Montreal, Canada, when she's not traveling. She works for a mission organization called SIM Canada.

When she was fourteen years old, Soula accepted Jesus as her personal Savior. She enjoyed following Him and learning about Him. One day, when she was sixteen, she learned a lesson she's never forgotten. Here's how she tells it:

As I was getting ready to go to my English class one afternoon [Soula's high school in Greece taught only French, not English], I went to my wardrobe, opened it, and tried to decide what I should wear that day. I started to think about who I would meet on the way to school. As different people came to mind, I wondered, Would they like to see me with this dress, or should I put on the other one?

I wanted to attract the attention of these people, so I was undecided. At that moment, the Lord spoke to my heart. I heard Him say, like a whisper, "Oh, you want to wear this dress to attract people's attention? I see!" That's all He said! I stood there like a piece of stone or wood. His words spoke deeply to my heart.

I changed my mind about the dress I was going to wear. At the same time, the Lord reminded me of other "clothes" He had dressed me with when this verse came to mind: "I delight greatly in the LORD; my soul rejoices in my God. For he has clothed me with garments of salvation and arrayed me in a robe of his righteousness, as a bridegroom adorns his head like a priest, and as a bride adorns herself with her jewels" (Isaiah 61:10). I took a piece of paper and wrote down this verse. I colored it and put it inside the door of my wardrobe.

I never forgot that day or the way God spoke to me about this area in my life. Many decades have passed since then, and I have put this lesson into practice all my life. I have often shared this story when speaking to women about the way we should dress as Christian women. And I still keep this verse inside my wardrobe!

YOUR TURN

- What goes through your mind as you get dressed every day? Is your focus on dressing in a way that will attract people's attention? Ask God to help you spend more time developing your inner beauty than your outward appearance.

- Just as Soula did, write out Isaiah 61:10 on a piece of paper, decorate it, and stick it inside your closet or wardrobe door as a daily reminder.

What are your thoughts?

Not Ashamed

BIBLE READING   *2 Timothy 1:8, 12*

TRUTH

When we suffer because of our faith, we don't need to feel ashamed.

Have you ever seen someone behave in a way that embarrasses the people around him or her but doesn't embarrass the person acting that way? For example, some young women wear clothes that show a lot of skin. They either get the wrong kind of attention or they make other people uncomfortable, but they don't seem to care. Some kids think it's cool to use dirty or disrespectful words that shock other people. Sometimes teenagers get in trouble at school for breaking the rules, but they just laugh about it.

Nowadays, people are proud to say which celebrities they admire, they're proud of the activities they participate in, and sometimes they're even proud of their sins. So isn't it strange that Christians are sometimes embarrassed to tell people that they believe in Jesus? We're shy to tell a friend about a prayer God answered. We're uncomfortable telling others that we go to church on Sunday mornings instead of sleeping in or going shopping.

Naturally, we worry that people will make fun of us if we share these things. That's because we forget how awesome and powerful God is! We don't need to feel shy about being His child.

DARE   Be confident in the One you believe in.

DOUBLE DARE

1. Think of a time when you were too shy to say that you believe in Jesus. Ask God to give you more courage the next time you have a chance to talk about Him. Someone may need to hear what you have to say!

2. Do you have a friend you've been wanting to invite to church? Do it this week!

PROMISE TO REPEAT

How did it go? What did you learn?

BIBLE READING   *Ephesians 4:3*

TRUTH

When Christians are united, we are stronger against the Enemy.

One of Aesop's fables is about four oxen that lived in a field together. Nearby was a hungry lion that would wander around the field, waiting for a chance to attack the oxen. But the oxen were smart. Whenever the lion got close, they would stand with their tails together. Each one would face a different direction so no matter what the lion did, he was always facing a pair of sharp horns.

But one day the oxen got into an argument with each other, and they all walked off to a different corner of the field. Seeing this, the lion was able to attack them, one by one, and soon there were no more oxen.

Christians are all members of the church (not one building or group of believers but the family of God all over the world). When we love one another, pray together, worship together, and serve God together, we are strong against the Devil's attacks. But when we start to argue over things that aren't important and forget to love one another, our hearts move apart. That makes us weak against temptation and can even make us hurt one another.

As we read today, we must make every effort to stay united through God's Spirit.

DARE   Be there for other Christians.

DOUBLE DARE

1. Do you know any Christians who aren't getting along (for example, in your church or family)? Pray that God will help them be united again.

2. Share today's story and Bible verse with a Christian friend. Talk about the importance of staying united.

PROMISE TO REPEAT

How did it go? What did you learn?

Serving with Love

BIBLE READING *Galatians 5:13*

TRUTH

Christians are free—not to be selfish but to serve one another.

Many people misunderstand what freedom means. They think it means you're allowed to do whatever you want, whenever you want. That's why so many kids say, "I can't wait until I'm older and can move out and have freedom!" What they really want is no rules and no one to tell them what to do. But that's not freedom. That's anarchy (a situation where there are no rules at all).

Can you imagine if there were no traffic laws and cars could drive in any direction at any speed without ever stopping or letting each other pass? That would be a disaster! What if there were no laws in a country to stop people from committing crimes? We would hear about many more robberies and murders, wouldn't we? Even games aren't fun if someone doesn't follow the rules.

God's freedom is from the power of sin and temptation in our lives. When He gives us strength to say no to sin, we are free to live the way He designed us to live: loving and serving Him and others. Life is beautiful when we help each other instead of just doing things for ourselves.

DARE Use your freedom to bless someone today.

DOUBLE DARE

1. If your mom asks for help today, remember that you're free to say no to the temptation to grumble. Stop whatever you're doing and help her humbly. You'll both feel good about it!

2. Has someone done something kind for you lately? Find a special way to say thank you!

PROMISE TO REPEAT

How did it go? What did you learn?

BIBLE READING *Galatians 5:26*

TRUTH

Christians should not envy one another.

A little blue jay once flew by a farm and noticed some beautiful peacocks. Their long, colorful tails made them look so elegant as they walked around the yard! The blue jay looked back at his shorter tail feathers with their simple blue and black stripes and wished he were a peacock. So he found some peacock feathers on the ground and tied them to his tail. Then he went into the yard and started to walk around as if he belonged there.

It didn't take too long for the peacocks to realize there was a fake among them. They all started to peck at him with their sharp beaks and pull out the feathers he had stolen. The disappointed blue jay had no choice but to go back to his own friends, but he learned a good lesson that day about not trying to be anything but himself.

Do you ever look at other girls and wish you had something they have—their hair color, their clothes, their parents? The Bible warns against envy because it stops us from loving others. Besides, you'll be happier if you try to be the best you instead of trying to be someone else!

DARE Take what's troubling you to God.

DOUBLE DARE

1. What are some ways girls might try to change themselves to fit in with others? Ask God to help you be grateful for who He made you and to love others instead of envying them.

2. Make a bookmark that looks like a peacock feather and write Galatians 5:26 on the back. Use it to remember today's devo.

PROMISE TO REPEAT

How did it go? What did you learn?

Sparkle Like a Diamond

BIBLE READING *2 Corinthians 4:17*

TRUTH

The more suffering a Christian goes through, the more she grows.

There's a saying that "diamonds are a girl's best friend." That's just an advertising slogan to encourage men to buy diamond jewelry for their wives or girlfriends, but real diamonds truly are beautiful.

There are two things you should know about diamonds:

1. Diamonds start out as carbon, a common material that is used for coal, in water filters, in soda (when it's mixed with oxygen), for fuel, and for many other uses. When carbon is put under extreme pressure at superhigh heat, it turns into diamond, the hardest material in the world.

2. A diamond rock has to be cut very carefully to be turned into a gemstone. One mistake can crack it and make it worthless. The more cuts a diamond has, the more brilliant and valuable it becomes.

There will be times in life when you'll feel a lot of pressure. You may be hurt, uncomfortable, confused, or stressed. You may wonder why God is letting bad things happen to you. But if you continue trusting Him, you, just like the diamond, will come out of your troubles sparkling! God knows exactly what you're going through and how much you can handle.

DARE Stay strong during hard times.

DOUBLE DARE

1. Ask your mom if she has a diamond she can show you. Look at it together and talk about how it started out as a lump of carbon. Pray together that God will give you both strength when life gets tough.

2. Memorize today's verse and try to remember it whenever you see a diamond.

PROMISE TO REPEAT

How did it go? What did you learn?

When Hayley was thirteen years old, she bravely shared a testimony at a Fellowship of Christian Athletes event in Fort Hood, Texas, where her family lived at that time. She talked about something that had happened to her less than three years earlier.

Her father, who was a soldier, was sent to Iraq in December 2005. Hayley didn't know it was the last time she would ever say good-bye to him. About four months later, her family got the news that he had been killed during a flight mission. Hayley told the audience, "We were all brokenhearted. All I could do that night was cry my heart out. Friends and our church family came for comfort. I stayed locked up in my room. I was asking God why He had done such a dramatic thing to me. *Why me, Lord? Why such a great man?*"

Hayley couldn't understand God and found it hard to praise Him, but her mother reminded her that Christians should praise God through good times and bad times. Hayley then said, "My mother was such a great role model through this time. She led us with encouragement. God was testing our faith for Him. When God puts you in a situation, you have to try your hardest to praise Him and make it."

A few months after her dad's death, Hayley, her mom, and her seven-year-old brother were given a special trip to California with other military families by an organization called Snowball Express. She told those listening to her story, "I came home from the trip overwhelmed by how much God has really blessed me by having ten years of memories to cherish. I know my dad loved me and I know my heavenly Father up above loves me. As long as you have faith, you'll be good, because faith is like a muscle. The more you use it, the stronger it gets … I can do all things through Christ who strengthens me if I have faith and trust and if I love God Almighty. I know for sure I'm going to see my dad and God someday in heaven."

YOUR TURN

- What did you learn from Hayley's story about trusting God in painful situations?
- Read Mark 10:15.

Some people who aren't Christian may think it's not a big deal if a child or a tween like you believes in God. In fact, because you do, they may think you're not as smart as they are and that you believe in God the same way some children believe in the tooth fairy or the Easter bunny. They may think that once you grow up, you'll see that God isn't real (like they believe).

As we see in Hayley's story, it can be really hard for a child to trust God if she doesn't understand why He lets some things happen—like letting a little girl's father die. So when a child makes the choice to believe in God, that's actually very special and wonderful. That's why Jesus said in the Bible verse you just read that people should have the kind of simple but strong faith children do.

- In your journal, write about a time when you had trouble understanding or trusting God. How did God help you in that situation?

DOUBLE DARE

Do you know any kids who have had a close family member die? Try to find a special way to encourage them and remind them that God loves them. If you've been in Hayley's situation and know what it feels like to have a parent die, then you have something special to offer to other kids because you know what they're going through and what they need. Pray that God will use you this weekend to bless someone.

What are your thoughts?

You Can't Take It with You

BIBLE READING *Jeremiah 9:23–24 and Ecclesiastes 5:15–16*

TRUTH

You can't keep your earthly riches forever.

What are your favorite board games? Have you ever played Monopoly, The Game of Life, Pay Day, or other games in which you have to try to collect money? If you're good at those games, it can be pretty exciting to see your money pile getting bigger and bigger while everyone else is losing money. When you finally win, you might yell out, "I'm rich! I'm rich!" It feels great, doesn't it?

But then what? When the game is over, you have to put the money back in the box along with the board and all the game pieces, right? Even if you kept it, could you do anything with the fake money? Nope.

Some people go through life as if they're playing a board game, collecting as much money and "stuff" as they can. It's almost as if they're waiting to say at the end, "Ha! I'm rich! I'm richer than all of you! I WIN!"

But the Bible reminds us that we can't take any of our riches with us when we die. So instead of chasing after wealth, we should chase after God and the things He wants for us.

DARE Don't boast about your riches.

DOUBLE DARE

1. Ask your family to play a board game this weekend. While you're playing, share today's devo with them and talk about what our attitude toward money should be.

2. Write a list of all your favorite stuff (clothes, books, and so on). Will any of them last forever? Ask God to help you not be too attached to things.

PROMISE TO REPEAT

How did it go? What did you learn?

Smoke Signal Prayers

BIBLE READING *Philippians 4:6*

TRUTH

God is always there, even in our worst situations.

A man who survived a shipwreck woke up all alone on a small island. He prayed desperately for God to help him, but as each day passed, no one came to rescue him. Finally, he built himself a little hut for shelter, using pieces of wood he found scattered around.

One evening, after scavenging for food, he came back to his hut to find it burning. His little shelter was on fire, and smoke was rolling high up into the sky. This was terrible! He was stunned and angry, and he cried out to God, "How could You do this to me?"

The next morning, the man woke up when he heard the sound of a ship's engine close by. Rescuers! The man asked them, "How did you know I was here?" They answered, "We saw your smoke signal!"

It's easy to feel sad or angry when things go wrong in our lives. That's because we forget that God is doing good work in us even when things seem painful or hopeless. So the next time you feel like your "hut" is burning, don't become anxious. Instead, keep praying and giving God thanks. You may be surprised by how He rescues you.

DARE Trust God when life gets you down.

DOUBLE DARE

1. Share today's story with your family. Then talk about some things you may be feeling anxious about and pray about them together.

2. Write today's verse on a piece of paper, and then cut out each word. Memorize the verse, and then see if you can put the words in the right order.

PROMISE TO REPEAT

How did it go? What did you learn?

BIBLE READING   *1 Corinthians 15:51–53*

TRUTH

When followers of Jesus die, they don't disappear. They metamorphose!

One day, there was a funeral in a little village of caterpillars. All the caterpillars dressed in black and sadly marched together, carrying the cocoon of their special friend who was gone.

Meanwhile, a beautiful butterfly fluttered above them, watching in disbelief. "What are you guys crying for?" he shouted. "I've been metamorphosed!" The little caterpillars didn't realize that their friend wasn't dead … He had just changed into a new kind of creature!

Metamorphosis is a word that comes from the Greek language, and it means pretty much the same thing as transformation (remember the Transformers toys?) or, more simply, changing from one thing into another.

The Bible tells us that when a Christian's life here on earth is over, he or she will be changed and given a new heavenly body. Just as God designed the caterpillar to become a beautiful butterfly that can fly up high, He will transform us in a way we can't even imagine!

For a Christian, death isn't a sad thing. It's just the time we leave the "cocoon" of our physical bodies.

DARE   Don't be afraid of death!

DOUBLE DARE

1. If you're not sure what will happen to you when you die, talk to your parents, your pastor, or another mature Christian. Ask them to explain what it means to receive Jesus as your Savior.

2. Ask your mom if you can buy something at the dollar store with a butterfly on it. Use that as a reminder about today's devo.

PROMISE TO REPEAT

How did it go? What did you learn?

Job Knew. Do You?

BIBLE READING *Job 19:25*

TRUTH

At the end of time, God our Savior will still be the Lord of everything.

If you think your life is tough, you should meet Job. That's pronounced "jobe" (rhyming with robe) and not "job" (rhyming with Bob). Many people in the Bible went through difficult situations. Joseph's brothers sold him. Daniel was thrown into a den full of lions. Esther was kidnapped. Jonah was swallowed by a huge fish. But no one had as many problems as Job had.

Job loved and obeyed God. He was a good husband, a loving father, and a hard worker. God was pleased with him. But the Devil wanted to prove that Job obeyed God only because he was rich and comfortable, so God let the Devil challenge Job. Job lost his riches, his home, his health, and even his ten children. His wife became angry with God. His friends told him he must have done something bad to deserve all these terrible disasters.

Do you know what Job did? He kept praising God. He loved and trusted Him so much that he accepted whatever God allowed to happen to him. And God honored Job for that, blessing him with even more than he had before he was tested. Job knew God was his Savior. Do you?

DARE Trust God even in the worst times.

DOUBLE DARE

1. Read Job 1 to get a better idea of what happened to Job. In your journal, write what you would do if you were in Job's place.

2. Make a plan to read Job 2 later this week. Ask God to help you trust Him the way Job did.

PROMISE TO REPEAT

How did it go? What did you learn?

Follow the Instructions

BIBLE READING *Ecclesiastes 12:13*

TRUTH

The only way to make life work properly is to obey God's commands.

Sometimes I whip up a batch of my famous brownies for special events. I've been asked many times how I make them so good, and that always makes me laugh. I told a friend that I just use a box of brownie mix, but she didn't believe me and begged me for my recipe!

So I started to wonder what made my brownies special. Then I remembered that I do something that some people think is strange. One of the steps in the instructions on the box is this: "Mix ingredients together, about fifty strokes." So when I mix, I count off every turn my wooden spoon makes in the bowl. "1, 2, 3 … 17 … 38 … 50!" And then I stop, even if the mixture looks lumpy or powdery.

I wonder if most people stir until the mixture is smooth. I don't because I know that whoever made the brownie mix knows exactly how much mixing is needed so that the brownies aren't too hard or too soft. I trust the instructions.

As Christians, we must remember that God made us, so He knows exactly what we need to have joy, peace, and a good life. That's why He gave us instructions in the Bible. We would be wise to trust Him and obey Him.

DARE Follow God's instructions.

DOUBLE DARE

1. Write five examples of things that work best if you follow the instructions. Ask God to help you remember to follow *His* instructions.

2. Write five commandments that God wants us to obey. Circle the ones you will work on getting better at.

PROMISE TO REPEAT

How did it go? What did you learn?

H.O.W. (Hero Observation Weekend) #10

HERO LIST

Choose ONE of these heroes to learn about this weekend:

Name	Bible Verses
Esther	Esther 3:1–11; 4:4–17; 5:1–8; 7:1–10; 8:1–11
Stephen	Acts 6–7
Ruth	Ruth 1–4
David	1 Samuel 17
Abigail	1 Samuel 25:1–42
Gideon	Judges 6–7
The Bleeding Woman	Mark 5:25–34
Joseph	Genesis 37; 39–41
The Widow of Zarephath	1 Kings 17:8–24; Luke 4:25–26
Noah	Genesis 6–8
Miriam	Exodus 2:1–10
Daniel	Daniel 6
Mary of Bethany	John 12:1–8
Abraham	Genesis 22:1–18

Your hero for this weekend: _____

QUESTION TIME

1. How did this weekend's hero show courage and faith in God?

2. What happened because of his or her courage and obedience?

3. What did you learn from this hero's life that will help you in your own walk with God?

DOUBLE DARE

Choose at least one of these ways to dig a little deeper into your hero's life this weekend:

1. See if you can find other Bible verses about him or her. Write the reference (or the "address" of the verses) here and also anything new that you learned.

2. Ask your parents or another Christian what they have learned from this hero's life and example.

Tell a friend or your family about your new hero!

BIBLE READING   *2 Timothy 4:2 and 1 Peter 3:15*

TRUTH

We need to always be prepared to tell others about Jesus.

I used to be in charge of the children's program at a missions conference in Montreal. Parents would bring their kids to me for a few hours of stories, crafts, snacks, and games.

For one game, I gave each child a paper bag and a pair of chopsticks, emptied a bag of candies onto the floor, and then gave them two minutes to collect as many goodies as they could. But they could pick up the candy only by using the chopsticks! One thing I didn't count on was having a Chinese boy in attendance and, wow, was he ever quick with the chopsticks! He collected much more candy than any of the other kids.

One child said, "No fair! He uses chopsticks every day at supper!" The smiling Chinese boy answered, "Not only supper … also breakfast and lunch!"

This boy had so much practice using chopsticks that he won the game easily. As Christians, we also need practice. We should know our Bible so well that we're always prepared to tell people about what we believe.

DARE   Be prepared to share the Word.

DOUBLE DARE

1. What are a few things that you're really good at because you practice often? Try to put as much effort into reading and studying the Bible so that you'll know it well too.

2. Share today's devo with your family or a friend, and then talk about how Christians can be prepared to answer people's questions about God.

PROMISE TO REPEAT

How did it go? What did you learn?

Me? An Evangelist?

BIBLE READING *2 Timothy 4:5*

TRUTH

Everyone can do the work of an evangelist. Even you!

What is an evangelist? Most people who hear that word think of preachers on TV or missionaries who go to foreign countries. Thousands of people listen to these kinds of evangelists preach about God. Because some evangelists are well known, we may forget that the Bible tells each one of us to be an evangelist!

Maybe you're thinking, *Me? What can I do? I'm just a kid!* No problem! When you love God, He helps you love others too. Start there. Here are four simple things to remember:

1. CARE—Get to know other people and show concern for them and anything they might be going through.

2. DARE—That's what this book is all about! Ask God to give you courage when you feel nervous telling others about your faith in Jesus.

3. SHARE—Talk about the ways God has helped you. You don't need to preach a sermon like a pastor. Just tell others about your own relationship with Jesus.

4. PRAYER—Take time to pray for others, asking God to work on the seeds of truth that you're planting in their hearts. The Holy Spirit will do the rest.

DARE Care. Dare. Share. Prayer!

DOUBLE DARE

1. In your journal, write the name of someone you want to talk to about Jesus. In the coming days and weeks, follow the steps above and write down what happens.

2. Write the words *care*, *dare*, *share*, and *prayer* on a card and keep it near your bed as a daily reminder.

PROMISE TO REPEAT

How did it go? What did you learn?

Domino Witnessing

BIBLE READING *Acts 1:8*

TRUTH

God can use you to touch many hearts with His truth.

Do you ever think about how many people there are in the world, in your country, in your city, or even just in your school and wonder, *How can I possibly tell all those people about Jesus? There are too many!*

Thinking about the domino effect may encourage you. Have you ever played with dominoes and stood them up on their short ends in a long, winding line—and then lightly pushed the first one? If you've placed the dominoes at just the right distance from each other, what happens next is really cool. The first one knocks over the second one, which knocks over the third one, and then z-z-z-z-zip! As if an invisible finger is moving over the line of dominoes, they all fall over from the first to the last.

Witnessing for God has to start by sharing your faith with one person. You can't talk to everyone at the same time. But each person you talk to has an influence on someone else's life. And that other person can influence someone else. And, like dominoes, when you share God's love and truth with someone, your effort may reach more people than you can imagine!

DARE   Be a domino for Jesus!

DOUBLE DARE

1. Think of one person you can talk to about Jesus. As you imagine a line of "domino" people standing behind this person, ask God to give you the courage to share His truth with him or her soon.

2. If you have a set of dominoes, use them to share today's devo with your family or a Christian friend.

PROMISE TO REPEAT

How did it go? What did you learn?

BIBLE READING *Deuteronomy 10:12–13*

TRUTH

True obedience doesn't take its time.

We live in a world where people expect things to happen instantly or automatically. You click a button and your TV comes on. You put a plate of food in the microwave and it's hot in about a minute. You type an email, click "send," and it arrives in someone's in-box in another country in just seconds. You get on a plane and arrive halfway around the world in less than a day.

The world has changed a lot in the last fifty to one hundred years. Back then, people had to do a lot of things by hand, wait for days to receive a message, or travel for months to go somewhere far.

It's strange, though, that we're so used to things happening instantly, because we are not like that. When we have homework or chores to do, we may put it off as long as we can. When someone asks us for help, we sometimes take our time thinking about it before saying yes. Worst of all, when it's time to obey God, we often are not willing to do it right away.

Waiting to obey God or doing it only because we have to (and not because we really want to) is the same as disobeying Him, because obedience is something we do in our hearts.

DARE Obey God without hesitating.

DOUBLE DARE

1. Can you think of times when your mom or dad asked you to do something and you didn't do it right away? What did today's devo teach you about how well you obey your parents?

2. Ask God to help you *want* to obey Him instantly.

PROMISE TO REPEAT

How did it go? What did you learn?

Can God Count on You?

BIBLE READING *Deuteronomy 4:40 and Joshua 22:5*

TRUTH

God blesses His children when they obey Him.

On the blank lines below, list five things (or people) you depend on to do what they're expected to do or have promised to do. I've given three examples to get you started.

Parents (to provide shelter and food)
Alarm clock (to wake you up at the time you set it for)
Rubber boots (to keep your feet dry)

_____

_____

_____

_____

_____

What if your alarm clock stopped working during the night? It wouldn't wake you up on time! Or what if you got a hole in your rubber boots? You'd probably have wet socks by the time you got home. If your parents stopped feeding you and told you to go live in the backyard, how would you feel? Would you feel like you could depend on them or trust them? Parents make a promise to take care of their babies from the day they're born, and they have to stick to that promise, no matter what!

When we become Christians, we make a promise too. We promise God that we will follow and obey Him. If we stop obeying Him, how can God count on us? We can't expect God to bless us if we break our promises to Him.

DARE   Obey God, no matter what!

DOUBLE DARE

1. How well have you kept your promise to obey God? If you know in your heart that He can't count on you, ask for forgiveness and for His help to be more obedient.

2. A big part of obeying God is obeying your parents. Find a way to show your parents today that they can count on you.

PROMISE TO REPEAT

How did it go? What did you learn?

Little Jimmy had a bad temper and a quick tongue. When his dad asked him to walk the dog and take out the trash, Jimmy said, "Why do I have to do so much work? It's not fair!" His dad grounded him. That made Jimmy angry, so he kicked the dog, hurting her leg. He didn't care that his mom had to take the dog to the vet or that she came home upset with him.

He was in such a bad mood that at school the next day, he pushed a girl out of his way. When she started crying, he laughed at her and called her a crybaby. When the teacher made him stay inside during recess as a punishment, he scribbled all over her desk with chalk. Boy, did he get into trouble after that!

After supper that night, Jimmy's dad gave him a hammer and a box of nails and took him over to the tree house in the backyard. He said, "Jimmy, every time you lose your temper, I want you to hammer a nail into the door of your tree house." Jimmy didn't understand why his dad asked him to do this, but he took the nails and hammer. Whenever he got angry, he went to the tree house and hammered a nail into the door. It didn't take long for the door to be full of nails! But a few weeks later, Jimmy's dad noticed that his son wasn't hammering in as many nails as before. He was learning to control his temper.

So Jimmy's dad said, "Now I want you to remove a nail every time you *don't* get angry or lose your temper." About a week later, Jimmy called his dad over to his tree house and said, "Look, Dad! All the nails are gone!" His dad was very proud of him for learning to control his temper, but he pointed to all the holes that had been left in the door.

He said, "Jimmy, I'm glad you've learned not to get so angry, but do you see the problem with having a bad temper? Just like the nails left marks in this door, our words can hurt people and leave a scar in their lives. Pulling the nails out was like Jesus forgiving you for the wrong that you did, but sometimes our actions leave marks that don't go away. That's why we need to control our temper."

YOUR TURN

- Read Ephesians 4:31–32.

- Do you have a bad temper? Do you easily get upset and say things without thinking when things don't go your way? Think back over the past week and try to remember any of your actions or words that may have hurt others. Write these down in your journal.

- Find something small that you can stick pins into, such as a pincushion, cork, or eraser. For each of the things on your list, stick a pin into your object. Then put the object on your desk, dresser, or nightstand. In the next week or so, try to make things right with the people you hurt with your words or actions. Apologize and ask for forgiveness. It will be hard sometimes, but if you pray first, God will give you courage! Each time you ask for forgiveness, pull out one of the pins. Keep doing this until there are no pins left.

DOUBLE DARE

If you're handy with a hammer and nails and your parents say it's okay, use a scrap piece of wood and nails instead. Then keep the wood, with the nail marks, as a reminder to control your temper.

What are your thoughts?

BIBLE READING *Psalm 37:23–24*

TRUTH

God guides the steps of those who love Him.

Missionaries have some of the best stories about scary or interesting experiences that showed them how powerful and great God is.

My friend Cheryl once heard a missionary woman speak about her time in Indonesia. She said it was pitch black at night there, and the people who lived there couldn't even see the road or the house next to their own. Most important, they couldn't see the poisonous snakes that lived in the area. They had to carry flashlights with them, and they tried not to travel after dark. The people made lights out of bottles by filling them with oil, putting a wick through the lid, and then lighting the wick.

One night, the missionary went to a prayer meeting that finished very late, and she had no flashlight. A poor family gave her the only light they had, which was a small medicine bottle that provided only a little light right at her feet. She was nervous because she couldn't see the road ahead of her, but she courageously made it home step-by-step, one foot at a time.

This lady learned that we only need to trust God one step at a time. He is our light, and He lights our way in life step-by-step.

DARE Trust God with what you can't see.

DOUBLE DARE

1. Share today's devo with your family. Discuss worries about the future that any of you have, and then pray together for help to trust God step-by-step.

2. Make a bookmark shaped like a flashlight and write today's verses on it. Give it to a friend who might need some encouragement.

PROMISE TO REPEAT

How did it go? What did you learn?

Say What?

BIBLE READING *Psalm 119:34*

TRUTH

When we understand God's laws, we can obey them.

It's fun to see signs or instructions that have been badly translated into English from another language. I feel bad for the person who didn't know how to translate the sentence properly, but the final result can be quite funny. Some make you scratch your head because they make no sense! For example:

- A hotel in Japan had this sign in a guest room: "Please not to steal towels. If you are not person to do such, please not to read notice."

- In Majorca, an island near Spain, a mall posted this notice: "English well talking here. Speeching American."

- An elevator in the country of Serbia had this sign: "To move the cabin, push button for wishing floor. If the cabin should enter more persons, each one. Driving is then going alphabetically by national order."

Imagine trying to build something or bake a cake when the instructions are all jumbled up. You might not know what to do, or you may end up with something you weren't expecting!

Do you ever read the Bible and feel unsure about what God wants you to do? No problem! God's Holy Spirit is there to "translate" for you and give you understanding. You just have to ask, like King David did.

DARE Ask God to "translate" for you.

DOUBLE DARE

1. Whenever you read something in the Bible that you don't understand, write it down in your journal. Then pray for understanding. Write your thoughts again when it starts to make sense to you.

2. Memorize today's verse and pray it as often as you can.

PROMISE TO REPEAT

How did it go? What did you learn?

What's the Difference?

BIBLE READING *Titus 1:15–16*

TRUTH

If you try to mix the world with the Word, you get a big mess!

There once was a farmer who was well known in his town for making the best cottage cheese and also delicious applesauce. Every week, he would take large tubs of his cheese and applesauce to the market to sell them.

The farmer always brought along two ladles (big spoons) to scoop out the cottage cheese and applesauce. But one day, he got to the market and discovered that he had brought only one ladle. He felt a little upset, but all he could do was use one ladle for both the cottage cheese and applesauce. This worked out okay at first, but after a while, it was hard to tell which tub had cottage cheese and which tub had applesauce.

It's like that in our Christian lives too. Sometimes we try to fit in with the rest of the world by listening to the same songs, dressing the same way, using the same language, and watching the same movies or TV shows. At the same time, we try to be good Christians by going to church and doing our devos. But you know what? In the end, it's hard to tell if we're in the world or with God.

DARE   Keep your "ladle" clean.

DOUBLE DARE

1. Do you find it tempting to try to fit in with your friends who aren't Christians? Ask God to give you the courage to obey Him even when it's tough.

2. Share today's devo with your family. Talk about the importance of not mixing the world with what we learn in God's Word.

PROMISE TO REPEAT

How did it go? What did you learn?

Inconceivable!

BIBLE READING *Romans 11:33–36*

TRUTH

God is so great that our minds can't even imagine it.

My favorite movie of all time came out in 1987, when I was fifteen years old, and it's still popular today. It's called *The Princess Bride*, and it's great because it has everything: adventure, romance, and humor. I have a few friends who also love this movie, and because we've all seen it so many times, we know half the lines by heart. If someone even mentions the movie, the rest of us start calling out famous quotes from it and laughing over the funny ones. Probably the most well-known line in *The Princess Bride* is just one word: "Inconceivable!"

One of the characters, Vizzini, always says that whenever something happens that makes no sense to him. Inconceivable means that something is impossible to understand or imagine.

The Bible talks about something that is truly inconceivable: God's riches, wisdom, and knowledge. There isn't a single human being who can understand how God thinks. None of us has anything to offer God that He doesn't already have. He made everything, He knows everything, and He controls everything.

You know what Vizzini would say to that? Inconceivable!

DARE Give God the glory He deserves.

DOUBLE DARE

1. Do you ever complain to God about the things He wants you to do? Ask Him to forgive you and to help you remember that He knows best.

2. In your journal, write each letter of the word *inconceivable* on a separate line, from top to bottom. For each letter, write a word that describes God's greatness. For example, C = creative.

PROMISE TO REPEAT

How did it go? What did you learn?

BIBLE READING   *Romans 1:11–12*

TRUTH

Christians can make one another's faith strong through encouragement.

Think about the last time you asked your mom if your friend could come over or if you could go to her house. Why did you want to see your friend and hang out together? Was it because ...

- You wanted to play and have fun?
- You felt lonely and wanted someone to keep you company?
- You were bored and needed something to do?
- You wanted to show her a new toy, game, bike, puppy ...?
- You wanted to see her new toy, game, bike, puppy ...?

Ask yourself this question: "Have I ever looked forward to spending time with a friend so that I could encourage her and help her grow as a Christian?" Hmm ... There probably aren't too many people who do that, right?

But Paul, the writer of the verses you read today, told the people in the church in Rome that that was exactly why he "longed" to see them. Paul wanted to help them get closer to Jesus and be stronger in their faith. And he knew that he, too, would be encouraged by spending time with them.

DARE   Encourage a friend's faith!

DOUBLE DARE

1. In your journal, write down a few ways you will try to encourage a Christian friend the next time you hang out together. (For example, share memory verses you've learned or tell her about the way God answered a prayer.)

2. Write down the names of people who often encourage you to grow as a Christian. Thank God for them, one by one.

PROMISE TO REPEAT

How did it go? What did you learn?

1. Cross out all the vegetables.
2. Cross out all the words beginning with *Q*.
3. Cross out all the words that rhyme with *wrong*.
4. Cross out all the eight-letter words.
5. Cross out all the words that end with *K*.
6. Cross out all the animals.

	A	B	C	D
1	CARROT	SONG	WHOEVER	JANITOR
2	QUICK	THINK	CUCUMBER	STRONG
3	DUCK	GIRAFFE	JUNK	QUIZ
4	HATES	CELERY	LONG	WORK
5	BASEBALL	QUEEN	COMPUTER	CORRECTION
6	FLAMINGO	IS	THINK	DOG
7	BROCCOLI	WEAK	STUPID	CHEETAH

Write the remaining words (reading from left to right) here:

Read Proverbs 12:1 to see the whole verse that these words come from.

What do you think is one of the hardest things for a human being to do? Lift one hundred pounds? Memorize the whole Bible? Become an astronaut? Climb Mount Everest?

Those are all difficult things to do, but there's something that people struggle with even more, and maybe you've experienced it too. It's accepting correction from others.

YOUR TURN

- Read Job 5:17.

- What are some times when people correct us? For example, your teacher at school will correct your math if you make a mistake. Can you think of a few other examples? Write them here:

- How do you feel when someone corrects you? Do you feel angry? Embarrassed? Stupid? The Bible says we don't need to feel stupid when someone corrects us. In fact, being thankful for correction shows wisdom! As we see in the phrase from the puzzle, we're only stupid if we hate being corrected. Why do you think that's true? It's because we can't learn and get better if we don't accept correction.

  I'm not in school anymore, but as a writer, my work still gets corrected or improved by editors with more experience than I have. If I did not accept their corrections, I wouldn't be able to become a better writer.

- Think of an example from your own life when listening to correction helped you. Write about it here:

  _____

  _____

  _____

  _____

- If you usually have trouble accepting correction from others, ask God to give you a more humble spirit so you can see how their advice and knowledge can help you. Remember that when people who love you correct you, they're not trying to make you feel bad. They're trying to help you be your best.

DOUBLE DARE

List some people in your life who have helped you in the past by correcting you:

This weekend, thank at least one of them and share how his or her correction helped you.

BIBLE READING *1 Timothy 4:4*

TRUTH

Thankfulness comes from our attitude, not our circumstances.

Have you ever noticed that some things seem to change color depending on the time of day or how the sun is shining into the room? I have an old rocking armchair covered with a velvet fabric that sometimes looks green and sometimes looks yellow. I'm really not sure what to call this strange color! But on a bright sunny day, the chair seems to be a cheery yellow. On dull gray days, the color looks more like the inside of a ripe avocado.

But the color never changes. What changes is the way my eyes see it.

A lot of things in life are constant—they just are whatever they are. But how we feel about them can change depending on whether our hearts and attitudes are dark or bright. For example:

- When you have to clean up your room, you can grumble about it or be thankful that you have clothes and toys to put away. Many children don't have any.

- When you have to do homework, you can complain or be thankful you have the chance to go to school. Many kids around the world don't.

God's Word tells us to be thankful in *all* situations.

DARE   Give thanks for everything!

DOUBLE DARE

1. Can you think of three more examples, like the ones given above, of how you can have an attitude of gratitude in a situation where you might be tempted to complain? Write them in your journal.

2. If you know you grumble more than you're grateful, confess this to God and ask Him to help you change.

PROMISE TO REPEAT

How did it go? What did you learn?

Walking in Someone Else's Shoes

BIBLE READING *Mark 12:31*

TRUTH

Loving someone means caring about his or her feelings.

Have you ever tried on your mother's high-heeled shoes and walked around in them? I admit that when I was little, and even as a tween, I would wait until my mom wasn't around and then try hers on. Of course, I couldn't walk in the high ones, especially since they were too big for my feet. But it was fun to pretend.

If you've ever seen a toddler stand in her mom's high heels or a little boy stomp around in his dad's boots, you know how funny it looks. It's fine when the parents are there making sure the children don't get hurt, but it could be dangerous if they really tried to walk in the wrong shoes.

When people talk about walking in someone else's shoes to understand the person better, literally putting on his or her shoes isn't what they mean. Walking in someone else's shoes means experiencing what another person goes through in life. Of course, this is impossible since we can live only our own lives, but when we care enough, we take time to listen and understand and try to imagine someone else's situation. When we love that much, we can treat others the way we would want to be treated if we were "in their shoes."

DARE Love the way you want to be loved.

DOUBLE DARE

1. When someone asks for your help, think about what you would want someone to do if you asked for help. Then do your best to help out cheerfully!

2. Write "Love your neighbor as yourself" on a sticky note and keep it on your mirror or in your planner.

PROMISE TO REPEAT

How did it go? What did you learn?

Beware the Leaf-tailed Gecko!

BIBLE READING *1 Peter 5:8*

TRUTH

The Devil doesn't warn you before he attacks.

Can you find the animal hidden in the photo? Do you see only leaves? Look again!

A few of those "leaves" are actually the body of a Satanic Leaf-tailed Gecko (or Uroplatus phantasticus), a species found only in Madagascar. This gecko's appearance is designed for camouflage, allowing it to sneak up on its victims. It can move through trees without being seen and, because it has a transparent covering over its eyes instead of eyelids, it can keep its eyes open at all times. Besides that, it can drop its tail to distract and confuse predators and, when it opens its jaws, frighten other creatures with its bright red mouth.

Although the leaf-tailed gecko probably does not deserve being called "Satanic," the word reminds us how dangerous and deceiving the Devil is. He doesn't announce his presence. He doesn't label the temptations he sends our way as sin. If he did, we would immediately move away or ask God for help. Instead, he creeps around us so that we think we're safe and can stop being careful.

But the Devil is more dangerous than a six-inch gecko, which is why the Bible gives us the strong warning in today's verse.

DARE Be alert and self-controlled!

DOUBLE DARE

1. What are some ways the Devil deceives people? Write out a prayer, asking God to give you wisdom and the spiritual "eyes" to spot temptation early enough to move away from it.

2. Ask your parents to help you research the Satanic Leaf-tailed Gecko. Print out or draw a picture of it and write today's verse beneath it as a reminder to be alert.

PROMISE TO REPEAT

How did it go? What did you learn?

Don't Gloat!

BIBLE READING   *Obadiah 1:12*

TRUTH

God's children must not be glad when others suffer.

What would you do in each of these situations? (Check off your choice.)

1. Your little brother gets into trouble for coloring in your new notebook.

    a.   You think to yourself, *Ha! He deserves it.*
    b.   You feel bad and promise to get him his own coloring book.

2. The most popular girl at school, who usually ignores you, falls down the stairs.

    a.   You and your friends start laughing.
    b.   You run over to help her and see if she's okay.

3. Your teacher asks you to make a new girl in class feel welcome.

    a.   You invite her to sit with you at lunch, but instead of trying to get to know her, you just talk about how popular you are at school.
    b.   You offer to show her around the school so she'll know where everything is.

In each situation, the first choice is exactly what today's Bible verse is talking about: gloating, or feeling glad when someone else goes through a bad experience. As Christians, we should be so full of God's love that we care about the feelings of everyone around us—even the people who aren't nice to us in return.

Just as we want people to be kind to us when we're down, we should care for others when they go through bad times.

DARE   Don't gloat!

DOUBLE DARE

1. Ask God to show you if you've been feeling glad about someone else's problems. Confess this and ask God to forgive you and to make you more caring.

2. Do you know someone who's in trouble or suffering right now? Take time to pray for him or her today.

PROMISE TO REPEAT

How did it go? What did you learn?

BIBLE READING *Isaiah 58:10–11*

TRUTH

God blesses us when we are generous toward others.

There's a secret for becoming rich really quickly. Want to know what it is? All you have to do is this: Remember all the people in the world who have much, much less than you do. No, really … it works!

When you know how many children in other countries would be happy to have a stale piece of bread to eat or a pair of old shoes to put on their bare feet, you suddenly realize that you have much more than you even need. The problem is most people in "rich" countries don't see these poor people except in pictures or on TV, so it's easy to forget they're real and to selfishly want more for ourselves.

The Bible tells us that we must not forget the poor. You and I may not be able to feed every single hungry child in the world, but we can make a difference for one person or for a family. The Bible also promises that when we give generously, we will never run out of what we need, because God will bless us and take care of us. Best of all, we will experience true joy!

DARE Share what God has given you.

DOUBLE DARE

1. If you get an allowance, pray for wisdom to know how to use it. Instead of buying things you don't need, try to save some of it to help others.

2. Ask your parents for ideas about how you can share your blessings with families who are going through a hard time.

PROMISE TO REPEAT

How did it go? What did you learn?

Planting the Seeds
That God Will Grow

Lilit is a young friend of mine who lives in Armenia, the country where my great-great-grandparents were born. I was able to visit this country for the first time in 2013. Although Armenia was the first nation to make Christianity its official religion and Armenian was one of the first languages the Bible was translated into, today many people in that country don't know Jesus and don't even believe in God.

But Lilit does believe in Jesus, and she loves to tell others about Him. Once, while studying at the university, she was able to tell her whole class about God! Here's her story:

It is not easy for a Christian to work or study with non-Christians. During my university years, I have had many arguments with my friends about Jesus or Christianity. Once, my professor gave us a topic to discuss. The topic was, "Is there a God or not?" I remember quite well the expression on one girl's face when she stood up and said, "What a question! Of course there is no God. There is nothing like that!"

I was surprised. I did not know I had been studying with an atheist [someone who believes there is no God]. The first thing that came to my mind was to say some harsh words to that girl. At that moment, I remembered this Bible verse: "For it is God's will that by doing good you should silence the ignorant talk of foolish people" (1 Peter 2:15). So I stood up and said to that girl, "How can you dare to say such a thing? God created you and me. There is a God."

To my great surprise, at the end of the lesson the professor came to me and asked me to be prepared for the next discussion. I would be leading the discussion and I could choose the topic for it.

The next day, I presented a good speech about the existence of God. I stood in front of the class and started to evangelize (tell the good news about Jesus) to the students. Sure, it was difficult for me at first. But before starting I prayed, and God reminded me of this verse: "Now, Lord, consider their threats and enable your servants to speak your word with great boldness" (Acts 4:29).

You know what happened? I saw tears in the eyes of most students. I was pleased, I was proud, and I felt good about obeying God. Anyway, I believe that "I planted the seed … but God has been making it grow" (1 Corinthians 3:6).

I just want everyone (especially girls, because I am a girl as well) to be bold and courageous enough to talk about God. God will take care of the rest. And let's always remember this: "Woe to me if I do not preach the gospel!" (1 Corinthians 9:16).

YOUR TURN

- What do you think you would have done if you had been in Lilit's situation and a classmate said, "There is no God"? In your journal, write about how Lilit's example encourages you to be bold in telling others about Jesus. Then pray and ask God to give you courage in these types of situations.

- Imagine *you* were going to talk to your class about God. What would you say? Take time this weekend to work on a "speech" that you could present. Ask your parents or another mature Christian for help if you get stuck. This will be good practice for future experiences.

- Read 1 Corinthians 3:6 again. Why do you think Lilit chose that Bible verse to share, and what do you think it means?

What are your thoughts?

Bulldogs and Skunks

BIBLE READING *2 Timothy 2:23–24*

TRUTH

Fighting doesn't do anybody any good.

Here's something to think about: A bulldog can beat a skunk, but is it worth the fight?

If you're like me, reading that might have created a funny cartoon in your mind of a big, growling bulldog with sharp teeth rolling around with a skinny, shrieking skunk. (I don't know whether skunks actually shriek, but that's how I imagined it!) Of course, the bulldog would quickly overpower the skunk, but what do you think the skunk would do? Yep! It would spray the bulldog and leave it smelling awful. A smart bulldog would just leave the skunk alone.

Sometimes humans start arguing and fighting without first thinking about what the outcome of the fight will be. Most of the time, everyone involved gets hurt and no one walks away happy, even if someone comes out the "winner." Even that person usually ends up with bad feelings.

The Bible cautions us to avoid silly disagreements that can lead to bigger arguments. God wants His children to be kind and humble toward others.

DARE Say no to arguing.

DOUBLE DARE

1. Think of someone you seem to argue with a lot. Ask God to help you have more patience with that person and to find a way to show him or her kindness.

2. Draw a picture of a bulldog being friends with a skunk and write today's verses somewhere on your page. Post the picture on your fridge as a reminder.

PROMISE TO REPEAT

How did it go? What did you learn?

The Problem with Pride

BIBLE READING *Proverbs 16:18*

TRUTH

Pride in ourselves can make us look foolish.

Once upon a time, in a pond behind a farm, there lived two happy ducks and their special friend, a frog. The three of them would spend hours and hours playing and laughing in their water hole, day after day. But during the hot summer, they noticed that their pond had begun to dry up. They knew they would soon have to move to another pond.

The ducks could easily fly to the next pond, but the frog would be stuck. After puzzling over what to do, they decided they would put one end of a stick in each of the ducks' bills and the frog would hang on to the stick with his mouth as the ducks flew.

The plan worked! In fact, it worked so perfectly that as they were flying, a farmer looked up at them and said, "What a clever idea! I wonder who thought of it?" The frog said, "I did!"

What do you think happened next? The frog, who was so proud of himself that he couldn't keep his mouth shut, fell down to the ground while the ducks kept flying!

The Bible warns us that pride can get us into big trouble too.

DARE Go to God when you are prideful.

DOUBLE DARE

1. In your journal, write about a time when you felt proud and then did or said something that you felt ashamed about afterward. Ask God to help you watch your pride.

2. Tell your friends the story of the ducks and the frog, and then talk together about how today's Bible verse can help you.

PROMISE TO REPEAT

How did it go? What did you learn?

BIBLE READING *Job 8:13–15*

TRUTH

Forgetting about God makes your faith as weak as a spiderweb.

Do you like spiders? I know a few people who hate spiders and start screaming and jumping when they see one. I have to admit that it makes me giggle because I actually like spiders. Well, not the big, ugly, hairy ones but the normal little ones we usually see. In fact, if I see a spider in the house, instead of killing it, I will take it outside.

I also really like spiderwebs, as long as they're not in the house, of course. It amazes me that such a tiny insect can create such a complicated, beautiful, and strong web that traps the spider's food but not the spider.

Spiderwebs are great for catching little bugs, but they're not strong enough to support a human. They're very delicate and easily broken. The Bible compares weak faith to a spider web. If we get lazy about spending time with God and obeying Him, we begin to forget things we've learned in the Bible. And then it gets harder to follow Him.

To keep our faith strong so that we can stand up against life's storms, we must stay close to God.

DARE   Don't forget God.

DOUBLE DARE

1. When you have a tough day, do you trust God, or do you fall apart? In your journal, write some ways you can grow in your faith this week.

2. On a piece of paper, draw a spiderweb. In bold letters, write the words of Job 8:13–14 over the web. Then put your drawing on the fridge as a reminder of this devo.

PROMISE TO REPEAT

How did it go? What did you learn?

Strength from God

BIBLE READING *Judges 6:7–14*

TRUTH

You can do great things when God gives you strength.

What do you think is the strongest animal in the world? The lion? The grizzly bear? The elephant?

What about the rhinoceros? No, but if that was your guess, you're close. Sort of. The strongest animal in the world—in relation to its size (that means that if it were as big as other large animals it would be much stronger than they are)—is the rhinoceros beetle. It grows to only about two inches long and weighs not much more than an ounce, so you wouldn't really think of it as a strong animal, would you?

Surprisingly, the rhinoceros beetle can lift up to 850 times its own weight, which comes out to about 53 pounds. That's like a person who weighs 155 pounds being able to lift a Boeing 737 (one of the largest airplanes) … or like you lifting up, all at once, 850 other girls your weight!

If that seems incredibly strong, just imagine that God is much, much, much stronger than the rhinoceros beetle. There is nothing He can't do. And God promises to help you when you need strength. Maybe He won't help you lift 850 girls, but He will help you get through tough situations.

DARE Ask God for strength.

DOUBLE DARE

1. In your journal, write about something you need to do that's making you feel afraid. Then ask God to give you His strength and courage.

2. Quiz your family about the world's strongest animal, and then share today's devo with them.

PROMISE TO REPEAT

How did it go? What did you learn?

BIBLE READING *Colossians 2:6–7*

TRUTH

We can be thankful even in bad situations.

Matthew Henry, a man who lived over three hundred years ago and was known for his great knowledge of the Bible, had his wallet stolen one day. He believed that it was important to give thanks in everything, so he thought carefully about what had happened to him and then wrote this in his diary: "Let me be thankful, first, because he never robbed me before; second, because although he took my money, he did not take my life; third, because although he took all I own, it was not much; and fourth, because it was I who was robbed, not I who robbed."

What a great attitude! Even though something bad happened to this man, he not only found a way to thank God, but he found four ways. He understood that things could always be worse and he was grateful they weren't.

How about you?

DARE Give God thanks always, no matter what.

DOUBLE DARE

1. Think of a difficult situation you or your family is facing right now. Write down at least one thing you can be thankful for in this situation. Can you think of three more?

2. Share today's devo with a friend and agree to help each other find things to be thankful for every day.

PROMISE TO REPEAT

How did it go? What did you learn?

HERO LIST

Choose ONE of these heroes to learn about this weekend:

Name	Bible Verses
Esther	Esther 3:1–11; 4:4–17; 5:1–8; 7:1–10; 8:1–11
Stephen	Acts 6–7
Ruth	Ruth 1–4
David	1 Samuel 17
Abigail	1 Samuel 25:1–42
Gideon	Judges 6–7
The Bleeding Woman	Mark 5:25–34
Joseph	Genesis 37; 39–41
The Widow of Zarephath	1 Kings 17:8–24; Luke 4:25–26
Noah	Genesis 6–8
Miriam	Exodus 2:1–10
Daniel	Daniel 6
Mary of Bethany	John 12:1–8
Abraham	Genesis 22:1–18

Your hero for this weekend: _____

QUESTION TIME

1. How did this weekend's hero show courage and faith in God?

2. What happened because of his or her courage and obedience?

3. What did you learn from this hero's life that will help you in your own walk with God?

DOUBLE DARE

Choose at least one of these ways to dig a little deeper into your hero's life this weekend:

1. See if you can find other Bible verses about him or her. Write the reference (or the "address" of the verses) here and also anything new that you learned.

2. Ask your parents or another Christian what they have learned from this hero's life and example.

Tell a friend or your family about your new hero!

What are your thoughts?

"But It Feels Good!"

BIBLE READING *Ecclesiastes 11:9*

TRUTH

God will judge those who live only for themselves.

Our world seems to think this rule is more important than any other rule: "If it feels good, do it." In other words, "If it makes you happy, if it makes you feel beautiful, if it helps you get what you want, don't worry about what other people think. You are in charge of your own life, so do whatever you want."

Every kid secretly wishes sometimes that she could do whatever she wanted without having to obey Mom and Dad's rules, but that's impossible, right? And if we're wise, we realize those rules are there for our own good.

The sad thing is, most people don't outgrow this feeling. When they're old enough to be on their own, they still think it would be cool to do whatever they want. That's why so many people don't follow God. They think it's boring or difficult to obey what the Bible teaches.

God gives us the freedom to do what we want, but He also warns us that there is a price to pay for our disobedience. Do you want to take that risk?

DARE Do what's right, not what feels good.

DOUBLE DARE

1. What are some things you would like to do if they weren't against the rules? Ask God to give you a heart that obeys Him out of love, not because you don't want to be punished.

2. Do your parents have any rules you don't understand or you think are not fair? Ask them (politely) to explain those rules so it will be easier for you to obey them.

PROMISE TO REPEAT

How did it go? What did you learn?

No Bones About It

BIBLE READING Ephesians 5:5

TRUTH

Greed is a sin.

When I was little, one of my favorite books was an old blue hardcover that contained a collection of fables by Aesop. I read those short stories, which always end with a moral lesson, over and over again. I've been sharing a few of those fables with you in *Truth, Dare, Double Dare.*

One is about a dog that was walking along, happily carrying a big bone in his mouth. As he walked by a lake, he saw his reflection in the water and thought he was looking at another dog. And he noticed that the "other dog" also had a big bone. He thought, *I want that bone too!* and barked at the other dog. Out fell his bone, which plopped into the lake and disappeared, leaving him with no bones at all.

Sometimes we're like that foolish dog. Instead of being thankful for what we have, we try to get more, and sometimes we miss out on what God has already blessed us with. More important, God hates greed, and the Bible warns us that it's a sin we must confess.

DARE Be thankful for what you have.

DOUBLE DARE

1. Write a list of some things you'd really like to have. Now write a list of things you already have that you're thankful for. Which list makes you feel richer? Ask God to forgive you for the times you've been ungrateful for His blessings.

2. Make a bookmark in the shape of a bone and write today's verse on it. Keep the bookmark in your Bible at Ephesians 5:5 as a reminder of today's devo.

PROMISE TO REPEAT

How did it go? What did you learn?

Serve with Your Heart

BIBLE READING *Ephesians 6:7–8*

TRUTH

When we serve others, we should do it as if we're serving God.

Check off any of these things that you have done (or know you would do):

❑ Your mom asks you to dust the living room, and you dust *around* things instead of *under* them.

❑ Your little sister asks you to fix her hair, and you quickly make an easy ponytail.

❑ Your dad asks you to water the lawn, and you do it for about three minutes, just getting the grass wet.

❑ Your teacher asks you to make a new girl in class feel welcome, so you invite her to sit with you and your friends at lunchtime but don't talk to her much.

In each situation, you could say that you're serving or obeying, but could you say that you're serving with your heart? It's easy to serve people with our *hands* by simply doing the actions expected of us. But serving with our *hearts* means that we do our very best to do a really good job. It means we try to do *better* than what's expected of us because we want to please the other person.

If we imagine that we are serving God when we serve others, we might do it a lot differently!

DARE Serve wholeheartedly.

DOUBLE DARE

1. Whenever you're asked to do something today, try to remember that God is watching and, in your heart, serve *Him* while you do your work.

2. Is there a chore you didn't do very well this week? Take time to do it again, but better this time. Use that time to talk to God.

PROMISE TO REPEAT

How did it go? What did you learn?

Never Give Up

BIBLE READING *Galatians 6:9*

TRUTH

God helps and blesses us when we continue to do good.

Once upon a time, a farmer's donkey fell into a deep, dried-up well that had been left uncovered. For hours, the donkey brayed and cried, but the farmer didn't know how to get the poor creature out. Finally he decided that since he didn't need the well and the donkey was very old, he would just fill the well with dirt and let the animal die. He called some neighbors over, and they started to shovel dirt into the hole.

At first, the donkey cried even louder, but after a little while he became quiet. Curious, the people looked down and got a big surprise! Whenever they threw dirt on top of the donkey, he shook it off and took a step up. As they continued to fill the well with dirt, the donkey kept shaking it off and stepping up. Pretty soon the dirt was high enough that he just stepped right out of the well!

Sometimes we face situations that seem impossible to get out of, or we feel like it's too hard to keep being good. The Bible encourages us not to give up! Like the wise donkey, we need to patiently "shake off" the things that hurt or scare us and keep praying and following Jesus. Pretty soon, we'll find that we've made it out.

DARE Don't give up!

DOUBLE DARE

1. Share today's story with a friend and memorize the Bible verse together. Promise to pray for each other for the courage to never give up.

2. Ask God to give you strength for whatever you're facing this week.

PROMISE TO REPEAT

How did it go? What did you learn?

BIBLE READING *Psalm 40:5*

TRUTH

It's impossible to measure all the great things God has done.

Have you ever seen those contests where there's a jar full of jelly beans, marbles, or coins and you have to try to guess how many it holds? You might try counting, but you'd give up pretty soon when you realize it's impossible. The best you can do is guess.

What about counting the stars in the sky? How high do you think you could count before you started mixing them up? Do you think you could count the blades of grass in a field? How about the bubbles in a soapy sponge? The fish in the sea? The sand on a beach? The words in a dictionary? You get the idea.

All these things are close to impossible to count or measure, right? But compared to the goodness of God, it would be easier to count all of those things! That's how wonderful our heavenly Father is.

DARE Count your blessings!

DOUBLE DARE

1. Ask your mom for an empty jar. Make a pretty label that says "Blessings" and stick it on the jar. Every time you think of something great that God has done, write it on a little slip of paper. Then fold the paper and put it in your jar. See how fast it fills up! Keep going until you can't stuff any more slips of paper into it. Whenever you feel down, read through some of the blessings.

2. After sharing today's devo with a friend (and showing her your jar!), work together to make a list of other things that would be almost impossible to count. Talk about how great God is.

PROMISE TO REPEAT

How did it go? What did you learn?

Created to Do Good Works

Read Ephesians 2:10.

If you had enough money and time, what hobbies or activities would you want to participate in? Here are some ideas: rock climbing, ballet, or photography. List your interests here:

Now think about the natural talents and abilities you have. For example, writing, taking care of animals, or swimming. List your talents here:

Did you know that your interests and your talents both come from God? They're not a random accident! God put you in the time and place you live in for a special reason, and you're His one-of-a-kind special design. He wants you to use your interests and talents to the best of your ability and not waste them. And He also wants you to use them for *His* glory.

We've got quite a few examples in the Bible of people who used their interests and abilities to serve God. Some of them needed courage to do what they did! If the reading in this devo is too much for you to do in one day, do the first one on Saturday and the other two on Sunday.

- Read Luke 7:36–50—The Perfume Lady.

  What interest or special offering did the woman in this story have?
  Why did her act take courage?
  What happened because she was willing to give her gift to Jesus?

- Read Luke 19:1–10—The Tax Man.

  What was Zacchaeus good at?
  What courageous thing did he do?
  What happened because he was willing to give money away?

- Read Mark 1:16–18; Acts 2:14; and Acts 2:40–41—The Speaker.

  What was Peter's interest or ability?
  What courageous thing did he do?
  What happened because he was willing to use his abilities for God?

DOUBLE DARE

Think of at least three ways you can use your special interests and talents to serve God. If you're not sure, ask your parents or another Christian adult to give you suggestions. Write your ideas here:

1.

2.

3.

Talk to God about how you want to use your talents to do good works and bless others. Ask Him to guide you and to show you how to do that. Try to remember to write about the results in your journal later.

Appreciate What You Have

BIBLE READING *Ecclesiastes 6:9*

TRUTH

When you're thankful for what you have, you'll feel satisfied.

The next time you go by an expensive jewelry store, stop to see if they have any pearls or diamonds displayed in the window. Smart store owners will usually place a valuable diamond ring or pearl necklace on black velvet cloth with nothing else around it. Do you know why? The plain black background makes the jewel or stone stand out brightly. If a diamond was added to a pile of other gemstones or jewels, would you be able to see it well? No, you'd be too distracted by everything else around it.

The blessings God gives us are precious gifts. But sometimes we don't notice or appreciate them because we're too busy complaining about all the things we think we're missing in life. You may look at other kids and think, *How come I don't have clothes like her? Why do his parents let him do whatever he wants? I wish I could go to that camp too. I can't believe my dad won't let me redecorate my room*, and so on.

When you do that, are you enjoying the things you do have? Probably not. You're also telling God you're not thankful for His gifts.

DARE   Want what you already have, not what you don't have.

DOUBLE DARE

1. At the top of a journal page, write the words "Wish List." Then, instead of listing things you want to get, list things you already have and are thankful for. Now enjoy them!

2. Do you complain a lot about things you don't have? Ask God to forgive you and make you more grateful.

PROMISE TO REPEAT

How did it go? What did you learn?

Generous Giving

BIBLE READING *Deuteronomy 15:10–11*

TRUTH

God blesses us when we are generous to others.

One morning, a mother was making pancakes for her two daughters who were five and three years old. The girls argued about who should get the first pancake.

Their mom thought, *This is a great time to teach them a lesson about living God's way!* So she turned to the girls and said, "You know, if Jesus were here, He would say, 'Let my sister have the first pancake. I can wait.'"

The little girls thought about this for a moment, and then the older one turned to her sister and said, "You can be Jesus."

She didn't get the point, did she? She pretended to be nice to her sister by saying, "You can be Jesus," but what she really meant was, "I still want the first pancake!" She wasn't generous because she was thinking only about what she wanted.

God told the Israelite people to be generous and to help those who had less than they did. He promised He would bless them if they gave from a willing and loving heart. He promises that to us too.

DARE   Put someone else's needs before yours.

DOUBLE DARE

1. At suppertime, when food is passed around the table, do you usually grab the biggest or nicest servings? At your next family meal, offer the best servings to others first. Later, write about how that made you feel.

2. Do you have more toys and clothes than you use? The next time you are tempted to ask for something new, try *giving* something to someone instead.

PROMISE TO REPEAT

How did it go? What did you learn?

With All Your Heart

- -

BIBLE READING *Deuteronomy 6:5*

TRUTH

God deserves the best of our love.

Here are some interesting facts about the human heart:

Many people think their heart is on the left side of their chest. Actually, it's in the center but tips a little to the left.

The average heart beats about one hundred thousand times a day. That's more than thirty-five million beats a year!

If you have a healthy heart, its muscles work harder than anything else in your body—twice as hard as your leg muscles when you are running fast.

God's design of the human heart is truly miraculous and is a gift we should be thankful for each day. We should also take care of it by eating wholesome food and getting lots of exercise. Every year, six hundred thousand people in the United States die from heart disease. That's one-quarter of all the deaths in the country!

But we shouldn't pay attention only to our physical heart. The Bible commands us to love God, our heavenly Father, with all our heart (and soul and strength!). That means giving our very best to God, not just a small effort or our leftover time. God has given you everything—including the gift of His Son, Jesus. What will you give Him in return?

DARE Love God with all your heart.

DOUBLE DARE

1. Draw a heart on a blank card and decorate around it. Write today's verse in the center and stick the card up in your locker at school as a reminder of this devo.

2. In your journal, write ten ways you can show God how much you love Him. Try to do one or two of those things today.

PROMISE TO REPEAT

How did it go? What did you learn?

When Life Gives You ...

BIBLE READING *Hebrews 13:5*

TRUTH

God will never forget about you.

Have you ever heard the saying "When life gives you lemons, make lemonade"? It's good advice to remember that when things go "sour" in life, you can either complain about it or try to do your best with what you have. Someone once changed the quote a little and said, "When life gives you lemons, keep them because—hey—free lemons!" That's not exactly the same, but it's still a positive attitude!

I enjoy sewing quilts, so I like this saying: "When life gives you scraps, make a quilt." It's the same idea: Take what looks like a failure and make something good out of it. Hebrews 13:5 tells us to "be content with what you have" instead of wanting more. For example, if your family is getting ready to watch a movie together and the power goes out, you can:

    a.   whine and complain
    b.   make the night even more fun with candles and board games or scary stories

If you don't get chosen for a part in the Christmas play, you can:

    a.   feel jealous of your friend who did get chosen and make her feel bad
    b.   use the time you would have spent at practices to help someone out

In any situation, you can keep a positive attitude when you remember that God is still taking care of you.

DARE Be content with what you have.

DOUBLE DARE

1. Think of something you felt disappointed about lately. Find a way to make "lemonade" or a "quilt" out of that situation.

2. Memorize today's verse and ask God to help you always have a positive attitude.

PROMISE TO REPEAT

How did it go? What did you learn?

Are You Robbing God?

BIBLE READING *Malachi 3:6–10*

TRUTH

When we are greedy about what we have, we're stealing from God.

Imagine you bake a batch of delicious chocolate chip cookies because your friend is coming over to play. When she arrives, you both go into the kitchen and you show her the plate of cookies, telling her to help herself. Your friend takes the plate of cookies, empties it into her bag, and doesn't leave any for you. How do you feel?

Now imagine that your parents buy you the shiny new bicycle you've been wanting all year. You know it was expensive and that they had to make sacrifices to be able to give it to you. When your dad asks you to ride your bike to the post office to mail some letters for him, you say, "No, the bike is mine. I want to use it only for myself!"

I'm sure you would never actually do those things, but that's how Christians sometimes treat God without realizing it. God has given us everything we need and more, and we usually give back very little to Him. We show Him we're not truly thankful for His gifts by not using them to serve Him and others.

DARE   Stop robbing God.

DOUBLE DARE

1. In your journal, list ten to fifteen gifts God has given you (such as good health, money, or a talent). Next to each one, write one way you can offer it back to God.

2. Have you been greedy with your money? Ask God to show you how to be generous and wise at the same time so that you can honor Him with what you have.

PROMISE TO REPEAT

How did it go? What did you learn?

You Did It to Me

Read each of the following situations and write what your reaction would be. Don't write what you think you *should* do but what you know in your heart you *would* do. (I won't see your answers!)

1. Your older sister never lets you go into her bedroom or look at her stuff. One day, when she's not home, you notice her door is wide open and her journal is on her bed. You …

2. Your best friend has been acting a bit strange lately. Today she yelled at you just because you forgot to give back the pen you borrowed yesterday. You …

3. On your way home from school with your friends, you notice the school bully sitting behind a tree, crying quietly. You …

4. Your dad is really tired after a hard week at work. In the kitchen, he sees the snack your mom made for you to have before bedtime (your favorite!). He starts eating it. You …

Read Matthew 25:31–46.

Now look at the answers you wrote for the situations above. How do you feel knowing that anything you've said or done to someone, you've said or done to Jesus?

We often say or do things without thinking about how we're hurting someone else. We do this because we don't love that person the way Jesus does. Your little brother may annoy you or your parents may frustrate you, but they are special people whom God loves, and He put them in your life for a reason. When you disrespect another human being, the Bible says you are disrespecting God.

On the bright side, when you love, respect, and show kindness to someone, you are loving, respecting, and showing kindness to God. What a great thing to remember!

Thinking about what you've just learned, how would you change your answers to the questions given earlier?

1.

2.

3.

4.

This weekend, try to pause and think before you say or do something. Ask yourself if you would act that way toward Jesus and how it would make Him feel. If you find this difficult, ask God to help you.

Remember, not doing something good when you should is just as wrong as doing something bad.

BIBLE READING *Deuteronomy 6:12*

TRUTH

God has done many good things that we should remember and be thankful for.

What are some things people do when they have to remember something important? We've given a few examples. Write your own on the blank lines.

use a sticky note   tie a string around a finger   set an alarm

_____

_____

Some things are very important to remember and other things don't matter too much if you forget them. Circle the things you think are very important to remember:

walk the dog   make Mom a birthday card   watch my favorite cartoon

tell Dad his boss called   pack a snack for school   study for my math test

The most important thing we should remember is the thing most people forget: what God has done for us. We're usually so busy thinking about school, our friends, our clothes, our families, sports, and other things that we don't take time to think about God. When we forget about God, we also forget to thank Him for our blessings. And when we forget about our blessings, we start to complain and feel selfish and unhappy. See why it's important to remember God?

DARE   Give God the attention and time He deserves.

DOUBLE DARE

1. In your journal, list twenty things you can thank God for. Go through the list and thank Him for each one, but not all at the same time! See if you can remember to come back to the list throughout the day and check off one or two at a time.

2. If you usually forget to thank God for blessing you, ask Him for forgiveness.

PROMISE TO REPEAT

How did it go? What did you learn?

Don't Explode!

BIBLE READING *Proverbs 16:32*

TRUTH

Patience and self-control are better than blowing up.

Have you ever opened a bottle or can of pop after it's been shaken? What happened? The drink probably shot out of the opening and spilled everywhere. Do you know why that happens?

Soft drinks are fizzy because they contain carbon dioxide, which becomes a gas in water. The drink in the can or bottle is put under a lot of pressure and then sealed. When you open the container, the pressure is released, and that makes the carbon dioxide gas escape as tiny bubbles. If you shake a can of pop, you put even more pressure on the carbon dioxide so it nearly explodes out of the can when you start to open it.

That reminds me of people who have bad tempers. Because they can't control their feelings, any kind of pressure makes them "fizzy." If you put a lot of pressure on them, they just about explode with anger. Do you know anyone like that? How do you feel when you see his or her feelings blow up?

The Bible warns us not to be out of control. When we invite God into our hearts, it's as if His Holy Spirit takes off the pressure. He can help us be more patient.

DARE Control your anger.

DOUBLE DARE

1. In your journal, write about a time when you felt very angry. What did you do? If you "exploded," ask God to forgive you and to help you control your anger.

2. Do you have a friend who often gets angry? With gentle words, share today's devo and Bible verse with her.

PROMISE TO REPEAT

How did it go? What did you learn?

BIBLE READING *Proverbs 30:33*

TRUTH

Making others angry always leads to problems.

Do you know where butter comes from? Unless you live on a farm, you might say, "Well, we just go to the store and buy it!" Long ago, people used to make their own butter. Basically, butter is made when cream is shaken up for a long time, a process called churning. This used to be done by putting the cream in a big barrel and pumping a plunger (a tool similar to the one used to unblock a sink) up and down in it. The churning makes the fat in the cream clump together and get hard.

Today's verse uses the example of churning to warn about the consequences of "stirring" up anger or, in other words, saying or doing things that make others angry. Just like butter doesn't make itself, sometimes we create problems that never would have existed if we hadn't been gossiping, lying, being rude, and so on.

The other example in this verse is also interesting! Can you imagine how painful it would be if someone twisted your nose hard enough to make it bleed? That's how bad stirring up anger is.

DARE Control the temptation to stir up anger.

DOUBLE DARE

1. Ask your parents to help you research how to make butter at home using heavy cream and a jar, and then make that a family project. While you shake the jar (it will take a while), talk about today's Bible verse.

2. Can you think of a time when you stirred up anger? What happened? Talk to God about it and ask Him to help you avoid doing that again.

PROMISE TO REPEAT

How did it go? What did you learn?

Does Your Inside Match Your Label?

BIBLE READING *Matthew 23:27*

TRUTH

A Christian who says one thing but does another is a hypocrite.

Can you think of three items that provide information about the item itself? Here are a few examples:

A price tag tells us how much something costs.

The back cover of a book tells us what the book is about.

The address on an envelope tells the post office where to send a letter.

Imagine you opened a can labeled "tuna" and found paper clips inside. Or you walked into a building that says "flower shop" on the sign and ended up in a dentist's office! We expect things to be what they say they are, right?

Sometimes people who call themselves Christians don't act or talk the way Christians should. Jesus warned the religious leaders about this. He said they made themselves look pure and good on the outside, but they were rotten on the inside. If we tell people we follow Jesus and then we lie or cheat or treat people badly, what will they think of Jesus? Will they want to follow Him too?

DARE Be who you say you are.

DOUBLE DARE

1. Think about this: If you've told people you believe in Jesus, can they see proof of that in the way you live and talk? If not, ask God to help you not to be like the Pharisees.

2. In your journal, write some changes you need to make in your life so that what is inside you matches your "label" better.

PROMISE TO REPEAT

How did it go? What did you learn?

BIBLE READING *Proverbs 11:6 and 2 Corinthians 11:14*

TRUTH

Sin can look beautiful on the outside but be deadly when you touch it.

You may already know that carnivores are animals that eat other animals, and herbivores are animals that eat plants. But did you know that there are carnivorous plants—plants that eat animals?

In Australia, there's a funny-looking plant called the sundew, which makes it sound very innocent. But it is actually deadly! The sundew has small, round leaves with short hairs sticking out that have shiny drops of liquid at the tips. The sparkly blossoms attract insects … and then the plant eats them for lunch!

If an insect lands on the pretty plant, it'll be surprised to discover that the shiny little drops on the leaves are stickier than glue. If the bug struggles to free itself, its flailing around will make the leaves close more tightly around it, trapping it in the tiny prison with no hope of escape before the sundew eats it.

Sin is a lot like the sundew. It can seem fun and attractive, promising us that we'll feel good or be popular. But sin always harms us, so we have to be careful to stay away from it. God can give us discernment (wisdom) to recognize sin before we go near it.

DARE Stay away from sin!

DOUBLE DARE

1. Write down some examples of sins that seem innocent at first but can actually be harmful to a Christian.

2. Tell God about the things that tempt you and ask for His help to say no the next time you're tempted to sin.

PROMISE TO REPEAT

How did it go? What did you learn?

Read Mark 2:17.

When I was around twenty-eight years old, I noticed a sharp pain in my lower back near my right side. At first I thought I had pulled a muscle, but this pain got worse over the next week so I decided to see a doctor about it. It turned out that I had a couple of large stones in my kidney. To explain it in a simple way, kidney stones can develop when there's too much calcium in your body.

Although the stones caused me pain and I needed treatment to get rid of them, analyzing what caused them helped my doctor discover that I had a condition called hyperparathyroidism. (Try saying that five times fast!) It's not a life-threatening disease, but it can lead to other problems if it's not treated. Since discovering this condition, I've gone through dozens of medical tests and X-rays and have had surgery a couple of times. I want to tell you about one of these tests because it got me thinking about how the Holy Spirit helps us.

One day, I had a scan called a sestamibi. This involved having a very mild radioactive dye injected into my blood and then waiting for the tiny gland that was causing me trouble to absorb the dye. During the scan, an X-ray picture of my neck was taken, and the gland that absorbed the dye glowed as a "hot spot," making it easy for the doctor to identify the problem and decide what to do next.

Pain isn't pleasant, but it tells us something is wrong. If it's serious or if we don't know what the problem is, we may need a doctor to check us out. We may even need to go through medical tests or operations to take care of the problem.

In the same way, there can be symptoms, or signs, that there are spiritual problems in our lives. If you feel anxious, angry, stressed, unhappy, or confused, there may be something going on that you need help with. Ignoring those symptoms or trying to make them go away on your own can make the situation worse. What you really need to do is go to God, the greatest "doctor" we have. When you give your life to Jesus, the Holy Spirit is there to help you identify the "hot spots" that can make you stumble and sin. When you admit that something in your life is unhealthy, infected, or broken, you can then ask God to remove the problem and to heal your spiritual disease.

Going to the doctor or hospital is not usually fun or comfortable, but it might help you feel better ... or even save your life!

YOUR TURN

- What are some symptoms in your life that might be signs that something is wrong?

- How do you think God can help with what's bothering you?

- Spend some time in prayer talking to God about your difficult situation. Ask Him to show you if there are any changes you need to make in your life or if there's someone you need to talk to. If you're really stuck, talk to one of your parents or another adult you trust.

BIBLE READING　*Numbers 32:23*

TRUTH

It's impossible to hide your sins from God.

I don't need to tell you that it's not wise to commit crimes. You know that it breaks the law, it's wrong, and it displeases God. But some criminals take foolishness to a whole new level! For example …

A man went into a store, put twenty dollars on the counter, and asked for change. When the clerk opened the cash drawer, the man pointed a gun and demanded that the clerk give him all the money in the drawer. The thief took the money and ran out of the store, leaving behind the twenty dollars. Know what? There had been only fifteen dollars in the cash drawer!

Another man broke into a house and stole many valuable items, but he forgot his cell phone in the house! The police were then able to go to this man's home, find him and everything he'd stolen, and arrest him.

Of course, many criminals never get caught because they're very careful. The point of today's devo isn't that we should be sneaky when doing wrong so that we don't get caught. God sees our sin even when others don't, and He will hold us responsible or will discipline us in some way.

DARE　Don't cover up sin. Avoid it!

DOUBLE DARE

1. Can you think of some wrong things you secretly did that you never got in trouble for? Admit those sins to God and ask Him to forgive you.

2. Memorize this phrase from today's verse: "You may be sure that your sin will find you out."

PROMISE TO REPEAT

How did it go? What did you learn?

What's the Most Dangerous?

BIBLE READING *Romans 6:23*

TRUTH

Sin, without God's forgiveness, leads to spiritual death.

What do these animals have in common with each other?

blue-ringed octopus	rhinoceros	shark
box jellyfish	African lion	mosquito
black mamba snake	polar bear	leopard
hippopotamus	crocodile	African elephant

These animals are all very dangerous. Some have deadly bites; others are so big and strong that they can crush you. But you may be surprised to know that the animal many scientists say is the *most* dangerous is the smallest one on the list.

Yep, mosquitoes can be deadly. That doesn't mean you need to be scared to go camping or sit in your backyard, but it's a good idea to use bug spray if you're going to be near a lot of mosquitoes. What makes these insects so deadly in some countries is that they carry diseases and infect almost seven hundred million people every year! About two or three million will die from those diseases.

Mosquitoes, sharks, and poisonous snakes can be deadly, but do you know what's even more dangerous? Sin. The Bible warns that sin kills us spiritually and separates us from God. That's why we all need a Savior—Jesus Christ—to forgive our sins, save us, and give us the gift of eternal life.

DARE Choose life.

DOUBLE DARE

1. Quiz your friends about the most dangerous animal in the world. Afterward, talk about the danger of sin and how Jesus can save us.

2. If you have any sins that you haven't confessed to God yet, do that today. Then thank Him for His gift of eternal life that you have because of Jesus.

PROMISE TO REPEAT

How did it go? What did you learn?

Who Likes Discipline?

BIBLE READING *Hebrews 12:5–11*

TRUTH

Discipline hurts for only a short time.

Violins need to have their strings carefully tuned, which is done by stretching them tightly. If the strings are hanging all loosey-goosey, the instrument will make a horrible sound.

Athletes need to train for hours a day and follow strict diets so they can be in good shape to compete in their sports.

Many things in life require discipline or an uncomfortable time of training and practice to make them better. When I was a tween girl taking piano lessons, my teacher used to make me stop every time I made a mistake and start from the beginning. That was so frustrating that sometimes I wanted to cry. But, knowing what a mistake would cost me, I was as careful as possible not to make another one.

In our Christian lives, we will have times of discipline. When we sin or when we don't follow God carefully, He uses different ways to get our attention and remind us to do better. If your parents punish you or if you feel bad in your heart, that's discipline. It may feel rotten, but you can thank God for it because it will help you become stronger and better.

DARE Be thankful when you're disciplined.

DOUBLE DARE

1. How do you usually feel and act when you're disciplined by your parents? Instead of fighting them, try to remember it is for your good.

2. In your journal, write Hebrews 12:11 in your own words. Then thank God that He loves you enough to discipline you.

PROMISE TO REPEAT

How did it go? What did you learn?

Look Up!

BIBLE READING *Isaiah 40:25–26*

TRUTH

No one is equal to God.

Michelangelo, an Italian artist who was born about 540 years ago, is probably most famous for painting the ceiling of the Sistine Chapel in Rome. For four years he painted pictures from Bible stories, such as Creation, Noah, Daniel, and the life of Jesus, covering an area measuring twelve thousand square feet. If you know how big a football field is, imagine one-third of that. That's how much Michelangelo painted!

Because the ceiling is so high, Michelangelo had to climb up on scaffolds to paint, even lying on his back sometimes. After spending such a long time looking up to paint the ceiling, Michelangelo's neck became very stiff and sore. In fact, he could no longer look down to read, so he had to lift things over his head to be able to read them. It was too painful to bend his neck downward.

Although this was a problem for Michelangelo, we can still learn something from his story. Many people go through life always looking "down" at their problems and at earthly concerns, such as money or clothes. Instead, we should always look "up" at God and heavenly things, such as joy, hope, and peace. That's where we'll find everything we need … and more! Nothing on earth is equal to God's greatness and goodness!

DARE Keep your eyes on the Lord.

DOUBLE DARE

1. Write ten things you spend a lot of time thinking about on most days (for example, your homework). Talk to God about the ones that trouble you.

2. Write a letter to God telling Him all the things you think are incredible about Him.

PROMISE TO REPEAT

How did it go? What did you learn?

Keep Your Eyes on the Master

BIBLE READING *Mark 14:38*

TRUTH

The best way to resist temptation is to keep looking at Jesus.

A writer named Leslie Dunkin once told a story about a lesson he learned from the family dog. To test the dog, Leslie's dad used to put a bit of meat or a biscuit on the floor near the dog and then say "No!" to the dog. The obedient dog knew it was not allowed to touch the treat. Leslie noticed the dog would not even look at it. Instead, it would keep staring at its master's face. It seemed to know that if it looked at the treat, it might be too tempted to obey.

That's an excellent example for us to remember. When we're tempted to do something wrong or to take something that isn't ours, the best thing to do is to shift our focus from the temptation to God.

For example, if your parents aren't home and you're tempted to watch a TV show you're not allowed to, it's better not to turn the TV on at all. Instead, go over a devo, talk to God, and do something positive that you know would please God and your parents. Keep your heart close to God until the temptation has passed.

DARE Keep your spiritual eyes on the Master, not your temptations.

DOUBLE DARE

1. What is a temptation you find difficult to say no to? Create a game plan for what you will do the next time you're tempted.

2. Draw a picture of the story about Leslie Dunkin's dog and write out Mark 14:38 at the bottom. Memorize the verse while you draw. Then post the picture where you'll see it often.

PROMISE TO REPEAT

How did it go? What did you learn?

HERO LIST

Choose ONE of these heroes to learn about this weekend:

Name	Bible Verses
Esther	Esther 3:1–11; 4:4–17; 5:1–8; 7:1–10; 8:1–11
Stephen	Acts 6–7
Ruth	Ruth 1–4
David	1 Samuel 17
Abigail	1 Samuel 25:1–42
Gideon	Judges 6–7
The Bleeding Woman	Mark 5:25–34
Joseph	Genesis 37; 39–41
The Widow of Zarephath	1 Kings 17:8–24; Luke 4:25–26
Noah	Genesis 6–8
Miriam	Exodus 2:1–10
Daniel	Daniel 6
Mary of Bethany	John 12:1–8
Abraham	Genesis 22:1–18

Your hero for this weekend: _____

QUESTION TIME

1. How did this weekend's hero show courage and faith in God?

2. What happened because of his or her courage and obedience?

3. What did you learn from this hero's life that will help you in your own walk with God?

DOUBLE DARE

Choose at least one of these ways to dig a little deeper into your hero's life this weekend:

1. See if you can find other Bible verses about him or her. Write the reference (or the "address" of the verses) here and also anything new that you learned.

2. Ask your parents or another Christian what they have learned from this hero's life and example.

Tell a friend or your family about your new hero!

What are your thoughts?

Learning from Mistakes

BIBLE READING *Proverbs 10:17*

TRUTH

When you don't learn from your mistakes, you set a bad example for others.

There are different kinds of mistakes. For example:

1. Foolish mistakes are things you do because you were careless, such as dropping your pizza on the carpet because you were trying to carry two full cups at the same time.

2. Simple mistakes are things you do because you didn't know any better, such as running out of cake at a party because you didn't expect so many people.

3. Irresponsible mistakes are things you do because you didn't make enough of an effort, such as getting to school late because you went to bed late and couldn't wake up.

4. Sinful mistakes are things you do even though you know they're wrong.

Some mistakes can be fixed, but many of them can't. There are two important things to do when you make a mistake:

1. Be humble if someone corrects or criticizes you and admit you were wrong.

2. Learn from the mistake and try not to do it again.

The Bible says if we don't accept discipline, we can lead other people down the wrong path. If you tell your friends that you love and follow Jesus, you have to make sure you're walking on the right path. Some of them may be following you!

DARE Learn from your mistakes.

DOUBLE DARE

1. In your journal, write about three mistakes you've made lately. What can you learn from each one? Ask God to help you to not repeat those mistakes.

2. Do you need to apologize to your parents for not accepting their correction? Do it today.

PROMISE TO REPEAT

How did it go? What did you learn?

Not Home Yet

BIBLE READING *Romans 8:18*

TRUTH

Our struggles on earth are only for a short time.

In a book I was reading many years ago, there was a conversation between a wise old Indian and his grandson, who was feeling angry about some things. The grandpa tried to explain that our time here on earth is kind of like a training period for eternity. To help his grandson understand, he gave an interesting example.

He said that if half the people in a building expect it to be a luxury hotel, they will grumble the whole time they stay there. But if the other half see the building as a prison, they will be thankful for any small comfort or nice thing.

In the same way, if we expect life here on earth to be perfect and wonderful—that we'll have lots of money, a fancy house, no sickness, expensive clothes, and so on—we will be disappointed. But if we remember that we're here for only a short time and then we'll go to heaven (where everything is perfect and wonderful), we'll always appreciate even the smallest blessings God gives us.

Which group of people would you rather be part of—the complainers or the thankers?

DARE Put your hope in heaven, not in the world.

DOUBLE DARE

1. Get two pieces of paper. On one, list things you sometimes complain about. On the other, write things you're thankful for. Which list makes you happier? Keep that one in your journal and throw out the other one.

2. Read Psalm 103:15–18. In your journal, write these verses in your own words (use a dictionary to help you with any hard words).

PROMISE TO REPEAT

How did it go? What did you learn?

Just Ask

BIBLE READING *Matthew 7:7–8 and James 4:3*

TRUTH

God welcomes you to ask for the things you need.

There once was a family with three young children. The parents loved their daughters and did their best to give them the best of everything they needed. But the three girls were very different.

Child number one never asked for anything. She expected her parents to always know what she wanted or needed.

Child number two sometimes asked her parents for special things, such as a toy or a favorite treat, but not for the things she knew they would give her every day anyway, though she was very thankful for those things too.

Child number three asked her parents for everything. She asked for milk, for soap, and for socks. She asked for a pony. She asked for new clothes every week. She asked to be driven everywhere, even if she could walk there.

Which child do you think the parents were most pleased with?

God knows what you need, so you don't have to ask Him for every little thing, but He wants you to go to Him with your special requests, as long as you're not asking out of selfishness.

DARE   Have the right motives when you ask God for something.

DOUBLE DARE

1. For one week, pay attention to (and, if possible, write down) all the things you ask for—from your parents, from God, from friends, and so on. At the end of the week, ask God to show you if you need to change the way you ask for things.

2. Memorize Matthew 7:7–8.

PROMISE TO REPEAT

How did it go? What did you learn?

A Leap of Faith

BIBLE READING *Isaiah 43:1*

TRUTH

Your heavenly Father made you, knows you, and watches over you.

Have you ever seen a Mandarin duck? The female is plain brown, but the male has many brightly colored feathers. What's really neat about Mandarin ducks is how brave the little babies are when it's time for them to leave the safety of their nest, high up in the trunk of a tree—at just two days old!

From the ground below, the mother calls them down with little encouraging noises. One by one, the babies nervously come to the edge of the nest, look down, and then …WHEEE! They jump out, spread their wings, and dive to the ground, sometimes bouncing or tumbling a little when they land. It looks a lot like kids jumping off a diving board into a pool, with their arms waving all over the place.

The ducklings are able to take this "leap of faith" because they trust their mom, who is calling to them. If they don't obey their mom, they will be stuck in that tree alone. Just like the ducklings, we can trust our heavenly Father when He asks us to obey Him. He loves us and will ask us only to do what's good for us, never something that would harm us.

DARE Take a leap of faith!

DOUBLE DARE

1. In your journal, write about a time when you obeyed God even though you were scared. What happened, and what did you learn from that situation?

2. Ask your parents to help you find the video "Fearless Baby Ducklings" on the Internet. After watching it together, talk about how we should trust and obey God.

PROMISE TO REPEAT

How did it go? What did you learn?

Will You Give It All Up?

BIBLE READING *Matthew 16:24–26*

TRUTH

When you give up everything in life, Jesus gives you a better life.

Read the sentences below and check off the ones that describe someone who is wise.

❑ Karen thought hats look dorky so she didn't wear one to school, even though it was snowing.

❑ Jessica took a babysitting job for two Saturdays. She couldn't go to the mall with her friends, but she earned enough money to buy a new art set.

❑ Derek sat with a new boy at lunchtime, even though his friends laughed at him because of it.

❑ Billy decided not to go to summer camp because he didn't want to miss his favorite TV shows.

Sometimes we make choices that feel right at the moment but horrible later on when we realize we were foolish. The Bible warns us about a much more important choice that we all have to make. Sadly, most people in the world will make the wrong choice.

Jesus told His disciples (and us) that if we want to follow Him, we have to first let go of all the other things we thought were important. We have to be willing to give up everything for Him. When we do, He will bless us with eternal life and blessings we can't even imagine.

DARE   Give it all up for Jesus.

DOUBLE DARE

1. What are some things you think you can't give up, even for God? Talk to Him about it and ask Him to help you trust Him enough to let go.

2. Memorize Matthew 16:26. If you don't understand it, ask an older Christian to explain what it means.

PROMISE TO REPEAT

How did it go? What did you learn?

Pandita's Passion

When I was a tween, I used to go to Camp Livingstone, a Christian summer camp in Quebec. I was seven years old the first time I went and didn't know anything about camp. I learned right away that each of the eight cabins (four for girls and four for boys) was named after a long-ago missionary. The eight cabins were known as:

Girls	Boys
Amy Carmichael	David Brainerd
Malla Moe	William Carey
Mary Slessor	Hudson Taylor
Pandita Ramabai	Adoniram Judson

I went to Camp Livingstone for seven years, and in that time, I slept in all the girls' cabins except for Mary Slessor. I remember the year I was in the Pandita Ramabai cabin and we had to come up with a cheer for our cabin. The eight of us put our heads together and came up with a silly rhyme, which we sang to the tune of "Row, Row, Row Your Boat":

Pandita, we're the best; we'll beat all the rest! We'll try our best to win the contest instead of taking a rest.

It's astonishing that I can still remember it after more than twenty-five years! The sad thing is I never learned anything about Pandita or the other missionaries the cabins were named for. But now that I've learned about Pandita's life, I think you'll find it interesting too.

Pandita was born in Karnataka, India, in 1858. Her father, a very wealthy man, was a faithful follower of the Hindu religion. Unlike most of the Indian girls of that time, Pandita was taught to read, and this ability changed her whole life. At a young age, she lost her entire family when there was a famine (not enough food). When she was sixteen, she walked across India and fascinated people when she read poetry in the Hindu temples. Actually, that's when she was given the name Pandita, which means "mistress of wisdom."

She got married when she was twenty-two, but her husband died sixteen months later and she was left alone with a baby daughter. She began to understand the difficulties other widows and orphans went through. And she began to do something about it. Even though she was young, she had the courage to build centers for widows to get help, and she began to teach them skills they could use to get jobs and earn money for their families. Because of her work, she met some Christian missionaries.

One day, Pandita accepted an invitation to go to England. She began to study the Bible, believed in Jesus, and was baptized. When people heard about this in India, they were very angry with her. So Pandita returned to India and, with God's help, showed the people that she still loved them and, more important, *God* loved them. She did her best to show them that the most important thing in religion is to love God and to love others.

YOUR TURN

- Read James 1:27 and 1 Timothy 5:3.

- Pandita was passionate about helping widows who were left alone and had no one to care for them. Modern life in North America is quite different from how it was 150 years ago in India (or even today). But that doesn't mean there aren't people who are lonely, poor, or helpless around you. They may be in your church, or they may live down the street from you. How do you think God might want you to help such people? Write your ideas here:

- Ask your parents or your pastor if they know someone who would appreciate some cheering up or a helping hand. In your journal, use a blank page and do the following:

  1. Write the person's name at the top.
  2. Pray for that person and his or her needs.
  3. Pray for wisdom so you'll know the best way to help.
  4. Write down some specific things you can do to cheer up this person.
  5. Check your list with your parents to get their advice on the best idea.
  6. Make a plan for how you will bring your idea to life.
  7. Do it!
  8. Write about it in your journal afterward.

What are your thoughts?

God Knows You Better

BIBLE READING *Luke 11:9–13*

TRUTH

God gives the best gifts because He knows you better than you know yourself.

Even though he died in 1977 (I was only five years old), singer Elvis Presley is still famous today. Elvis sang many gospel songs, but he is better known as the "King of Rock and Roll."

But when Elvis was young, he could not have guessed how famous he would become. On his eleventh birthday, Elvis wanted a bicycle. But, knowing his talent was special, his mother bought him his first guitar.

If Elvis had gotten his wish, what might have happened to him? Would he have developed his musical talent? Who knows?

It's easy to feel confident about the things we wish for, thinking we know what is best for us or what will bring us the most happiness. But Jesus reminds us in the Bible that He knows what we really need and what will satisfy our hearts. All we have to do is humbly ask Him.

And just like Elvis's mother, He'll give us what's *best* instead of what's just *good*.

DARE   Ask God for His best for you.

DOUBLE DARE

1. Write a letter to God telling Him about all the things you wish for. Then ask Him to bless you with what *He* wants for you and to help you trust Him if His plans are different from yours.

2. Today, surprise a friend or someone in your family with something that would make him or her happy. For example, play with your little sister longer than you usually do, wash the dishes without being asked to, or give your friend an extra hug.

PROMISE TO REPEAT

How did it go? What did you learn?

Money Isn't Everything

BIBLE READING *Luke 12:15*

TRUTH

Life is about more than how much we have.

If someone offered you one billion dollars, would you take it? What if she told you she'd give you one billion dollars in single one-dollar bills but only if you agreed to count each bill? You might think, *Sure, what's the big deal about that?*

It's hard to imagine how much one billion is, so you might be surprised to know that it could take you fifty to sixty years to count all those dollars, even if you counted for eight hours a day, every single day of the year! You would be old and probably quite sick by the time you finished, and you would not have enjoyed the money at all.

This is an extreme example, but, sadly, there are people who would be more willing to give up their health, time with their families, a peaceful life, and even eternal life with God than they would to give up money and riches.

But the Bible tells us that life is about much more than money and "stuff," and it warns us not to be greedy. Instead, we should trust God to provide all the things we need because He knows what's best for us.

DARE Tell greed to take a hike!

DOUBLE DARE

1. Do you ever wish you had a lot more money than you do? Talk to God about it and ask Him to help you trust Him to provide for all your needs.

2. In your journal, list twenty things that don't cost money but bring joy to your life. For example, sunshine, your eyesight, a hug from your mom.

PROMISE TO REPEAT

How did it go? What did you learn?

Where's Your Treasure?

BIBLE READING *Luke 12:32–34*

TRUTH

What we do with our money shows what's in our hearts.

One day, a Sunday school teacher was telling her class of ten-year-olds about a family of missionaries who were serving God in a faraway country. She asked her students, "Would you give one million dollars to the missionaries?" The children all yelled, "YES!" The teacher asked, "Would you give one thousand dollars?" Again they yelled, "YES!" So the teacher asked, "How about one hundred dollars?" They all screamed, "YES!" Finally, the teacher asked, "Would you give just one dollar to the missionaries?"

This time, when all the children yelled "yes," the teacher noticed that Brittany was quiet and was holding her purse tightly. "Why didn't you say 'yes' this time?" the teacher asked Brittany. With a sad face, Brittany said, "Because I have a dollar."

It's easy for us to make promises to God about big things we know He doesn't expect from us right now. But what about doing the small things that we can do? It's like telling your parents that when you're older and have lots of money, you'll buy them a beautiful new house. But if you're not willing today to help them wash the car or put away the laundry, your promise isn't worth much, is it?

DARE Be generous with whatever God has given you.

DOUBLE DARE

1. What is your favorite thing to do with money when you have some? What does that say about what's important to you? Write about it in your journal.

2. Write the words of Luke 12:34 on a sticky note and keep it in your wallet as a reminder of today's devo.

PROMISE TO REPEAT

How did it go? What did you learn?

BIBLE READING *Mystery! Solve the puzzle to find it.*

TRUTH

God's thoughts are greater than we can understand or measure.

Use the code below to solve this puzzle and find today's Bible verse. Using the letters in the first line of the code, find the corresponding letter in the second line to complete the puzzle. The first word is done for you.

HOW _____

_____

_____

"ESM HQXYUSLJ PS RX ZQX NSLQ PESLVEPJ, VSA! ESM OZJP UJ PEX JLR SD PEXR! MXQX U PS YSLIP PEXR, PEXN MSLGA SLPILRCXQ PEX VQZUIJ SD JZIA—MEXI U ZMZTX, U ZR JPUGG MUPE NSL" (HJZGR 139:17–18).

Code: Z C Y A X D V E U F T G R I S H Q J P L O M N K
A B C D E F G H I J K L M N O P R S T U V W Y Z

Do you ever feel like no one cares or thinks about you? Even if you know that your parents love you, there may be days when they seem too busy and distracted to listen to you, or maybe they're not feeling well and don't have the energy to help you with something. If you have a best friend, you know she enjoys hanging out with you, but sometimes she might not be able to or she might not feel like it. It's easy to feel lonely on days like that.

But God *never* stops thinking about you, and He *always* wants to spend time with you. When King David thought about this, he was astonished. Our awesome Creator, who is more powerful than anything in the universe, thinks about *you*!

DARE Share your time and thoughts with God.

DOUBLE DARE

1. Put a teaspoon of sand (or sugar or salt) into a bowl and try to count the grains. When you give up, thank God that His thoughts for you are more than all the grains of sand in the world!

2. In your journal, write about how it feels to know that God cares for you so much.

PROMISE TO REPEAT

How did it go? What did you learn?

Super-stretchy Love

BIBLE READING *Psalm 136:1*

TRUTH

God's love lasts forever.

Compared to a smartphone, spacecraft, or washing machine, a rubber band doesn't look like much of an invention, does it? It's just a small circle of rubber, usually in a boring beige color. And yet, because of its stretchiness, a rubber band can be very useful. It can tie your hair back, bundle papers together, and, if you're creative, do all kinds of other things. (For example, if a candle is wobbling, wrap a rubber band around the bottom before putting it in the candleholder. Ta-da!)

Some rubber bands are so big and stretchy that they seem like they can stretch forever. But even the biggest rubber band will break at some point. Not God's love! When we sin God is disappointed, but He still loves us—and He helps us make things right and do better the next time. When we're sad, God doesn't ignore us like our friends sometimes do. He comforts us and gives us strength. When we're scared, God doesn't laugh at us or tell us to grow up. He holds our hand and reminds us to trust Him. And then He walks with us through the scary situation.

If someone made a rubber band that could stretch all the way from Earth to the moon, that would be nothing compared to God's love. God's love stretches forever.

DARE Thank God for His incredible, stretchy love.

DOUBLE DARE

1. Memorize today's verse. Put a rubber band around one of your wrists, and whenever you see the rubber band, review the verse.

2. Thank God for ten ways He shows He loves you.

PROMISE TO REPEAT

How did it go? What did you learn?

Pop Quiz #2

After almost a whole year of doing Bible devos, do you think you know the Bible pretty well? Let's see how you do with these questions. The answers are found in the answer key at the end of the book.

Set A

1. Who broke all ten commandments in one day?

2. Which Bible character had no parents?

3. Where is baseball mentioned in the Bible?

4. How many animals did Moses take onto the ark with him?

5. How long was Noah in the belly of the big fish?

6. Is the book of Josiah in the Old Testament or the New?

7. What about the book of Hezekiah?

Go check your answers, and then come back to finish this devo.

So … how did you do? (Okay, I admit it: I'm giggling a little right now!) Now that we've had some fun, let's do a real quiz. Let's see how much you can remember from the past year's devos.

Set B

1. What were the names of the two sisters Jesus visited with His disciples? (Hint: one of them listened to Jesus while the other one worked in the kitchen.)

2. What was Naaman, the man with leprosy, told to do so that he could be healed? (Hint: he hesitated because he thought it didn't make sense.)

3. What kinds of things does the Bible say our thoughts should be focused on? (Hint: remember the acronym REPLANT.)

4. Jesus told a parable about three things that were lost. What were they?

5. What are the three ways God answers our prayers?

6. What are five helpful things to look for when you study the Bible? (Hint: remember the acronym SPACE.)

7. What are five things to remember to make sure your words don't hurt others or displease God? (Hint: remember the acronym THINK.) "Are my words …?"

DOUBLE DARE

Ask your parents if you can have a Bible trivia book or game or if they can find a Bible quiz website to help you remember important facts from the Bible. Try to make time at least once a week to quiz yourself. See if a family member or friend wants to join you.

Keep up the good work!

Are You a Polar Bear?

BIBLE READING *2 Corinthians 3:18*

TRUTH

The closer we get to God, the more people will see Him when they look at us.

List five things that reflect light (such as a window):

1.

2.

3.

4.

5.

Do you have polar bears on your list? No? Did you know that polar bears, the world's largest land predators (animals that hunt and kill other animals for food), aren't actually white but *look* white because they reflect the sun's light? Each hair on a polar bear's body is a clear, hollow tube that reflects light, just like snow and ice do. Cool! (Here's another piece of trivia: 60 percent of the world's polar bears live in Canada.)

As Christians, we should be a bit like the polar bear. Can you guess why? The Bible says we should reflect the light of Jesus to the world around us. That means that just as a polar bear reflects the sun and appears white, we should reflect purity and other qualities of Jesus to other people when they look at us.

How can we reflect Jesus's light? By spending time with Him and in His Word.

DARE Let people see Jesus in your life.

DOUBLE DARE

1. Think about how easy it is for people to figure out that you are a Christian. Can they see it in your actions, or do they have to wait until you tell them? Ask God to help you be a better reflector of His light.

2. In your journal, try to write today's verse in your own words. Then write down two ways you will try to be a "polar bear" for Jesus.

PROMISE TO REPEAT

How did it go? What did you learn?

Our Great God

BIBLE READING *Isaiah 40:28*

TRUTH

There is no beginning or end to God.

When I was little, I liked going to the park with my cousin and playing in the sandbox. I've always enjoyed being creative, so it was fun to build things out of wet sand or to take a stick and draw pictures in the sand. Sometimes my cousin and I would take our little plastic shovels and just start digging and digging. Do you remember doing this when you were younger?

We wondered how deep we could go and what we might find. Sometimes kids think that if they dig a deep enough hole in a sandbox or in their backyard, they'll end up on the other side of the world. This isn't possible, but if it were, do you know where people in the United States would end up? No, not in China. They'd be in the Indian Ocean! If people in China dug straight through, they'd end up either in Chile, Argentina, or the Pacific Ocean. People in New Zealand would pop up in Spain, and people in Hawaii would end up in Botswana.

Our earth is so big that it's hard to imagine. What's more astounding, though, is that God created it and He is much, much greater than the distance from one end of the earth to the other.

DARE Worship God's greatness!

DOUBLE DARE

1. Read Isaiah 40:18–28 and write down, in your own words, the remarkable qualities of God mentioned in these verses.

2. Draw a picture that contains all the things you're glad God created. While you draw, talk to God silently about how much you love Him.

PROMISE TO REPEAT

How did it go? What did you learn?

BIBLE READING *John 14:6*

TRUTH

You can't get to God without Jesus.

Optical illusions—things that trick your eyes into seeing something that isn't really there—can be really fun. Want to try one?

Hold your two index fingers in front of you so that their tips are touching in a straight line. Slowly bring your fingers closer to your face at the level of your eyes. As they get closer, something strange will happen. A mini–hot dog will be floating between your fingers!

Now slowly pull your fingers apart. What happened? The hot dog disappeared, right? (By the way, don't do this trick too many times or your eyes will start to hurt.) Actually, there was never a hot dog floating in front of you. It was an illusion.

The Devil tries to trick us too. He tells people they don't need to believe in Jesus to go to heaven, or that there is no heaven, or that it's okay to believe in Jesus when they're older and just have fun now. But those are all lies. Jesus said that believing in Him is the only way to go to heaven and be with God. And since none of us knows when we're going to die, we need to trust in Him today, not just in the future.

DARE Trust Jesus, not illusions!

DOUBLE DARE

1. What are some wrong things people believe about Jesus? Ask God to help you courageously share the truth with people who need to hear it.

2. Get a friend to try the floating hot dog illusion. Then tell her about today's Bible verse.

PROMISE TO REPEAT

How did it go? What did you learn?

Take My Life

BIBLE READING   *1 Corinthians 6:20*

TRUTH

Jesus gave His life for you.

I love singing traditional old hymns in my church. Many of them have beautiful melodies and, more important, meaningful words that help me worship God. But sometimes it's hard to sing the songs if I really pay attention to the words, because I have to make sure I mean what I'm singing!

One hymn that has challenging words is called "Take My Life and Let It Be." A few of the lines say this:

> Take my hands and let them move
> At the impulse of Thy love.
> Take my feet and let them be
> Swift and beautiful for Thee.
> Take my voice and let me sing,
> Always, only for my King.
> Take my lips and let them be
> Filled with messages from Thee.

In other words, "God, please use my hands to do what You want them to do, let my feet go only where You want them to go, and let me use my mouth to say only the words that You give me."

Those are big requests, aren't they? But the Bible teaches us that we must be willing to honor God with every part of us. He deserves it!

DARE   Give your life to Jesus.

DOUBLE DARE

1. Look for the complete words to this hymn on the Internet or in a church hymn-book. Copy them in your journal and try to make each line a true request that you can pray to God.

2. List as many things as you can think of that God has done for or given to you. Then list what you've done for or given to Him. Write down any changes you think you should make in your relationship with God.

PROMISE TO REPEAT

How did it go? What did you learn?

BIBLE READING *2 Corinthians 8:11 and Acts 20:24*

TRUTH

God has a job for each of us to complete.

Each of the following words has something to do with finishing, but each is missing one letter. Fill in the missing letters and write them, in order, in the spaces below to find an encouraging message.

1. VICTOR_   2. C_MPLETE   3. CONCL_SION   4. EN_ING

5. ACCOMPL_SH   6. SUCCEE_   7. ACH_EVE   8. _ERMINATE

Answer: _ _ _   _ _ _   _ _!

Do you ever start a project or chore and then not finish it or stop when you think you've done enough? When I was a tween, I took piano lessons. I was supposed to practice every day, but sometimes I got *sooooo* bored with it. I would practice a song a few times and then stop. My mom would yell from the kitchen, "Do it again!" She wasn't being mean (even if it felt like it to me!). She knew if I didn't learn the music properly, I was just wasting my time (and my parents' money) on the piano lessons.

It's foolish to start a project and then give up before we're done, but it's even worse if we get lazy as Christians and stop following or serving God. You've done a great job working through these devos for a year. Now keep going with your Bible studies and prayer times and finish well!

DARE Finish what you've started.

DOUBLE DARE

1. In your journal, write about how your life has changed in the past year as you've read your Bible daily and dared to live out what you've learned.

2. How are you going to continue growing in your relationship with Jesus? Write your plan in your journal and ask God to help you finish well.

PROMISE TO REPEAT

How did it go? What did you learn?

Read Matthew 25:22.

Can you believe this is our last weekend devotional after hanging out together for more than 360 days? If you've completed all the daily and weekend devos in *Truth, Dare, Double Dare*, I'm sure that God would say to you, "Well done, good and faithful servant!"

But the end of this book is not really *the end*. When you've done the last devo and put this book away on your shelf or in a box, I hope you won't stop reading your Bible. And I hope you won't stop being a *double-dare dynamo* who courageously lives out the things God has taught you in the past year.

YOUR TURN

- This weekend, take time to think back on this past year and all that you've learned. Try to remember yourself twelve months ago. How much have you grown by daring to trust and obey God? Flip through the devos in this book to read some of the notes you wrote and remember the dares you completed.

- Write out a prayer asking God to help you continue being daring for Him in the year ahead.

- On the opposite blank page, write down the most important things you want to remember from the past year of devos. It can be Bible verses, truths, dares, or anything else you learned.

DOUBLE DARE

I'd love to hear about how God helped you grow in your faith this past year! You can send me a note by regular mail or email at the addresses below. I promise to keep your note private and to pray for you when I hear from you. I can't promise to answer every letter, but I will do my best!

Ann-Margret Hovsepian
5941 Park Avenue
Montreal, Quebec, Canada
H2V 4H4

Email: ann@annhovsepian.com

Your parents can also find me on Facebook at www.facebook.com/ann.hovsepian.author.

Now go and be a *double-dare dynamo*!

WANT TO KNOW MORE ABOUT HOW TO BECOME A CHRISTIAN?

God created everything in this universe: the planets, the stars, the sun and moon, the world we live in, the animals, and, best of all, human beings. God made everything perfect, and He loved the people He made very much.

Sadly, the first humans who existed (Adam and Eve) rebelled against God and sinned. Since then, humans have always been born with a sinful nature that separates us from God and heaven. The Bible says that the punishment for sin is death (hell).

But there's good news!

About two thousand years ago, God came down to earth in the form of a human named Jesus (that's what we celebrate at Christmas). Jesus was God, but He loved us so much that He was willing to come to earth to help us find God. He was also willing to die on a cross to be punished for our sins (instead of us) and to make a way for us to live forever in heaven with Him. There's even more good news: Because Jesus rose from the dead three days after He was killed (which is what we celebrate at Easter), we know we can also have eternal life after we die!

The Bible says, "For God so loved the world that he gave his one and only Son, that whoever believes in him shall not perish but have eternal life" (John 3:16).

THE A-B-C-DARE

1. Admit that you are a sinner.
2. Believe that Jesus died on the cross and came back to life three days later.
3. Confess your sins to God and ask Him to forgive you.
4. Dedicate your life to Him and promise to love and obey Him.

You don't need to go through a complicated ceremony to become a Christian. Simply believing in the truth about Jesus and asking God to come into your heart will get you started on your new life and your new relationship with Him. After that, three things will help you grow stronger in your faith:

1. Studying your Bible
2. Praying
3. Going to church to worship God with Christian friends who can encourage and support you

If you still have questions, talk to a pastor, Sunday school teacher, or youth group leader (or your parents, if they're Christians). You can also write to me at ann@annhovsepian.com.

427

Matthew 11:29							G	E	**N**	T	L	E		
1 Kings 1:46								R	**O**	Y	A	L		
1 Chronicles 12:21									**B**	R	A	V	E	
1 Timothy 3:2	R	E	S	P	E	C	T	A	B	**L**	E			
Ruth 3:11			C	H	A	R	A	C	T	**E**	R			

Jennifer	Jonathan	Emily
Sophie	Andrew	Alison
Megan	Joshua	Thomas

Psalm 150:2	"Praise him! Praise him! Jesus, our blessed Redeemer!"
Psalm 29:2	"To God be the glory, great things he hath done!"
Luke 23:49	"Jesus, keep me near the cross."
Exodus 33:22	"He hideth my soul in the cleft of the rock."
Mark 8:36	"Take the world, but give me Jesus."
Hebrews 3:15	"Jesus is tenderly calling you home."
Hebrews 10:22	"Draw me nearer, nearer blessed Lord."
Ecclesiastes 12:6–7	"Some day the silver cord will break."

Kintsugi, page 158

Origami = folding paper
Shibori = dyeing cloth
Bonsai = growing miniature trees
Temari = wrapping balls with thread
Amigurumi = knitting or crocheting tiny stuffed animals

God's Great Love, page 187

"THE LORD IS GOOD TO THOSE WHOSE HOPE IS IN HIM."

Is Church a Chore?, page 204

"LET US NOT GIVE UP MEETING TOGETHER."

Pop Quiz #1, page 216

in a day
get out of the kitchen
shouldn't throw stones
I'll tell you no lies
cherries
new tricks
try, try again
feeds you
The last proverb doesn't have an ending in everyday use, but it comes from Matthew 21:16! People wrongly use the phrase to simply mean that little children always say the truth, even if it's embarrassing.

"I Want to See," page 275

"The Lord gives sight to the blind."

"I Know How You Feel," page 277

1. empathy
2. sympathy
3. empathy
4. sympathy

Learning to Accept Correction, page 352

"WHOEVER HATES CORRECTION IS STUPID."

God's Thoughts, page 414

"How precious to me are your thoughts, God! How vast is the sum of them! Were I to count them, they would outnumber the grains of sand—when I awake, I am still with you" (Psalm 139:17–18).

Pop Quiz #2, page 416

Set A

1. Moses, when he smashed the stone tablets on the ground (see Exodus 32:19).
2. Joshua. He was the son of Nun (see Joshua 1:1).
3. In Genesis 1:1 (in the "big inning").
4. None. It was Noah!
5. He wasn't. It was Jonah!
6. Neither. There is no such book.
7. Ditto!

Set B

1. Mary and Martha (see Luke 10:38–42).
2. Dip himself in the Jordan River seven times (see 2 Kings 5:1–15).
3. Right, excellent, praiseworthy, lovely, admirable, noble, true (see Philippians 4:8).
4. A sheep, a coin, and a son (see Luke 15:3–31).
5. Yes, no, or not right now.
6. Sins to confess, promises to keep, actions to avoid, commands to obey, and examples to follow.
7. True, honest, inspiring, necessary, or kind.

Finish Well!, page 423

YOU DID IT!

Notes

Monday – God Sees and Knows Everything, page 51

1. "World's Top Ten New Species," Community Research and Development Information Service, May 29, 2005, http://cordis.europa.eu/news/rcn/30827 _en.html.

Tuesday – Spread the Good News, page 148

2. "Who Dares Wins—Success Through Intelligent Risk," Business Case Studies, http://businesscasestudies.co.uk/coca-cola-great-britain/who-dares-wins-success -through-intelligent-risk/a-story-of-global-success.html#axzz33R9Es6Cn.

Friday – Words That Become Wildfires, page 215

3. "Wildfire Causes," Wildfire and Aviation Management, http://www.nps.gov/fire /wildland-fire/learning-center/fire-in-depth/wildfire-causes.cfm.

Thursday – Twenty-Four Hours, page 238

4. "Who Needs Chiropractic Care?" Chiropractic Life Center—Kingston & Sydenham, Ontario, http://kingstownchiropractic.com/old/who-needs-chiropractic-care.shtml.

Dare to Let the Truth Change Your Life

Spark a fierce faith that will transform your life through these
devotions that not only feature powerful Scripture and godly messages,
but daily challenges to take the truth to heart and live it.

David C Cook
transforming lives together